RITUALS *of* RESISTANCE

RITUALS *of* RESISTANCE

AFRICAN ATLANTIC RELIGION

IN KONGO AND THE

LOWCOUNTRY SOUTH IN

THE ERA OF SLAVERY

JASON R. YOUNG

 Louisiana State University Press
Baton Rouge

Published by Louisiana State University Press
Copyright © 2007 by Louisiana State University Press
All rights reserved
Manufactured in the United States of America
Louisiana Paperback Edition, 2011

Designer: Laura Roubique Gleason
Typeface: Minion Pro
Typesetter: Newgen–Austin

Library of Congress Cataloging-in-Publication Data

Young, Jason R.
    Rituals of resistance : African Atlantic religion in Kongo and the lowcountry South in
the era of slavery / Jason R. Young
        p.   cm.
    Includes bibliographical references and index.
    ISBN 978-0-8071-3279-1 (cloth : alk. paper)
    1. Africans—South Carolina—Religion.   2. Africans—Georgia—Religion.   3. Congo
(Democratic Republic)—Religion.   4. America—Civilization—African influences.
5. African diaspora.   6. Africans—Migrations.   I. Title.
    BR563.N4Y683 2007
    305.896'009—dc22

                                                                                        2007006809

ISBN 978-0-8071-3719-2 (paper : alk. paper)

Dedicated to

The Butterfly
who, like Icarus, ventured too close to a burning sun
who, like the Ibos, returned home

and to

The Beautiful Ones Not Yet Born

CONTENTS

TABLES AND ILLUSTRATIONS

Tables

Maps

Figures

ACKNOWLEDGMENTS

It is true, as many have noted before, that writing is a corporate enterprise. And so there are individuals and institutions, foundations and family members who deserve my sincerest thanks for the crucial roles they played in helping me bring this project to fruition. But with my mind on Deuteronomy 5:15 and Ntozake Shange's *Sassafrass, Cypress & Indigo,* I would like to start by thanking *the slaves who were ourselves.*

Sterling Stuckey served as my dissertation advisor, and his guidance and expertise have been indispensable. Indeed, Stuckey inaugurated, through his unwavering faith in the power and importance of slave folklore, a new way of thinking not only about the conditions of slavery but also about the lives of slaves. I mean my own work to be a reflection of the path that he set.

Several people read drafts of the work at various stages. Margaret Washington and Jane Landers kindly agreed to travel to Buffalo to participate in a book manuscript workshop. They took time out of their very busy schedules and prepared detailed comments and questions that helped me revise the project in its later stages. Then, as now, I have only my deepest thanks to offer, though I wish I could give so much more. I want to thank Michael Gomez especially for his comments. He has shown a genuine interest in my academic and intellectual development since we first met during my undergraduate years in Atlanta, Georgia. From that time to this, he has been a consistent and reliable source of support.

At various stages, I have received support from the Ford Foundation, the Gilder-Lehrman Institute for American History Research, the Schomburg Center for Research in Black Culture, the Nuala McGann Drescher Fellowship, the Julian Park Publication Fund, and the Baldy Center for Law and Social Policy (SUNY, Buffalo). Many thanks also to SUNY, Buffalo for funding several research trips. These institutions have certainly been important to me for the very necessary material resources that they have provided. But even more, the support offered by these institutions has had the added benefit of introducing me to larger bodies of interested people who have since become not only colleagues but also dear friends.

Others have helped in incalculable ways. These include Marcellus Barksdale, Alton Hornsby Jr., and Augustine Konneh, each of whom in their own way introduced me to the discipline of History. Sterling Stuckey, Ray Kea, Sharon Salinger, and Ralph Crowder guided me through graduate level training. Jermaine Archer, Jennifer Hildebrand, Frans Ntloedibe, Karen Wilson, Frederick Knight, Walter Rucker, Kwakiutl Dreher, Rahel Kassahun, Millery Polyné, Lisa Gail Collins, Akil Houston, Eric Taylor, Christopher Span, Susan Cahn, Kari Winter, Erik Seeman, Pat and Sheila McDevitt, Felix Armfield, Lillian Williams, and Surrendra Bhana have all supported and encouraged me.

The staff at several research institutions were vital in the researching of this project, especially those at the Schomburg Center for Research in Black Culture; the Georgia Historical Society; the South Carolina Department of Archives and History; the South Caroliniana Library; the Avery Research Center in Charleston, South Carolina, especially Sherman Pyatt; and the South Carolina Historical Society, especially Jane Aldrich, Mike Coker, Mary Jo Fairchild, and Lisa Hayes.

To my father, Michael; my mother, Geneva; my sister, Alicia; my nephew, David; and the rest of my family, I owe a debt that I will never be able to pay. For true inspiration, I thank you, Idris. To the butterfly, I offer my deepest thanks and, as always, a Love unconditional.

I hope to repay all of you for all that you have done for me, *Insha'Allah.*

RITUALS *of* RESISTANCE

Introduction

I am remembering Reema's boy—the one with the pear-shaped head.[1] Once a child of Willow Springs, he returned to the small island off the coast of Georgia and South Carolina after having graduated from a mainland college. He came back toting notebooks, a tape recorder, and a curled, pensive lip. Even more than that, he carried about his person a rattle of a tongue, blathering of ethnography, cultural preservation, unique speech patterns, and the like. Perhaps because he was a child of the island—or maybe even in spite of it—the people of Willow Springs indulged him as he went about studying the people and place of his youth. One resident, Winky, sat for hours chewing up the expensive tobacco the boy had bought, spitting it into a can so that Reema's boy could record the cadence and tone of it.

Months passed, and in return for their kind cooperation, Reema's boy sent everyone signed copies of the newly published monograph based on his extensive fieldwork conducted at Willow Springs. According to Reema's boy, the people of Willow Springs did not know very much at all about themselves: "Being [they were] brought here as slaves, [they] had no choice but to look at everything upside-down. And then being that [they were] isolated off here on this island, everybody else in the country went on learning good English and calling things what they really was . . . while [they] kept on calling things ass-backwards. And [Reema's boy] thought that was just so wonderful and marvelous, etcetera, etcetera."[2] To be sure, the researcher had not gone so far as to call the residents of Willow Springs dumb. He assured readers that they were "'asserting [their] cultural identity,' 'inverting hostile social and political parameters.'" In the end, few in Willow Springs ever got beyond the introduction of that book, and others simply marveled at "the people who ran the type of schools that could turn our children into raving lunatics—and then put his picture on the back of the book so we couldn't even deny it was him."[3]

1

The tragedy of Reema's boy, and of his work, rests in the certainty that had he truly wanted to know the people of Willow Springs, he needed only to ask—of their curved spines, their moss-filled shoes—and listen. But for Reema's boy, true objectivity (if ever such a thing existed) required distance. So ever between him and his subjects, he insinuated the mechanisms of modernity: tape recorders, microphones, and wires. Then again, "someone who didn't know how to ask wouldn't know how to listen."[4]

I suspect that I have more in common with Reema's boy than I would like to admit. Like him, I too am possessed of an inquisitive spirit and at least some certainty that questions, if sufficiently researched, can be answered. Like Reema's boy, I too have chosen a vocation that presumes that cultures and histories are such as may be adequately transcribed. We are both confined, to a greater or lesser degree, to a particular discipline, a certain category of sources, and a prescribed methodology.

Reema's boy reminds us of others—anthropologists, historians, missionaries, and colonial agents—who devoted themselves to laying bare the "other." They described the loin cloth in detail, the hide and sinew of it, the stitch and strap. They revealed the nakedness of the so-called native, who becomes not only a naked body but also the embodiment of nakedness. They defined the community in its lack, in the thatched rooftops and devilment. But the tribe is also described in its excess, in the dance and sex and sin of it all. Frantz Fanon argues that this near-constant bombardment assaults the observed, who becomes "beaten down by tom-toms, cannibalism, intellectual deficiency, fetishism, racial defects, slave-ships, and above all else, above all: 'Sho' good eatin.'"[5] In the meantime, the observer maintains distance, revealing nothing of the smoke and mirrors that constitute this particular portrait. The observer transcends gender and class and race, shielded in the methodology of the discipline, hidden behind the camera's lens, funded by the foundation. Writing in *The Practice of Diaspora*, Brent Edwards warns, "Reading the archive must not serve to buttress the pretensions and mystifications of the present self or the current community."[6] I would rather admit at the outset the imprecision that marks my own endeavors. This project reflects my own motivations, interests, gifts and deficits, and in the midst of a narrative about brutality and resistance, racism and religion, I am left, somewhere, swirling all about it.

Rituals of Resistance has several aims. I examine the relationship between the religious traditions of precolonial Kongo and those of the Lowcountry region of coastal Georgia and South Carolina.[7] The choice of these two sites reflects the historical trajectory of the transatlantic slave trade, which for centuries transplanted Kongolese captives to the Lowcountry through the ports of Savannah and Charleston. I am interested in both marking the resonances and dissonances in the religious traditions of these two sites and historicizing those links. That is, *Rituals of Resistance* treats the manner in which the historical exigencies of the slave trade conspired to send not only men and women but also cultural meanings, signs, and symbols around the Atlantic rim. Because change, innovation, and creativity were crucial to the development of black cultures around the Atlantic, each chapter in this study offers a comparative analysis of how Africans on the continent and their contemporaries and progeny enslaved in the Americas responded to the dynamics of slavery and the slave trade. African culture did not ride Atlantic waterways as vestigial survivals or retentions but as the product of cultural memory, mediation, and creation. New World slaves *remembered* Africa intentionally and deliberately, creating new and vibrant cultures informed by memories of Africa. For this reason, the cultural, political, and social life of West-Central Africa is treated in depth in each of these chapters, not in an attempt to mine the ultimate sources of black American culture but as a way of understanding the relationships that pertain between different African Atlantic locales. This book adopts a methodology that offers an ongoing treatment of Kongo, positing the political economy of that region as a central component in understanding the cultural production of American slaves. Kongo figures throughout the project not as a monolith but as an ever-changing political, cultural, and commercial landscape that gave character to New World ritual in particular ways at different times.

In recent years, some have articulated varied oppositions to that manner of anthropological (and for present purposes, historical) investigation that attempts to demonstrate that African culture survived the passage across the Atlantic, creatively adapting itself to its new environment in the process. David Scott, writing in "An Obscure Miracle of Connection," presents one of the most engaging and challenging positions on this issue. He does not argue, as have some, that black American cultures carry little or no trace of African antecedents, nor does he contend, as have others, that these cultures are so marked by hybridity and/or creolization as to make any search for origins futile.[8] Instead, he is concerned that studies in this field have been largely "verificationist" in their epistemology; that they have answered questions as to "whether or not or to what extent [the black cultures of the Americas] are authentically African; and whether or not and to what extent [black peoples in the Americas] have retained an authentic memory of their past."[9] From the outset, these studies responded to a set of older assertions that maintained that the violence and horrors of the Middle Passage erased any semblance, among the enslaved, of distinctively African practices. Convinced that slaves had been culled from the lesser stock of African men and women, and presuming blacks to be naturally more childlike (and thus more pliable) than whites, many scholars argued that blacks were a people "without a past."[10] Scott worries that to enter "this debate—to make, for example, a counter-claim about identity—you were virtually *obliged* to provide the counter-evidence . . . to demonstrate that as a people your cultural sources were *not* (or not *only*) European ones."[11] In this, one had to engage the debate on its own terms by presuming, on the one hand, that pasts are such as can be identified in their authenticity and, on the other, that the special task of an anthropology of peoples of African descent consists in "providing the theoretical and methodological apparatus for corroborating such pasts in the present."[12]

So one notes the importance of Melville Herskovits, who expressed an opposition, "*within the terrain of positive (i.e. Scientific) evidence,* to the Eurocentric rationalist claim that [blacks throughout the Americas] were a people without history and therefore a people without culture."[13] For Herskovits, *The Myth of the Negro Past* represented "the documentation of an hypothesis, developed in the course of two decades of research," detailing the substantial, significant, and continued influence of African cultural elements in the histories, lives and cultures of blacks through-out the Americas.[14] Herskovits wrote vehemently against a longstanding academic practice that discounted any suggestion that African cultural elements could be identified in black American societies.[15]

Ultimately, Scott contends, these studies rest on the assumption that "peoples of African descent in the New World require something like anthropology, a science of culture, to provide them with the foundational guarantee of an authentic past."[16] Scott imagines a very different engage-ment: "And suppose then that we were, instead of laboring to find the ethnographic counter-evidence that would settle the matter of our identity once and for all, to dispense with the preoccupation as a whole of finding in ourselves the authoritative proof of an alternate authentic origin?"[17]

So Scott adopts "tradition" as a term denoting a discursive field "not merely about received wisdom or . . . an inheritance, something that you *get*," but about "an active relation in which the present calls upon the past." In this sense, Scott understands diaspora as "an attempt to signal the *ideological* convergences and divergences in the way that cultural practices across the black Atlantic put 'Africa' and 'Slavery' to use." He notes, for example, that while "dreadlocks" are "a recognizably black Atlantic 'hair style/politics,'" the uses to which that style is put differ quite markedly in New York City, Kumasi, or Kingston.[18] That enslaved Africans imagined Africa in creative and innovative ways should not be read to mean that the Africa they constructed was a mere fiction. As Stuart Hall writes, Africa "is not a mere phantasm ... it is *something*—not a mere trick of the imagination. It has its histories—and histories have their real, material and symbolic effects."[19]

Scott acknowledges, in reference to the monumental work of Kamau Brathwaite, that citing the "African" character of an African American cultural practice is never the terminus, that these investigations are "always on their way *elsewhere,* always folded into another project."[20] By noting the historical relationship between African and African American cultural practices, *Rituals of Resistance* is not aiming to authenticate black identity in the Americas but to historicize and contextualize the religions, cultural patterns, gestures, and lexical traditions that comprise the African Atlantic. These connections are forged, ultimately, out of the historical crucible of the transatlantic slave trade and slavery. I attempt to advance the discussion beyond comparisons of similarities that one might find between this essentially "African" ritual form and its subsequent reappearance, even if significantly altered, in the plantation Americas. That manner of research has been incredibly useful, and I am supported by the work of earlier scholars who, in the face of tremendous opposition, resolutely proclaimed the critical importance of Africa to the study of American slavery.[21] Their work is reflected in my own.

However, I want to build on that work by mining extant sources to develop an understanding of the historical movement of those signs, symbols, and meanings across the Atlantic. Historical change, both in Africa as well as in the plantation Americas, is part and parcel of my configuration and is part of the story to be told here. I seek to add dimension to the cultural continuities that exist between Africa and the Americas by drawing, in historical outline, the warp and woof from which African cultural forms were dispersed throughout the New World. More than a narrative detailing the dispersal of African cultural elements in the New World, this project also details the uses to which enslaved Africans put Africa; that is, the manner in which slaves called upon, remembered, and engaged Africa as part of the critically important work of cultural resistance.

Writing in *Central Africans and Cultural Transformations in the American Diaspora,* Linda Heywood argues that "general interest and knowledge of the history and cultural impact of Central Africans in the African Diaspora lag far behind that of West Africa."[22] And yet West-Central Africa is among the best documented of all regions in Africa, especially for the precolonial period. Some estimate that scholars, travelers, political officials, religious authorities, and others have devoted as many as half a million pages to the societies, languages, customs, and cultures of West-Central Africa for the period 1500–1800.[23] In this way, investigations into the history of West-Central Africa and its influence in the slave societies of the Americas serve to enhance our understanding of American slavery and encourage greater balance in our assessments of the varied roles that both West Africans and West-Central Africans played in the burgeoning plantation economies and cultures of the Americas.

That scholars have devoted relatively more attention to West Africa than West-Central Africa does not mean that scholars have wholly neglected the latter. To be sure, American scholars have addressed the cultural and linguistic contributions that West-Central Africans have made in the United States, the Caribbean, and South America.[24] Perhaps less attention has been devoted to this issue for the United States in line with a general perception, established during the early and mid-twentieth century by Melville Herskovits and others, that black Caribbean and South American cultures exhibited greater incidences of "Africanisms" relative to the black cultures of British North America. These arguments rested, in part, on the distinct demographic conditions of slavery in the United States, where the slave community (1) never enjoyed a numerical majority and (2) reproduced itself at a relatively early stage not by direct importation of captive Africans but through natural increase. By contrast, African imports regularly replenished the slave societies of Latin America and the Caribbean, which generally failed to reproduce through natural increase. In these societies, blacks predominated demographically, constituting, in some cases, 80 to 90 percent of the overall population.

Some scholars argued that the Catholicism to which captive Africans were exposed in Latin America and some areas of the Caribbean, with its pantheon of saints, elaborate festivals, and varied religious implements, proved more amenable to African spiritual practices.[25] In this way, en-slaved Africans manipulated the religious structures and hierarchies in Catholicism to create wonderfully complex and subtle religious practices, as in Candomblé in Brazil, Santería in Cuba, and Vodou in Haiti. Even outside the purview of Catholic practice, enslaved Africans were presum-ably better able to engage in cultural and religious practices more on the order of African practice in the British Caribbean, as exhibited in Myal and Obeah in Jamaica or in the Spiritual Baptist movement in Trinidad. When argued most stridently, these claims imply that enslaved Africans in Latin America and the Caribbean remained more authentically black/African than their counterparts enslaved in British North America. Indeed, Herskovits established a fairly strict hierarchy to that effect:

> It is quite possible on the basis of our present knowledge to make a kind of chart indicating the extent to which the descendants of Africans brought to the New World have retained Africanisms in their cultural behavior. . . . We may say that after Africa itself it is the Bush Negroes of Suriname who exhibit a civilization which is the most African. . . . Next to them would be placed their Negro neighbors on the coastal plains of the Guianas. . . . Next on our scale we should undoubtedly place the peasants of Haiti . . . [and] in a lesser degree, would come the inhabitants of neighboring Santo Domingo. From this point, when we come to the islands of the British, Dutch and Danish West Indies, the proportion of African cultural elements drops perceptibly. . . . Next on our table we should place such isolated groups in the United States as the negroes of southern Georgia, or those of the Gullah islands of the Carolina coast . . . , and then the vast mass of Negroes of all degrees of racial mixture living in the South of the United States. . . . Finally, we should come to a group where, to all intents and purposes, there is nothing of the African tradition left, and . . . who only differ from their white neighbors in the fact that they have more pigmentation in their skin.[26]

Herskovits's tabulation of "Africanisms," implying a continuum of racial as much as cultural assimilation, has been thoroughly revised and recon-sidered in the last half-century by scholars whose increased sensitivity to the subtleties of race and culture have led to more nuanced views.[27] Still, some of the basic presumptions that fueled Herskovits' writing persists, particularly the notion that the historical connections and relationships between Africa (and for present purposes, West-Central Africa) and the United States are more contingent, fugitive, and fleeting than in other American locales.[28]

The present study eschews the notion that blackness is such a quantity that might be compared and evaluated from one context to another. I am not interested in measuring the relative "blackness" of enslaved Africans in different parts of the African diaspora. I am interested, however, in developing a corrective to the prevailing view of African cultural continuities in the Americas; namely, that in order to be regarded as viable and valid, these connections need be preserved in some sort of formal praxis, easily compared and analyzed against a presumed African precedent, whether formalized in material culture, as in weaving and basketry, enacted in behavior, gesture, and dance, or articulated in lexical traditions and songs.

Sidney Mintz and Richard Price, writing in the *Birth of African American Culture*, advise scholars to maintain a skeptical attitude toward claims that many contemporary social or cultural forms represent direct continuities from Africa. Mintz and Price find the mere presence of this or that seemingly African trait in the Americas largely unimportant, arguing that direct formal continuities from Africa "are more the exception than the rule." They suggest that the historical connections between Africans and their contemporaries and progeny in the New World are, more often than not, "simply inferred from a small number of formal similarities, with lexical items, for example, playing a major role in 'documenting' alleged relationships."[29] Writing similarly, Jon Butler argues that the conditions of American slavery caused the "destruction of traditional African religious systems as *systems*. . . .What survived, then, were not African religious systems but discrete religious practices."[30]

These arguments, when taken further, have led some scholars to do away with the very notion of cultural origins, opting instead for a view of culture based in theories of creolization and hybridity. Joseph Roach argues that because memory (read: history) is constituted by a process of nonlinear and continual surrogations, the search for origins is a futile, if not misguided, enterprise: "What is found at the historical beginning of things is not the inviolable identity of their origin; it is the dissension of other things. It is disparity."[31] In this way, all presumed points of origin represent merely the resolution of contested and multiple options. They are marked not by their presence at the beginning of things but by all that preceded them. Like Roach, Saidiya Hartman questions the role that cultural memory played in the lives of New World slaves. She suggests that these "traces of memory [Africanisms] function in a manner akin to a phantom limb," a once viable and functional member, now irrevocably ripped away and unrecoverable; what is felt is no longer there.[32]

In contrast, James Sweet, in arguing for the persistence of African cultural practices in Brazil, challenges widely held notions that "African slaves were unable to replicate specific African institutions in the Americas."[33] As Sweet maintains, some communities of slaves maintained the functional and structural integrity of specific African rituals and beliefs from Africa in the Americas. More than the broad contours of West-Central African rituals remained intact in Brazil; "uniquely Angolan implements of spiritual invocation made their way across the Atlantic."[34] Rather than the product of creolization, black culture among enslaved Africans in Brazil, especially during the seventeenth century, witnessed the use of lexical structures and material implements for which no analogous words or practices existed among the Portuguese. For Sweet, the culture of enslaved blacks in Brazil carried the stamp of West-Central African provenance. Indeed, some ritual practices made their way across the Atlantic "in a nearly pure structural form," while other rites may be regarded as "classically. . . Kongolese."[35]

I am concerned that, like Herskovits's defiant declaration half a century earlier (that the cultures of West and West-Central Africa were critical in the subsequent development of black culture in the Americas), Sweet's argument is bound by terms not of his choosing. In response to the claim that "the diversity of African languages, cultural beliefs, and social structures in the slave populations of the Americas" necessitated the creation of new (creole) communities, Sweet provides the counter evidence to support his contention that the cultures of Kongo-Angola arrived in Brazil largely intact, pure, and "essential[ly] 'African.'"[36]

I am critical of theories of creolization and hybridity not because they overstate the degree of cultural interaction in the Americas (the basis of Sweet's opposition) but because they fail to adequately historicize the nature of that interaction. The notion that black creole cultures forged in the plantation Americas are ultimately "new," that they are composed of a dynamic mix of soluble cultural elements whose interactions render each cultural component contingent on the others and individually indecipherable, renders impossible any historical investigation of those cultural components. Instead, I regard black cultural formation as composite, composed of separate elements that, though not hermetic, were neither subsumed into a hazy cultural mist. Such an approach allows for investigations into particular and ongoing relationships between Africans and their contemporaries and progeny in the Americas while still regarding culture as multiple and dynamic.

The pioneering scholars in the field of African cultural influences in the Americas concentrated much of their effort on those cultural practices easily subject to direct comparison: this basket woven in South Carolina against its (presumed) prototype in Africa or that syntactical structure against Bantu grammar.[37] While these efforts made explicit the longstanding influence of Africa on the lives of blacks enslaved in the Americas, and inaugurated an entire field of study, I am arguing that other, more implicit sets of relationships and connections were equally important, though not as easily subject to direct formal comparison. As I detail the relationships between the cultures of West-Central Africa and those of the Lowcountry, the reader will note that some practices, methods, implements, and forms are strikingly similar in both locales. This is true, for example, in chapter 3 in relationship to the construction and use of a certain set of ritual objects prevalent in West-Central Africa and the Lowcountry. These objects contained many of the same materials and ritual experts manipulated them to quite similar ends. In other instances, however, the immediate, formal similarities may not be obvious, though they are connected by the principles and beliefs that undergird them. This is most obvious in chapter 2 with respect to Christian conversion in Kongo and the Lowcountry of coastal Georgia and South Carolina, where enslaved Africans from West-Central Africa managed, manipulated, and crafted recombinant forms of Christian ritual and theology even as they adhered faithfully to a broad set of religious principles and concepts first developed in Kongo. This cultural ingenuity may have been the most important African cultural inheritance. As Richard and Sally Price suggest, this "readiness to extrapolate new forms from old reflects a maintenance of the internal dynamism . . . that constitutes one of the most striking features of West and Central African cultural systems."[38]

So I return to the notion of "tradition," mentioned above, as an ongoing praxis based not only on an *inheritance*—that which one receives from ancestors—but also on *memory*—the manner in which we call upon our ancestors and put them to use in our constructions of ourselves. This approach enables us to analyze the cultural relationships and dialogues that crisscrossed the Atlantic during the era of slavery and the slave trade, without having to entrench ourselves in dour dialectical debates burdened by the need to prove or disprove Africa's role in the development of black identities in the Americas. In this way, this study promises to enhance both our understanding of slavery in the United States and our awareness of that which constitutes a viable and meaningful connection and relationship between West and West-Central Africans and their contemporaries and progeny enslaved in the New World.

The study of religion offers a unique opportunity to conduct the manner of historical investigations outlined above. Christian missionaries first arrived in Kongo at the end of the fifteenth century, and since that time the Kongolese have sought to resolve the mandate of Christian conversion with their own religious traditions. This centuries-long engagement with Christianity prefigured similar negotiations enslaved Africans of Kongolese descent made throughout the Americas in general and the Lowcountry in particular. Even outside the realm of Christianity, as in the use of ritual objects or the enactment of funerary ritual, the ritual landscape of precolonial Kongo remained conversant with ritual practice in the slave South.

The central thesis of this book is that religion operated as a central form of resistance not only against the system of slavery but also against the very ideological underpinnings that supported slavery in the first place.[39] That the dispossessed used religion and culture to mitigate the more deleterious effects of oppression is certainly not novel. Indeed, scholarship treating just this sort of resistance is quite extensive, and I rely on it in this project.[40] Some of the best work in this regard focuses on enslaved Africans who created cultural practices to encourage community formation. Sterling Stuckey, for example, argues in *Slave Culture* that the ring shout was the "key to understanding the means by which [slaves] achieved oneness in America."[41] Out of the multitude of African cultural and religious practices, Stuckey reveals the multiple ways in which enslaved Africans mobilized around the varied rituals of circular movement common to many in the development of a more cohesive black American culture. Building on the work of Stuckey, Michael Gomez details the process by which enslaved Africans moved away from distinct ethnic identities in favor of a larger racial identification that contributed to the rise of African American culture.[42] By coming together around a series of religious and social institutions, enslaved Africans built a more cohesive, even if stratified, community based on race. Likewise, Margaret Washington demonstrates that "resistance against white power and hegemony was conspicuous in the Gullahs' sense of cultural autonomy, authoritative, creative community-building, and their spiritual disengagement from the slaveocracy's version of Christian teachings."[43] Taken together, these arguments make clear that enslaved Africans eschewed their own ethnic and cultural particularities in the larger process of creating communities unified through race and culture as a way to mitigate the violence and brutality of slavery. As a defensive strategy, this culture and community building proved quite successful in the development of an autonomous worldview and moral ethic not modeled on the example of the master class.

While building on this work, I argue further that slave cultural resistance was not only defensive in nature, as it helped slaves shield themselves from some of the horrid conditions of enslavement, but also offensive, enabling them to attack directly the ideological underpinnings of slavery. That is, slave cultural practice may be read as something of a political tract denouncing the varied justifications that members of the master class expounded in support of slave labor. James Scott, writing in *Domination and the Arts of Resistance,* adopts the idea of "hidden transcripts" in detailing the "often fugitive *political* conduct of subordinate groups."[44] In his formulation, cultural practices, including religious rituals and rites, helped slaves and other subordinates put forth disguised critiques of power outside the purview of the master class. Taken together, these forms of "ideological insubordination" comprise the "infrapolitics of the powerless"—a realm of discrete political action operating alongside the more formal political engagements of the State and civil society.[45] In this sense, the varied cultural practices treated throughout *Rituals of Resistance* are best regarded as immanently political in nature. Unlike Scott, who argues that the "infrapolitics of the powerless" very rarely reaches the eyes and ears of the dominant class, I argue that slaveholders not only acknowledged but also responded to the political implications of slave cultural practice.[46] The cultural resistance of slaves exhibited in the realm of material culture, folklore, and religion directly affected the larger political discourse in the country in general and, in particular, the ways in which the powerful justified their control over the mechanisms of oppression and violence. This is certainly evident throughout this book as members of the master class responded to the prevalence of ritual medicines and poisons or to the slaves' particular interpretation of Christianity. That religion and culture served as a salve for the wounds inflicted by slavery and functioned as a sword for battling the ideological framework upon which justifications of slavery rested promises to expand our understanding of the potency of religion and culture.

My notion of resistance is based on my understanding of slavery as a variously defined system. Slavery is, on the one hand, a mechanism for the forced extraction of labor. Any tactic that slaves undertook to disrupt this forced extraction may be deemed resistant as in absconding, rebellion, work slowdowns, feigned illness, and/or the destruction of tools. These forms of resistance have enjoyed wide coverage in the historiography of slavery and they are treated throughout this study.[47] At the same time, however, slavery transcends the sum of the mechanisms used to forcibly extract labor; it is more than the shackle, stocks, and auction block, and its scope extends beyond the reach of the whip. Slavery reflects an ideological engagement that relies on the religious, economic, political, and philosophical sanction of the society that supports it. It requires the ideological consent of society at large, a consent that must be written into law, justified in the church, rationalized in the schoolhouse.

Ideally, slaveholders regarded the slave as but a body, a vehicle for labor and capital accumulation. Writing in *Scenes of Subjection,* Saidiya Hartman figures this relationship as enjoyment, which entailed "the exercise of a right; the promise and function of a right, privilege or incorporeal hereditament. Comfort, consolation, contentment, ease, happiness, pleasure and satisfaction. Such includes the beneficial use, interest, and purpose to which property may be put, and implies rights to profits and incomes therefrom."[48] More than this, the subjection of the slave to all whites defined his condition in civil society such that the enslaved could potentially be "used and abused by all whites."[49] Similar systems of labor relations operated elsewhere—as in the rise of the British factory system, for example—but are perhaps most pronounced in American slavery, in which the body was in fact a commodity in and of itself.[50] Members of the master class perceived of the slave as a tool, an instrument and extension of his own will, and demanded utter obedience.[51] Indeed, Anglo-American jurisprudence on this question maintained the status of slaves as objects of property. Yet everyday experience revealed the fantasy of absolute submission as slaves regularly exerted their own will and, in innumerable ways, resisted their enslavement.[52] So the adherents of slavery—whether slave holders, overseers, or the varied instruments of the state—violently imposed their will on the body of the slave: in the brand burned into the skin, the raised scars strewn across her back, the amputated limb, her violated body. Moreover, one notes all of the quotidian ways that the master class exerted itself on the enslaved: an endless and palpable dehumanization, a disgusted glance, a grin.[53]

During the eighteenth century notions about the legal basis of slave status in civil society combined with Enlightenment thought and an impending modernity by which many found crucial avenues to rationalize and regulate American slavery and the transatlantic slave trade. In espousing the superiority of a new scientific order, the planter elite began increasingly to manage plantations with newly esteemed rational methods.[54] Along with methods of scientific management, the Age of Reason promised an increased rationalization and secularization of modern life. In what Max Weber calls the "disenchantment of the world," the ruling and industrial classes of the West came to regard the rituals, customs, and beliefs of the working classes as backward (read: premodern) and therefore subject to repression and eradication.[55] Thus the bodies of slaves were subject to violence and slave culture and religion were decried as primitive.

When the slave acted outside the parameters of this new order; when she became more than a vehicle for profit and more than a discrete and secular object as in transmigration, spirit possession, and conjure, she attacked not only the condition of being a slave but also the systems of modernity and scientific rationalism that supported slavery.[56] In opposition to the demands of the master class, slaves utilized their own bodies through the idioms of ritual and rite to redress their pains and oppressions; and in place of master-class imperatives toward obedience and submission, slave spirituality afforded a space for dance and divination. Indeed, slave spirituality played a critical role in the resocialization of the slave body and behavior away from the brutalities of the master class.[57] In effect, slaves looked—at least in part—to the realm of the spirit to express their discontent with slavery's collusion with the dawn of a new era of juridical and philosophical thinking that formalized and justified the exercise of violence. This does not mean, however, that slaves represented the somehow risibly curious and quaint reminders of an old-fashioned and outmoded way of life. If enslaved Africans rejected some aspects of an impending modern age, they certainly did not reject all of it. As argued by Paul Gilroy, black people were part of modernity and have expressed—"sometimes as defenders of the West, sometimes as its sharpest critics—... their sense of imbeddedness in the modern world."[58] *Rituals of Resistance,* then, posits the slave body as both a site of violence as well as a vehicle of resistance, enabling enslaved men and women to resist both the physical assailments of slavery and its ideological assault.[59] If, as others have argued, the ubiquity of slave escape stands in direct defiance of master-class imperatives restricting slave mobility, then the persistence of autonomous slave ritual opposed master-class narratives regarding the vacuity of the slave spirit, memory, and humanity.

The African Atlantic Defined

While Atlantic studies have gained some considerable currency and popularity in recent years, no general definition or broad theories have as yet arisen that might cohere all of the different investigations conducted under its rubric. One result of this is the development of numerous terms—"black Atlantic," "circum-Atlantic," "Atlantic world"—that have been used variously to define the field and to describe the relationships, both past and present, that existed (and presently exist) between Europe, Africa, and the Americas. Anthropologists, historians, literary critics, and scholars of cultural studies have presented theoretical models that attempt to address the field as a valid unit of analysis, replete with its own internal dynamism and structures of organization. This process continues.[60]

Notably, much of the current scholarly work in the field of Atlantic studies builds on a much earlier tradition of scholarship that focused on the early development of the African diaspora.[61] While the work conducted under this rubric reflects the invaluable contribution of early scholars in the field, its use of the term "diaspora" calls to mind the Jewish dispersal as described in Deuteronomy 28:25, emphasizing, on the one hand, a movement from a homeland outward to varied parts of the world and, on the other, an elevation of that homeland as the principal arbiter of cultural, religious, and political authenticity. Writing in *The Making of the African Diaspora in the Americas,* Vincent Bakpetu Thompson uses the term "diaspora" as a synonym for dispersion, arguing that the forces that drove Africans into the plantation societies of the Americas were "not dissimilar to those which dispersed the Jews."[62] As Michael Gomez notes, the African diaspora is "primarily concerned with massive movements and extensive relocations . . . resulting in the dispersal of Africans and their descendants throughout much of the world."[63]

As construed in *Rituals of Resistance,* the African Atlantic emphasizes the roles that blacks around the Atlantic rim played in the development of ongoing networks of engagement. As Isidore Okpewho argues, "Given the fluid movement of persons and of ideas from both sides of the Atlantic, and in light of the shifting political and economic relations between Africa and west Atlantic society . . . it becomes clear that *diaspora* represents a global space, a worldwide web, that accounts as much for the mother continent as for wherever in the world her offspring may have been driven by the unkind forces of history."[64] Writing similarly, Kristin Mann maintains that the cultural influences between Africa and the Americas "moved not only back and forth between specific regions of Africa and the Americas but also between different parts of Africa and of the Americas. Indeed, they circulated in flows of differing reach and proportion all around the Atlantic basin."[65] In this sense, I regard each sector and region of the African Atlantic as on par with other regions, highlighting their interconnections and relationships.

The term "African Atlantic" is used here to denote a certain set of composite relationships that developed around the Atlantic rim during the era of the transatlantic slave trade and New World slavery. Rather than perceiving of the African Atlantic as a unidirectional space whereby the peoples and cultures of West and West-Central Africa were dispersed throughout the plantation Americas, informing the cultures of enslaved Africans, *Rituals of Resistance* posits the African Atlantic as a constellation of sites with each point ever conversant with the others. I am thinking here of Paul Gilroy's use of ships in motion as a symbol that crystallized the connections between different African Atlantic locales. Ships call to mind the Middle Passage and the forced migration of millions to the New World, the "varied projects for redemptive return to an African homeland," as well as the circuitous movement of materials, cultures, and ideas around the Atlantic rim.[66] Julius Scott details the existence of wide ranging networks of communication and resistance around the Atlantic rim as the movement of ships, goods, and seamen "not only offered opportunities for developing skills or escaping, but provided the medium of long-distance communication and allowed interested Afro-Americans to follow developments in other parts of the world."[67] In the end, this system of communication created crucial transatlantic connections between free blacks, slaves and nonslaveholding whites.[68]

More than a simple scattering of dispersed bodies, the African Atlantic operated as a system of theoretical and intellectual engagement whereby Africans on the continent and enslaved in the Americas redressed and resisted the trauma and violence of slavery and the slave trade. As a heuristic device, the notion of the African Atlantic as a constellation helps explode discrete national boundaries. Indeed, I insist in this book that the latitude and lens of black cultural formation must be extended; they must be transnational.[69] As Edouard Glissant states, "We are the roots of a cross-cultural relationship. Submarine roots: that is floating free, not fixed in one position in some primordial spot, but extending in all directions in our world through its network of branches."[70] Such a panoramic orientation is crucial for any study of the relationships that pertain to the cultural formation of blacks both bound together and set asunder by Atlantic waters. The cultures of West and West-Central Africa are related to the cultures of the Caribbean and mainland Spanish America, and to the cultures of plantation slaves in Brazil and South Carolina. In the Americas, one observes these similarities in many realms of slave life, including material and artistic culture, lexical traditions, and religious practices, to name but a few. And yet the slave cultures throughout the Americas were not essentially analogous. I have no intention of eliding the very crucial distinctions and differences that mark the African Atlantic. The sociopolitical and commercial landscapes of various New World plantation societies differed significantly, a matter that necessarily affected the subsequent development of black Atlantic cultures. Still, the dynamism, innovation, and difference constitutive of black cultural formation in the plantation Americas functioned within the framework of the African Atlantic. Writing in "How the West Was One," Robin D. G. Kelley notes that "forced labor, racial oppression, colonial conditions, and capitalist exploitation were global processes that incorporated Black people through empire building. They were never uniform or fixed, but did create systems that were at times tightly coordinated across oceans and national boundaries."[71]

As a system of theoretical and intellectual engagement, the African Atlantic enabled—to a degree—the resolution of cultural difference toward broader-themed convergences, including ongoing relationships with Africa, persistent engagements with racial identification and racism, and resistance to the violence of slavery and the slave trade. Regarding religion, Deborah Gray White asserts that "one thing all the religions of the Black Atlantic seem to have in common is their existence at the nexus of political resistance and cultural expression."[72] The African Atlantic provided a shared vocabulary of religious experience and resistance to which different slave societies referred in the creation of dynamic and innovative communities. When combined, the connections established between and betwixt the African Atlantic comprise a terribly complicated, dense, and potent palimpsest of cultures, languages, religions, and lives. Though ever aware of the larger webbed matrices that compose the African Atlantic, *Rituals of Resistance* investigates but one strand in this network, namely, the relationship between the spiritual and religious lives of West-Central Africans and the ritual practices and beliefs of their progeny enslaved in the coastal regions of Georgia and South Carolina.

This book is a study both of cultural recuperation, as captive Africans drew on a wellspring of memory and experience of an African past, and of cultural generation, as slaves in the New World mediated their differences into viable slave communities in the New World. The project is divided into four case studies. Chapter 1, "Kongo in the Lowcountry," treats, in broad outline, the political economy of Kongo and the Lowcountry during the period of slavery and the slave trade and contextualizes the historical connections between the two locales. This chapter acquaints readers with two historical locales that challenge some generally held presumptions about slavery and the transatlantic slave trade. Regarding Kongo, the reader is introduced to an urbane and highly complicated society that, at its height, was comparable in size to present-day California; whose nobility was largely literate and multilingual; and whose diverse religious landscape included Christian practice as early as the late fifteenth century. In the Lowcountry, one notes the establishment of a highly autonomous black community whose cultural, linguistic, and religious lives continued to be deeply connected to Africa throughout the period of slavery. Chapter 2, "Saline Sacraments, Water Ritual, and the Spirits of the Deep," addresses the nature of cultural continuity in the realm of Christianity and marks the Christian faith as a critical site for community construction for New World slaves. In addition, the chapter reveals the process of Christian conversion as a ritual death, the submersion of the faithful beneath murky baptismal waters as a literal plunge into the otherworld. It not only probes the often elusive and subtle question of conversion but also reveals fresh avenues and insights regarding those points and processes that helped to create the African Atlantic. Chapter 3, "*Minkisi,* Conjure Bags, and the African Atlantic Religious Complex," focuses on community construction outside the purview of the master class, in the clandestine consulting rooms of root doctors and conjure men as ritual experts called on the powers of the dead to effect change in the here and now. This chapter treats the development and dispersal of a certain set of ritual objects found in Kongo and throughout the African Atlantic. The treatment is comparative, noting both the similarities and differences between the two traditions and emphasizing the importance of innovation and creativity in the maintenance and operation of ritual objects and their attendant practices. Moreover, the chapter establishes these objects as central to resistance both in Kongo against the demands of the slave trade and in the slave South, against the imperatives of plantation slavery. Lastly, this chapter notes the relationship between these objects and the limits of modernity. In chapter 4, "Burial Markers and Other Remembrances of the Dead," we are witness to cemeteries and song at the site of burial mounds throughout the Deep South as well as the North. Through a treatment of grave decoration and funerary ritual, this chapter investigates the manner in which the burial ritual informs and reflects the African Atlantic. It proposes something of a generalized biography of the dead, charting the movement of the postmortem body and soul from this world to the next.

Death permeates these pages. Each of the rituals discussed in this book reflect the struggles of enslaved men and women who navigated their way through a landscape littered with the lifeless bodies of others. One thinks here of the uncounted numbers of men and women who, captured, shackled, and driven from the African interior westward toward the Atlantic, never made it to coastal ports of call; of bodies thrown overboard, swallowed by the sea; or of broken bodies bound to the lash in the plantation Americas. Writing in *Slavery and Social Death,* Orlando Patterson claims that slavery always arises as a substitute for death.[73] In exchange for life, the slave is wrested from his social and political existence to perform the will of the master class. The specter of death accompanies the enslaved, whose lives, if found to be an affront to the state, may be stamped out in perfect harmony with the law. No wonder then that so many of the rituals performed by slaves explored the possibilities of transcending not only the physical death of the body but also the metaphoric death that is slavery. In baptism, burial, and conjure slaves mobilized, manipulated, and, in some instances, embraced the specter of death attendant on their daily lives. Writing in *The Souls of Black Folk,* W. E. B. Du Bois makes the point clear:

Of death the Negro showed little fear, but talked of it familiarly and even fondly as simply a crossing of the waters, perhaps—who knows?—back

to his ancient forests again. Later days transfigured this fatalism, and
amid the dust and dirt the toiler sang:

Dust, dust and ashes, fly over my grave,
But the Lord shall bear my spirit home.[74]

A Note on Sources and Method

Each chapter in this book makes extensive use of the slave arts, including material culture, folk tales, oral traditions, and slave (auto)biography
as crucial tools necessary for understanding how slaves perceived their
world and created innovative cultures.[75] This source material is critical for
the study of slave culture inasmuch as it reveals slave communities that
are resistant, ever aware of their position in the world as oppressed, but
determined to affect the course of their own lives, resolute in their own
resistance.[76] To take but one example, every victory that Br'er Rabbit had
over wolf, tiger, and bear represented a victory for the community at large.
Indeed, "his exploits mimicked the survival strategies of the slaves who
elaborated these tales."[77] Enslaved Africans could, at one and the same
time, identify with Br'er Rabbit's varied exploits against powerful oppres-
sors while claiming that the stories were merely innocuous.[78] In the formal
structure of the tales, in their antiphony, rhythm, and lexical tradition,
one notes the presence of African-derived words and ritual practices that
link the tales to a broader African Atlantic.

Folk art operated as a living, breathing cultural expression that connected the cultural practices of American slaves with those of other black
cultures around the Atlantic rim. One thinks here, for example, of Anansi
tales told throughout the Caribbean.[79] Because slaves were excluded from
other systems of political, social, and economic redress, they conferred on
the very songs they sang and the tales they told critical information regarding their beliefs, lives, and aspirations. As a form of corporate memory,
folklore represents a great distillation of generations of experience and
expectation, passed from lip to lobe, often in direct opposition to members
of the master class, who touted slavery as a benign system. Contrary to
the sanitized picture of an Old South, replete with contented servants and
benevolent masters, slaves mobilized folklore and art as an oppositional
narrative of the past, an inherently resistant process.[80] As others have noted
in a similar context, "oral traditions, due simply to their means of transmission, offer a kind of seclusion, control, and even anonymity that make

them ideal vehicles for cultural resistance."[81] The study of slave folklore also provides an active repository from which contemporary visual artists and novelists draw. One finds the folklore of slaves embedded in some of the most highly acclaimed African American contemporary art. *Rituals of Resistance* treats folklore as a way of understanding events of the past even as it highlights the prevalence and persistence of folk forms in the present day. In this way, novels, photographs, sculpture, and the like are treated in their relationship to the folk arts that preceded them and as a way of understanding the continued development of the slave arts into new idioms.

Through extensive treatment of slave folklore, I investigate the power of magical medicines, the movement of ancestors in ritual dance, and the conversations that the living had with the dead. Taken together, these phenomena reveal a ritual landscape that belies much of modernity's assumptions about the rational order of the known universe, where the dead certainly do not possess the limbs and lips of the living, compelling them to dance and sing. In analyzing the slave folk tradition, many have sought to either seek rational explanations for these phenomena or reduce them to that set of irrational flailings presumably common among untutored and ignorant peoples. Indeed, Reema's boy, with whom this chapter opened, took this approach. But this book eschews this approach in favor of treating this material as the articulation of a subtle and imaginative spiritual complex replete with its own notions of spirit, the body, and its movement. When we ignore this fact, we do the ritual (not to mention knowledge about the ritual) a serious disservice. Writing in a similar context, Wyatt MacGaffey maintains that "there is, or should be, nothing shameful about our [scholarly] agendas, but we should be willing to suspend them from time to time, and to recognize the *irreducibility* of these testimonies to life in another world and to imagine in our turn a reality based on very different assumptions about personhood, agency, life and death, and the nature of power."[82]

In addition to folklore, I make extensive use of Protestant missionary reports, which have been invaluable as a source for studying slave ritual practice and belief in the American South and as a tool for understanding how whites commonly perceived of these beliefs. Significant tensions marked the relationship between Christian missionaries and their would-be converts, principally because planters, in the main, opposed the religious instruction of slaves on the grounds that it would make them rebellious. As missionaries lamented the varied failures of slave conversion, they decried the persistence of what they deemed superstitious and primitive beliefs, creating in the process a valuable record of slave ritual practice, though marred by an intense ethnocentrism. In much the same way, the reports of travelers through the antebellum South shed light not only on the slave practice but also on the various engagements whites had with slave belief and ritual.

The substantial set of slave narratives is also mobilized here as a way of highlighting firsthand accounts of the cultural lives of enslaved Africans in the South. Written, in many instances, at the behest of abolitionist advocates, some narrators emphasized the readiness of African Americans for fuller participation in American life, for which they regarded Christianity an important prerequisite. In this sense, the spiritual lives of enslaved men and women outside the purview of Christianity remains more elusive in these texts, though one still finds in the antebellum slave narrative tradition critically important information about slave ritual practice. To a lesser extent, *Rituals of Resistance* utilizes slave narratives collected during the early twentieth century as part of the Works Progress Administration (WPA). The difficulties and benefits inherent in using these materials have been well documented by historians and will not be repeated here except to add that these sources are treated in this book in correlation with historical material contemporary to the period under investigation.

Criminal court records are among the most difficult, though fruitful, source materials for the study of slave life. Though slaves were traded as chattel and denied access to most arenas of social and political engagement (voting, marriage, taxation), southern whites did acknowledge slave agency in one area of public life, namely, its criminality. Indeed, some maintain that southern society recognized the slave as human "only to the degree that he is criminally culpable."[83] These sources reveal much about the ubiquity of slave resistance and the pervasiveness of white fears of black rebellion.

As the Kongo region figures prominently in this project, primary source material from that region is used extensively. This material includes the reports of missionaries stationed in Kongo during the era of the slave trade as well as accounts of travelers through Kongo's districts and provincial states. As is true of the American case, these sources require careful reading for several reasons, not the least of which involves the varied biases that missionaries brought with them as they detailed their experiences.

Moreover, the Catholic mission in Kongo was perpetually undermanned and largely ill equipped, a matter that colored the reports sent to papal authorities. Lastly, Catholic missionaries in Kongo early on allied themselves to various political interests in the country, an issue that became increasingly important in the second half of the seventeenth century. A full treatment of Catholic missionaries in Kongo must address the larger political landscape within which they operated.

Unlike other regions of precolonial West and West-Central Africa, Kongo is unique in that the royal court developed literacies in European languages quite early. This resulted in a rather extensive epistolary exchange whereby Kongo nobility wrote to papal authorities, European monarchs, and their own provincial nobility. These sources afford a rare view into Africans' own responses to slavery and the slave trade. This book also draws on a wide range of interdisciplinary sources from anthropology, linguistics, ethnography, and art history, some of which were produced during the late nineteenth and early twentieth centuries. While these sources cannot be simply read backward to precolonial Kongo, the information can be useful, especially when treated alongside contemporary accounts.

1

Kongo in the Lowcountry

Writing in *Slaves in the Family,* Edward Ball details the arrival, in 1736, of a young woman in South Carolina. She had been sold as a slave in West-Central Africa and would be sold again once she arrived at Charleston. She was bought by the Ball Family, owners of the Comingtee plantation, where she came to be known as Angola Amy. She served the Ball family for more than fifty years until 1790, when she died, having given birth to seven children. Her descendants became the single largest clan on Ball's rice plantations.[1] Angola Amy's movements reflect the larger flow of human beings, beliefs, and histories, traveling from West-Central Africa, across Atlantic waters, to the rice, indigo, and cotton plantations of the Lowcountry region of Georgia and South Carolina. More than a century earlier, in 1619, West-Central Africans had been among the first shipments of Africans to arrive in British North America. Later, West-Central African traditions of warfare and battle proved critical in the Stono slave uprising of 1739.[2] Indeed, the culture, customs, and language of West-Central Africa have left indelible marks on the lives and cultures of the Lowcountry region in particular and throughout the Americas in general.[3]

As illustrated in table 1, West-Central Africans constituted the single largest ethnic cohort of all Africans imported into the Lowcountry. But they were far from alone. The cultural landscape of the Lowcountry included West Africans from various regions, especially Senegambia and Sierra Leone. This book focuses on the role West-Central Africans played in the development of Lowcountry culture, but this should not be read to mean that other regions did not play critically important parts in that culture. The geographical origins of enslaved Africans in the Lowcountry were varied, even if governed by certain trends and identifiable tendencies. The culture of enslaved Africans in the region drew upon a wellspring of cultural influences and factors derived from African, Native American, and European elements, each one affecting the others. Enslaved Africans found, among their neighbors, British colonists, a diverse group of Africans, both slave and free, Spanish settlers in Florida, and Native Americans with whom they occasionally sought refuge. Thus identity formation among slaves in the region was a dynamic process, with each constituent group participating in the composition of slave culture in the region.

Table 1. Number of Africans from various regions imported to the Lowcountry in various periods

Region of origin	1700–1740	1741–1787	1788–1808	1700–1808
Benin	0	1,875	652	2,509
Biafra	2,619	6,745	2,135	11,499
Gold Coast	385	10,841	5,842	17,068
Kongo-Angola	10,375	12,609	26,667	49,651
Senegambia	2,440	18,872	3,087	24,399
Sierra Leone	0	10,393	6,764	17,157
Southeast Africa	0	239	473	712
Windward Coast	62	8,366	4,829	13,257
Unknown	12,780	7,845	15,062	35,687
Total	28,661	77,767	65,511	171,939

Source: Data from David Eltis, Stephen Brehendt, David Richardson, and Herbert Klein, eds., *The Trans-Atlantic Slave Trade: A Database on CD-ROM* (New York: Cambridge, 1999).

The Kongolese presence in the region should not be regarded as hermetic in any way. Neither should black culture in the region be perceived as exclusively Kongolese. As Maureen Warner-Lewis argues in another context, "In respect of certain practices, one is dealing with mutual reinforcement in [the New World] of certain widespread African cultural morphologies."[4] This is true all the more in light of cultural variation within Africa itself, not to mention its diaspora. In this sense, any given cultural practice likely took various forms both on the continent as well as in the diaspora. Certain aspects of African religious and spiritual culture were broad and general enough to be understood and elaborated by enslaved Africans from various regions. As some have argued, slave culture most probably relied on these commonalities in the creation of slave culture.[5] To acknowledge this level of cultural interaction does not detract from the singular contributions that West-Central Africans made to the religious and cultural landscape of the Lowcountry. Indeed, a broad sense of the varied elements that composed the cultural landscape of the Lowcountry highlights all the more the particular and significant contributions of West-Central Africans.

Kongo

From the mid-fifteenth century until the mid-seventeenth century, Kongo held sway over much of West-Central Africa, with zones of influence that extended from the north in the Bateke plateau southward to Benguela. Though the formal boundaries of the nation shifted between the fifteenth and seventeenth centuries, the general outline of the kingdom followed the Atlantic Coast in the west, the Congo River to the north, the Kwango River to the East, and the Loje River to the south (see map 1). Beyond its formal boundaries, Kongo dominated many outlying areas and smaller kingdoms by levying tribute and extending its territorial claims.

John Thornton has detailed the basic structural division of the kingdom into two sectors: the town *(mbanza)* and the countryside *(lubata)*. Each of the two sectors operated a complete social system with its own systems of production, distribution, and exchange; its own structure of status and power; and its own means of control and continuity. In addition, each sector had its own economy and was thus affected by different economic factors. In the countryside, kinship networks regulated peasant production from which local rulers collected rent, passing the surplus on to the royal bureaucracy at Mbanza Kongo, capital of the kingdom. In the towns most production rested on slave labor to the benefit of landlords, who used the surplus as a source of wealth and luxury.[6]

Even as the two sectors were motivated by their own internal forces, they were also interwoven into a single, noble directed centralized system replete with a national tax, extensive markets, international trade, and fully developed monetary system. Kinship ties, both marital and lineal, connected one village to the next in the rural sector, and the same manner of connection linked the royal and noble sectors of the town. The town centers and the outlying rural areas were also connected by shared customs, cultures, language, and cosmological conceptions.[7]

Kongo was highly centralized, the king occupying the highest position atop a large redistributive network from which matters political, economic, religious, and social originated. From his ritual throne, the king oversaw the

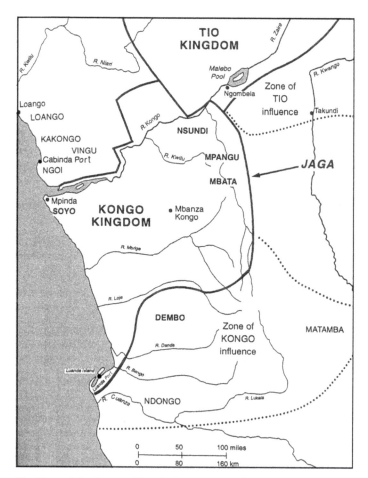

The Kongo kingdom and bordering states in the sixteenth century
Adapted from General History of Africa, *vol. 5, abridged ed., ed. B. A. Ogot*
(Berkeley: University of California Press, 1999), 274.

functioning of lesser priestly chiefdoms and a network of lineage descent groups that formed the bureaucracy of the nation. He appointed governors (often related either through lineage or marriage) who served both at the town centers as well as in provincial regions. Because noble status was not inherited, the king also appointed, dismissed, or relocated officials in order to prevent them from building oppositional factions and parties.[8]

Kongo ideologies of kingship maintained that all power and authority in this world derived from the otherworld.[9] Power was justified through access to the spiritual realm, and only those with special spiritual access were qualified for leadership. Kongolese subjects addressed the king as a sacred being due to his supreme ritual access to otherworldly power. Ceremonies and rituals of royal investiture expressed and solidified this sacredness. Only the king's divine access to the spirit world ensured Kongo's bounty, rain, and prosperity. Through the king, royal officials enjoyed that access to otherworldly powers necessary for the justification of their own authority. In addition to affording spiritual gifts, the king also dispersed material gifts to his nobility and a centralized monetary system rendered noblemen incumbent upon the king for the varied luxuries of noble life. Thus a small priestly bureaucracy under the authority of a sacred king resided at Mbanza Kongo. The nobility, except those who served as the provincial governors of rural regions, typically lived in urban centers. This bureaucracy collected rents, enforced the rule of law, and managed life in town centers as well as in outlying village settlements. Like noble status, the throne was not inherited. Instead, a royal council elected the king from a set of noblemen, each with his own claims to the throne based on lineage, marriage, and status. Because they were connected by marriage and lineage, the nobility formed a cohesive social unit, though competition and aggression marked the relationship between various noble families, especially in cases of royal succession.[10]

As for social organization, three well-defined social strata existed: nobility, villagers, and slaves. War captives made up the latter group, though not all slaves were subject to the transatlantic slave trade. Instead, the Kongolese drew distinctions between domestic slaves and trade slaves, the former being attached to noble houses or Catholic missions.[11] Domestic slaves were not subject to export and generally resided within their own clans. They could be liberated over time and they often came to be regarded as family members. Trade slaves, on the other hand, were acquired through wars or at market and were subject to sale and export. In fact, many used slaves as a form of currency, a mobile and easily transferable unit to be traded for goods and services.[12]

In its earliest development, the trade in slaves between Kongo and Portugal remained modest. Portuguese traders procured relatively few captives during the late fifteenth and early sixteenth centuries. For Kongo's King Afonso, these slaves were legally captured and could be used rightfully for monetary exchange. Afonso monopolized the commodity exchange with the Portuguese, effectively locking other titleholders and provincial lords out of the trade. As a result, Afonso's inferiors (royal officials and lords) depended on the monarch for Western trade goods. For their part, Portuguese traders, few in number in Kongo at this point, depended on Afonso to supply slaves.[13]

Beginning in the sixteenth century, the Atlantic slave trade became an increasingly important function for Kongo's government. Steadily increasing demand from New World plantations along with the growing influence of European merchants in the body politic and commercial in Kongo rendered ultimate control of the trade difficult for Afonso. Individual Kongo traders in the town center as well as in the provincial areas circumvented the king by providing slaves directly to the Portuguese, thereby securing better terms than had been possible under Afonso's monopoly. The direct trade between Portuguese and Kongo traders threatened Afonso's centralized network and weakened his position. Without a royal monopoly, slave raiding in Kongo's outlying areas increased unchecked, a matter of great concern for the monarch.

As the volume of the trade increased, and when African traders illegally captured and sold members of his own family along with other nobles to Portuguese merchants, Afonso vociferously opposed the Atlantic trade. In a 1526 letter to Portuguese heads of state, Afonso railed against Portuguese traders in the region, noting their brutality and licentiousness. He attempted to make the trade illegal in Kongo and expressed his conviction that as far as the Luso-Kongo trade was concerned, Kongo had need only of priests, teachers for the schools, and materials necessary for sacraments.[14] Afonso's words fell on deaf ears, however, and the trade imposed itself to an even greater degree in the country. Eventually, Afonso redoubled his efforts to develop a royal monopoly over the trade. He appointed a council comprised of several members of the nobility whose purpose was to assure that all slaves sold to Portuguese traders were legally captured and rightfully subject to sale.[15] Afonso's council proved ineffective in preventing the escalation of illicit commerce, however, and Portuguese traders showed themselves adept at evading the council and its officers. Throughout the sixteenth century and certainly well into the seventeenth, Kongo kings wrote to papal authorities as well as to European heads of state in unsuccessful attempts to rectify the harmful effects of the slave trade.[16] In the end, the trade in slaves perverted indigenous forms of forced labor, causing the transport of hundreds of thousands westward to the Americas.[17]

The high demand for labor on American plantations during the seventeenth and eighteenth centuries had the overall effect in Kongo of exacerbating the social and economic differences between the nobility who were enriched by the trade and the villagers and slaves who were its victims. European traders, missionaries, and officials, first Portuguese and Dutch, then English and French, allied themselves with leading clans in the country, which came to form what may be termed militaristic-political parties competing not only for influence at royal court but also for access to profits garnered from the slave trade. They established factories along the coast from which they negotiated terms and secured captives.[18] Military and political alliances shifted throughout the period as Kongolese traders, including many from Kongo's lesser nobility, played the various powers off of one another. These developments played an important role in the gradual decentralization and reorganization of Kongo's political and social structure, especially during the second half of the seventeenth century.

In the end, the Kongo throne failed to maintain its stance at the top of the redistributive network. Foreign invasions from Kongo's eastern boundary, civil war, succession battles, and outside pressure from European interests, especially the Portuguese, who established colonies south of Kongo in Angola, led the country into a period of prolonged war in the mid-seventeenth century that left the capital abandoned. The slave trade contributed greatly to the decentralization of the Kongo state, and the national interest of the country, as it were, ceased to exist throughout much of the eighteenth century.[19] Instead, local and regional factions emerged and competed with each other for wealth, prestige, and power.[20] The control of caravan routes, markets, access to foreigners, and the circulation of prestige goods such as slaves and ivory created intense and violent conflict. Slave exports rose throughout the eighteenth century and remained high until the mid-nineteenth century.

While the Portuguese controlled the southern port at Luanda, British traders, who entered the fray in West-Central Africa relatively late, focused their attention northward at Loango, where, between 1660 and 1793, an estimated one million slaves were sent to varied New World locations.[21] Competition escalated throughout the period as other ports, including Malemba, Boma, Cabinda, Cape Lopez, and the Gabon Estuary, entered the trade. The slave trade became formalized during the seventeenth and eighteenth centuries such that trade networks extending well into the West-Central African interior were supported by well-established pricing structures and professional traders. Closer to the coast, existing legal and political systems were perverted in order to maximize the number of captives available for sale and transport, and raiding and kidnapping occurred on the slaving edge.

West-Central Africa in the Lowcountry

The importation of West-Central African captives into the Lowcountry began in earnest during the eighteenth century and continued not only until the end of legal trading in 1808 but also through the nineteenth century via illegal slaving. The importation rates for captive Africans during this period reveal periodic shifts in volume and concentration. Thus while the aggregate numbers and percentages of enslaved Africans into the region for the entire era of slaving are important, the historical exigencies of that trade—its waves, peaks, and flow—is perhaps best understood by dividing the trade into three successive periods.

Slave importation into the Lowcountry during the early period, 1700–1740, coincided with the initial settlement of the region. The earliest settlers in the Lowcountry arrived from Barbados and Jamaica and included planters who wanted to establish West Indian-style plantation slavery in British North America. To begin the work of clearing lands and planting fields, these planters brought their slaves from the Caribbean. Direct importation from Africa began in the early eighteenth century and increased during the 1720s and 1730s. During this early period, West-Central Africans predominated among Lowcountry slaves as British traders established themselves along the coast of West-Central Africa, providing a steady supply of captive Africans (see table 1). Indeed, English slaving vessels delivered more West-Central Africans to the Lowcountry than to any other American locale, including Jamaica and Barbados, during the second quarter of the eighteenth century.[22]

Charleston served as the primary port for all Africans brought to the Lowcountry, and an estimated 60 percent of Charleston's African imports during the 1720s and 1730s were from Kongo's Cabinda port.[23] This trend continued during the 1730s and 1740s, when nearly half of all imports into South Carolina originated from West-Central Africa. The 1730s and 1740s witnessed tremendous importation of labor from Africa coupled with little natural increase. As a result, by 1739 less than half of South Carolina's black population had been in the New World for more than ten years.[24] Moreover, the five-year period between 1735 and 1740 witnessed an astonishing predominance of West-Central African importation, with 70 percent of all African imports into the Lowcountry coming from that region.[25] Enslaved Africans in the Lowcountry achieved an early numerical majority in South Carolina, and by 1740 the black population was roughly twice the size of the white population.[26] The effect of the increasing numbers of Africans in the region can be surmised by a statement made by Samuel Dyssli, a Swiss settler, who suggested in 1737 that Carolina "looks more like a negro country than like a country settled by white people."[27]

During the middle period of African importation into the region, 1741-1787, planters came to rue the high concentration of West-Central Africans among South Carolina's slave population. This period began soon after the 1739 Stono Rebellion, which erupted only twenty miles from the commercial and political capital at Charleston. When colonial officials discovered that the leadership and much of the membership of the rebellion featured West-Central Africans, they deemed it prudent to reduce the numbers of Africans in the colony and levied a series of duties to decrease the numbers of direct imports from Africa.[28] These measures, however, enjoyed only mixed success. African importation into the region slowed considerably for approximately ten years, but the trade resumed during the 1750s, when rice production exploded and indigo plantations emerged. Margaret Washington and Peter Wood argue effectively that during the middle period of slave importation, South Carolina's planters drew on a more diverse group of Africans, especially those from Senegambia and Sierra Leone, whose experience with rice cultivation proved critical in the production of South Carolina's first cash crop. Planters increasingly expressed preferences for Africans from the rice-producing regions of West Africa. At the same time, they expressed uneasiness regarding the importation of West-Central Africans, due in no small measure to the fearful memories many planters held of the Stono uprising.

Indeed, during this period, Senegambians comprised nearly 27 percent of all Africans of known origin imported into the Lowcountry (see table 2). Moreover, captives from Sierra Leone and the Gold Coast were also well represented among the colony's enslaved population during the second half of the eighteenth century. While Africans from rice-producing regions were desired for their productive capacities, they contributed much to the cultural and social landscape of the Lowcountry. For example, Margaret Washington detailed the special role West Africans played in the early spread of Baptist theology and conversion in the region.[29]

Table 2. Percentage of Africans from various regions imported to the Lowcountry in various periods

Region of origin	1700–1740	1741–1787	1788–1808	1700–1808
Benin				
% of all imported Africans	0.00	2.39	1.00	1.46
% of imported Africans of known origin	0.00	2.66	1.29	2.49
Biafra				
% of all imported Africans	9.14	8.67	3.26	6.69
% of imported Africans of known origin	16.49	9.65	4.32	11.43
Gold Coast				
% of all imported Africans	1.34	13.94	8.92	9.93
% of imported Africans of known origin	2.42	15.50	11.98	16.97
Kongo-Angola				
% of all imported Africans	36.20	16.21	40.71	28.88
% of imported Africans of known origin	65.33	18.03	52.86	49.37
Senegambia				
% of all imported Africans	8.51	24.27	4.71	14.19
% of imported Africans of known origin	15.36	26.99	6.12	24.26
Sierra Leone				
% of all imported Africans	0.00	13.36	10.32	9.98
% of imported Africans of known origin	0.00	14.86	13.41	17.06
Southeast Africa				
% of all imported Africans	0.00	0.31	0.72	0.41
% of imported Africans of known origin	0.00	0.34	0.94	0.71
Windward Coast				
% of all imported Africans	0.22	10.76	7.37	9.98
% of imported Africans of known origin	0.39	11.96	9.57	13.18
Unknown				
% of all imported Africans	44.59	10.09	22.99	26.19

Source: Data from David Eltis, Stephen Brehendt, David Richardson, and Herbert Klein, eds., *The Trans-Atlantic Slave Trade: A Database on CD-ROM* (New York: Cambridge, 1999).

Planters were not able to rid themselves entirely of enslaved Africans from the Kongo-Angola region, who constituted a sizable minority during the middle period, though the actual number of Kongolese captives imported during the period decreased significantly. Because of the early demographic dominance of West-Central Africans, neither the increased importation of Africans from Senegambia and Sierra Leone nor the planters' reticence about importing Kongo-Angolans eliminated the West-Central African contingent, which remained the single largest geographical cohort among all slaves in the Lowcountry.[30]

During the late period of slave importation, 1787–1808, planters once again increased slave importation in response to the introduction of large-scale production of short-staple cotton in the late eighteenth and early nineteenth century, and Kongo-Angola emerged, once again, as the primary source for enslaved Africans. During the first decade of the nineteenth century, one-third of all enslaved Africans brought to the Lowcountry came from West-Central Africa.[31] During the three-year stretch from 1804 to 1807, more than half of the slaves imported into South Carolina were from the Kongo-Angola region.[32] Nearly 40 percent of Africans enslaved and brought to South Carolina between 1733 and 1807 came from Kongo-Angola.[33] While the actual numbers of enslaved Africans imported into the Lowcountry during the period of illegal slave trading is difficult to assess, many of the captives taken during this period were West-Central Africans.[34] In 1858, the slave ship *Wanderer* took on a cargo in West-Central Africa of five hundred captives. The four hundred survivors of the trip arrived in Georgia and made their owner, Charles Lamar, quite a profit. Though Lamar was arrested for carrying and selling his illicit shipment, he was eventually acquitted of all charges due to the reluctance of an all-white jury to convict one of their own. Lamar subsequently repurchased the *Wanderer* at public auction and resumed his slave-trading ventures until his death during the Civil War.[35]

West-Central Africans constituted a demographic majority in the Lowcountry throughout the period of legal slaving. Though this majority was especially pronounced in the early period and the late period of slave trading, Kongolese captives were still well represented during the middle period, despite slaveholders' stated preferences for Africans from the rice-producing regions of West Africa. But demography does not, in itself, resolve the critical questions related to cultural formation. As units of historical analysis, demography and culture are not coterminous. One may not reduce cultural formation to a mere matter of percentages, deducing, for example, that because West-Central Africans constituted nearly one-third of all Africans shipped to the Lowcountry, they therefore contributed one-third of the cultural elements and practices exhibited in Lowcountry black culture. While demography is critically important, this study situates it within a larger discussion of the subtle and elusive nature of culture and identity formation for slaves in the antebellum period.[36]

The Lowcountry

The country into which African captives were brought was incredibly rich and diverse, a point to which early observers made extensive reference. Francis Asbury, noted Methodist minister, observed the oaks, palmettos, and junipers that dotted the landscape and was awe struck by the "beautiful deep sands . . . lofty pines and twining Jessamine flinging its odours far and wide."[37] The Georgia and Carolina coastal plain comprises a region of low-lying pineland that runs parallel to the beaches of the Atlantic Coast. As one approaches the coast from these woodlands, the Lowcountry emerges, bound on the north by Georgetown, South Carolina, with its deep swampy region, through Port Royal and St. Helena, down through Savannah to Brunswick, Georgia, in the south (see map 2). A maze of rivers and streams cut into and across the coastline, which over the course of time have carved out a set of islands that lie just off the coast proper. Harvesting the famed "sea-island" cotton produced in the region, and before that, extensive rice fields, Lowcountry planters—some of the wealthiest planters of the antebellum period—called this region home. Rice production required intensive labor and, subsequently, a relatively large number of workers such that even the more modest rice plantations claimed upward of thirty slaves. Larger estates often housed hundreds of bondsmen.

Rice production, Carolina's first cash crop, flourished in the swampy regions of the Lowcountry, but planters preferred to take up residence in nearby urban centers, considering it essential to their health, especially during the summer, as a protection against miasma—the environmental condition thought to cause malaria.[38] As noted above, Charleston and Savannah served as the commercial centers of these plantations and imported enslaved Africans throughout the period of slavery.[39]

The consistent presence of a black majority, the continual and extended importation of captive men and women from Africa and the Caribbean, and the geographic isolation of the Sea Islands have led some scholars to render a portrait of the Lowcountry as unique in comparison to other areas in the American South.[40] Writing in *Rehearsal for Reconstruction*, Willie Lee Rose notes that the "special peculiarities of topography and

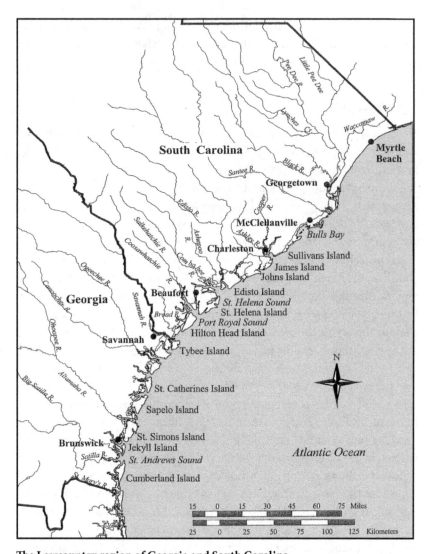

The Lowcountry region of Georgia and South Carolina

Adapted from William Politzer, The Gullah People and Their African Heritage *(Athens: University of Georgia Press, 1999), 5.*

climate had served over the years to isolate the island country from the mainland."[41] Some scholars regarded this isolation as something greater than a matter of mere topography and climate. Well into the twentieth century, the Lowcountry was regarded by some as not only separated from the mainland by a crosshatch of rivers and streams but also isolated in time, stuck somewhere in a yesteryear of antebellum mansions, wealth, and leisure. Writing in 1940, Mason Crum noted: "About these modest islands there is a serene beauty almost beyond description. One who visits them with a view to finding sophisticated pleasures or, indeed, anything modern meets nothing but disappointment. No signs of progress are evident. The islands are like lavender and old lace; and he who does not love old things and the mellowing process of time should not visit them. The Carolina Sea Islands are backward looking; they have no interest in the future."[42]

When, in the early twentieth century, the study of black culture, folklore, and language enjoyed increasing popularity among academics, some anthropologists, historians, linguists, and others, approached the Lowcountry as a "laboratory" in which black men and women—former slaves and their descendants—could be studied in a presumed natural and pure state. Indeed, some considered blacks part of the natural environment of the region. As one observer noted, "[The Negro] is authentic Southern atmosphere."[43] Even more, some interested researchers deemed Lowcountry blacks less diluted, assimilated, and acculturated than blacks elsewhere in the country. They were perceived as more African, more authentically and genuinely black. C. R. Tiedman, when writing in the 1930s about the Lowcountry for the WPA, concluded:

> The isolation of these sea island plantations in a great measure helped to preserve the characteristics that mark the Gullah Negro so indelibly as a group apart from all others. They lived together, segregated in their own quarters, seldom if ever coming into contact with any one beyond the plantation overseer and the family to whom they belonged. Thus, their whole body of traditions, superstitions, language and mental background were handed down practically unchanged. . . . [They] are easily distinguishable from Negroes of any other locality, not only by their speech but they retain to a marked degree the character of their origin, being a picturesque type of rather low mentality . . . steeped in the art of black magic and superstitions practiced by their ancestors . . . untouched by a changing world."[44]

The notion that Lowcountry blacks represented perfect anthropological subjects, frozen in time, led to a concern for documenting these "authentic plantation Negroes" and their way of life. Folklorists transcribed tales, ethnograhers recorded spirituals, and linguists transliterated Gullah—a newly defined language. Indeed, the very term "Gullah" has been the source of considerable debate for historians, folklorists, linguists, and anthropologists interested in black culture in the Lowcountry. For some, "Gullah" is an abbreviated form of "Angola," which would be consistent with the import data of enslaved Africans. For others, the term refers to the Gola tribe of the Windward Coast, a notion more consistent with planters' expressed preference for slaves from rice-producing regions.[45] The debates related to the term's origin are critical because they may be wielded to both validate and invalidate claims regarding black culture in the region. For present purposes, I am less interested in etymological debates and more inclined to suggest that both sources—Gola and Angola—contributed to the development of "Gullah." This stance is consistent with the fact that Gullah vocabulary and syntax includes elements from various West African locales, from Senegambia in the North southward into Kongo-Angola.[46]

Many of the early studies of the region were attended by a sense of urgency and a concern with preserving a cultural heritage presumably on the verge of collapse under the impending weight of modernity.[47] Dubose Heyward, who wrote extensively on black culture in the Lowcountry, lamented what he saw as an inevitable cultural loss: "And the plantation Negro, too, will pass. The rhythm of our National life, so alien to him at first, will eventually possess him. . . . For the Negro in the mass, the call of the city has already been heeded. The migration has commenced. The old, uncomplicated pattern of life is broken. The forces of advancement are at work and will prove irresistible. They will be taken from our fields, fired with ambition, and fed to the machines of our glittering new civilization."[48] Indeed, the very pace at which these changes were being wrought shocked some observers, who felt that the progress of a thousand years had been collapsed into a few generations. One observer noted, "We catch glimpses of a transit in three generations from unlettered superstition to responsive and discriminating play of intelligence. We watch the shift from conjuror and charms to island doctor and nurse and clinic."[49]

Some recent scholarship has complicated our understanding of Gullah culture as distinct and unique. In contradistinction to the image of the Lowcountry in general and the Sea Islands in particular as isolated, Ras Michael Brown argues that the extensive network of streams and rivers that ran through the region "united the entire seaboard into a single, cohesive realm."[50] In fact, most aspects of life in the Lowcountry were oriented toward the waterways that fed the Atlantic and linked every planter to the bustling ports of Charleston and Savannah. Extensive roadways connected plantations by land, and even failing access to roads, slaves proved adept at traveling through the dense woods that separated the seaboard from the interior.[51]

Ironically, many of the anthropologists, historians, folklorists, and ethnographers who recorded the lives and cultures of blacks in the Lowcountry depended on the special and unique character of the region to bolster the importance of their own scholarly work. The question of the singular authenticity of the Lowcountry was certainly an important matter for E. C. L. Adams, a well-known physician turned folklorist whose collections of black folklore contains some of the richest material yet transcribed. Much in the antebellum plantation tradition, Adams often entertained guests in his home with varied sorts of "Negro entertainment," performed not by professionals but by "local blacks who knew how to put on an unprettified Congaree show."[52] One reviewer of Adams's first collection of black folklore, *Congaree Sketches,* makes clear the importance of authenticity, noting that "here we have, at last . . . etched with dry point and to the palpitating life, the real Negro of the field and swamp. He is not the made up Negro, the masqueraded and synthetic Negro." For this reviewer, blacks, as presented by Adams, could be easily differentiated from other, presumably "synthetic" types often described in the collections of other folklorists. Adams's Negro was

> not the Negro of the Black Border, the Gullah; nor the Negro of Harris, nor of Julia Peterkin, nor of Dubose Heyward. To see him one must plunge into the slime and mud of the Congaree Swamps, or creep about their tangled edges, and then know what to look for—the Negro brutalized into a semi-civilization yet not purged of his African inheritance of voodoo and fetish and cunjuh. Let this Negro forget, as he would in a week, his little scrappy English speech, and throw him back into the Kongo jungles—and he would hardly know he had ever left them. He is still a portion of Africa, torn from her side, the flesh still dripping with dark blood.[53]

Julia Peterkin, a well-known southern writer, won fame for her works of folklore and fiction, which presented presumably authentic renditions of black life. Indeed, many regarded the singular perspective of southern whites as absolutely essential in penetrating, translating, and ultimately transcribing the supposed opacity of black life. Writing in reference to *Green Thursday,* a collection of short stories and folktales compiled by

Peterkin, one reviewer noted that the author "lives on a plantation, isolated from the white world, surrounded only by negroes. She has always known them; she looks at them with marvelous sympathy." Lest the reader of that review presume that Peterkin's proximity to her subjects ruined her objective and dispassionate rendering of black life, however, the reviewer continued, noting that "her viewpoint isn't warped by the hysterical Boston attitude—bastard of the abolition days—that, if anything, niggers are better than white people. She penetrates their childishness, their superstitions, and their basic savagery, but does not forget their amiability."[54] At least one reviewer of Peterkin's work highlighted the paradox of her professional endeavors. In reference to Peterkin's fiction, famed poet and literary critic Sterling Brown wrote, "One merely has the uncomfortable suspicion that she has harvested what she preferred, and that there are teeming fields still awaiting the sickle. . . . She has carefully studied a certain section of Negro life, restricted in scope and in character, and she has revealed skillfully and beautifully and from a single point of view the results of her study."[55] Responding to *Roll, Jordan, Roll,* a collection of folklore based on the lives of the black men and women who labored on Peterkin's plantation, Brown notes further that "in her personal dealings with the people on her plantation she is in all likelihood a kindly mistress. But kindliness is not enough. These people pay for their quaintness by their—at best—semi-enslavement. And even for quaintness, this is too much too ask."[56]

By drawing critical attention to the presumed exceptionality of Lowcountry life and culture, I do not mean to ignore the distinguishing elements of the region. That the demography, climate, and historical trajectory of the region contributed to the development of particular cultural elements in the region is well established. I am less convinced than some, however, that these conditions created not only certain historical particularities but also historical peculiarities as compared to the rest of the slave South. Rather than treating black culture in the Lowcountry as a historical anomaly, we might regard it otherwise, namely, as reflective of a larger African American culture that developed in the United States during the antebellum period. In this way, conclusions drawn from the Lowcountry, rather than reflecting the historical oddities of an outlandish place, may help us understanding black cultural production and identity formation throughout the region under investigation. How, for example, should our knowledge of Lowcountry burial rites affect our interpretation of the Negro Burial Ground in New York City? Or how might investigations of Sea Islands folk medicine contribute to our understanding of the same in Florida, Mississippi, or Louisiana? To regard Lowcountry slave culture as isolated and quaint is to delimit any discussion of the manner in which it might be related to other American and Atlantic locales. In its transnational orientation, the notion of an African Atlantic religious complex disrupts the idea that slave cultures and national boundaries are coterminus, highlighting instead linkages across various regions and nations.

2

Saline Sacraments, Water Ritual, and the Spirits of the Deep

CHRISTIAN CONVERSION IN KONGO AND ALONG THE SEA ISLANDS OF THE DEEP SOUTH

Sarah was a slave; and a dutiful one at that. When Sarah spoke, she comported herself with all of the deference demanded by the master class: "'Your servant, massa; your servant missus.' Then a pause, and the hands meekly folded before her."[1] She was well liked and highly regarded by members of the master class:

> Sarah was not, and from the circumstances could not have been, a romantic or sentimental creature, full of fancies and vagaries, and artfully seeking to impose her visions and dreams upon more simple and credulous people. Such a physiological embodiment as hers never developed much fancy, and such a life-history of toils and hardening processes would have effectually eliminated any tendencies to cultivate the romantic, had her nature been by any possibility receptive. Her face was altogether honest, with its deeply marked lines of suffering; and her whole expression clearly evinced those plain, practical, sensible qualities which had gained her so good a reputation.[2]

Still, Sarah's Christian faith was peppered with occasional paroxysms, which she termed "mazes." During one incident, Sarah rose from her quarters during the midnight hour and, in a fit of screams and shrieks, entered the "Big House" and burst into the bedroom of the plantation's owner, minister Charles Raymond. He recalled Sarah's screams as the most "agonizing groans ever vented by tortured humanity." Sarah stood dazed, with her eyes glassy, her hands extended before her, and her visage shrouded with a lifeless hue. In a moment she collapsed prone on the floor and said, "O Lord, I'm damned! O master, I'm in hell! O Jesus, do save me." So she continued for thirty minutes, "bathed in a cold sweat, and with pulse scarcely perceptible, until at last her agony ceased from utter prostration." Morning arrived, and once again fully in control of her faculties, Sarah reported, without suspense or apology, that she had simply had one of her "mazes."

Given Sarah's usual disposition, Raymond could scarcely make sense of the outburst: "So quiet! So sensible! So undemonstrative! How had good old Sarah ever been the subject of such a vagary?" When the second maze hit Sarah in broad daylight, Raymond was forced to concede that the fits were "no somnambulistic feat, growing out of disordered digestion or incipient dyspepsia. The physical theorists upon the subject were nonplussed." If the theorists were confused, the same may not be said of Sarah, who knew that the mazes were directly related to the unconverted condition of her soul. When Sarah's mistress attempted to educate her in the manner of proper Christian conversion, to assure her that "mazes" played no part in the path of religious redemption, Sarah responded curtly that white folks were different from "colored" persons. Only after Sarah's third maze did she finally came through jubilantly with the certainty that, having seen hell, she had been taken to Jesus to have her sins forgiven: "Sins all gone, bress de Lord! Leff um down dere under dat tree. Amen! Bress de Lord! Took 'emself right out'n 'emself." So was Sarah converted, and her bouts with the mazes ceased.[3]

Recounting her own experience, Elizabeth Roberts, a former slave of the Georgia coastal islands, reported that it was the water that washed the sins away, and so, she said, baptism must be performed when the tide is going out. Roberts recalled that as converts congregated along the river bank for the ritual, they did not direct their prayers to the Father, Son, and Holy Spirit; rather, the preacher prayed to the river, asking that all sins be taken away, noting that the water washed all sins away.[4]

This chapter focuses on the complexities and subtleties that often attend ritual belief and practice. It does not posit conversion as a clear and discrete movement from a precessional realm of belief to a successional one. Indeed, conversion rarely entails the complete abandonment of former belief systems, nor does it imply a total embrace of new spiritual theologies. The notion of conversion as discrete movement wrongly suggests that older beliefs are too rigid to negotiate a changing spiritual environment and presumes that new belief systems are impregnable, unaffected by older notions. Instead, the "new" belief system is understood largely through the context of the "old." That is, the precessional belief system does not simply replace the successional, and the former is not simply discarded. Rather, a notable adaptability of belief most marks conversion whereby older belief systems affect the newer and vice versa. This notion of conversion is complicated all the more when one considers that even religions that differ quite widely may contain significant similarities with respect to notions of God, the afterworld, or ritual. Different religions, in fact, may overlap in important ways such that clear distinctions between one realm of belief and another, between an old belief system and a new one, may be difficult to locate.

The Christian conversion of Sarah and her fellow slaves reflect one instance in a broader African Atlantic negotiation with the Christian faith that occurred at various times and in varied locales throughout the Atlantic world.[5] Through a comparative analysis, this chapter addresses the manner in which Africans in Kongo as well as their counterparts in the New World interacted with Christianity and baptism, navigating similar issues of coercion, conversion, and belief. On both sides of the Atlantic, the faithful proved adept at resolving and amending Christian doctrine and dogma in line with their own cosmological conceptions and with the immediacy of their own condition. Religious doctrine and practice in the two locales reveal such malleability that under the general rubric of Christianity, one witnesses widely variant rituals and rites. One notes in this chapter at least five different forms of Christian practice, including (1) European missionary efforts in Kongo under the aegis of papal authority; (2) Kongolese Christianity, which acted as a state-sanctioned and urban-based ritual movement associated with the royal court; (3) rural-based peasant practice in Kongo, which operated as a theology of resistance and ritual protection against the slave trade; (4) Protestant missionary efforts in the Lowcountry, which worked in concert with slaveholding interests; and (5) a slave theology, which developed in the antebellum period in coastal Georgia and South Carolina and sought to mobilize the slave body and behavior away from the pains and oppressions of the master class.

Throughout the eighteenth and nineteenth centuries, the dynamics of the slave trade and related historical events connected each of these articulations of Christianity. Writing in reference to the religion of slaves along coastal Georgia and South Carolina, one scholar maintains, "The mere fact that a people *profess* to be Christians does not necessarily mean that their Christianity is of the same type as our own. The way in which a people interpret Christian doctrines depends largely upon their secular customs and traditions of the past. There is an infinite difference between the Christianity . . . of whites and colored, due in the main to their different modes of life and social backgrounds."[6] To be a Christian or a convert in such a complicated religious landscape is neither simple nor obvious.

There are no clear binaries that may be used to explain the religious faith or practice of any of the peoples treated in this chapter, no Manichean distinctions between the converted and the unconverted, the faithful and the heretic. As a result, our notions of what it means to be a Christian, or to be converted, must be malleable.

As noted above, Kongo and the Lowcountry were intimately linked for centuries by the dynamics of the slave trade, and many of the victims of the trade in Kongo found themselves enslaved along the coastal region of Georgia and South Carolina.[7] Catholic missionaries in Kongo had exposed at least some enslaved Africans to the tenets of Christianity through their work in Kongo. In fact, Protestant missionaries in South Carolina occasionally described black spirituality as a curious superstition reminiscent of Catholicism. Thomas Turpin, one such missionary, encountered a relatively isolated group of slaves along the South Carolina Sea Islands in 1834, whereupon he noted that they had "societies organized among themselves; and that those societies were very corrupt, and appeared to be very much under the influence of Roman Catholic principles; and . . . they did penance."[8] Christian Oldendorp, a Moravian clergyman and poet, interviewed hundreds of West Indian slaves during the late eighteenth century and noted that "the Negroes from the *Congo* nation who came to the West Indies have, for the most part, a recognition of the true God and of Jesus Christ" due to the role played by Portuguese and Italian missionaries.[9] Jane Landers documented similar developments in Spanish colonial Florida, where enslaved West-Central Africans, fleeing the plantations of Georgia and South Carolina, reported their exposure to Catholicism while in their homelands.[10]

The prior experience and exposure of some Africans to Christianity in Kongo undoubtedly colored their interactions with Protestant missionaries in the Americas. They likely drew upon a vocabulary of Christianity and of Christian conversion that developed in Kongo as early as the late fifteenth century and persisted through the era of the slave trade and into the antebellum period in certain New World plantation communities. This vocabulary of Christian conversion became significant when large numbers of Kongolese, held captive along the Sea Islands of the Georgia and South Carolina coasts, developed their own responses to Christianity in the New World. An understanding, therefore, of the experience of Christian conversion and baptism in Kongo is essential to any investigation of similar themes in the American South.

Christianity and the Kongo Court, 1491–1645

Christianity came to Kongo during the late fifteenth century, when Franciscan priests baptized King Nzinga a Nkuwu as João I in 1491. In the months and years immediately following the conversion of the king, many members of the royal court and nobility also adopted the faith. A Catholic church was constructed at Mbanza Kongo, capital of the country, and a number of European missionaries arrived in Kongo, offering sacraments and conducting mass. Still, European missionaries had some difficulty maintaining the faith in its early phases as many clerics perished in Kongo's tropical climate. Those hardy enough to withstand the climate suffered from a chronic shortage of priests with which to conduct effectively the business of conversion and maintenance of the faith. In fact, King João's conversion was rather short lived, and by the turn of the century, he ceased to practice as a Catholic, returning to indigenous Kongo beliefs.[11] Many members of the Kongolese elite again followed suit. The history of Christian conversion in Kongo may very well have ended there had it not been for João's son, Afonso. As it stands, however, the story of Christian conversion in Kongo has very much to do with Kongo rules of royal succession, visions in the sky, and the intervening hand of God in the lives of ordinary men.

Kongolese succession rules were not governed by primogeniture. Instead, candidates from competing royal clans sought endorsement from the court and provincial nobility. This support proved crucial because it ensured arms and men to fight the bloody battles that occasionally attended vacancies at the throne. Candidates able to amass larger and more powerful networks tended to win these battles and, eventually, the throne. These skirmishes could last for weeks and months as several would-be kings struggled for possession of the kingdom. In the interim, the throne remained vacant. Rather than compromising the ultimate stability of the kingdom, these battles proved decisive, affording newly invested monarchs significant power over recently defeated rivals.[12]

Evidence suggests that for Afonso, the battle for succession to the throne served as a testing ground between his own Christianity and the "pagan" ways of his brother. Unlike his father, Afonso remained steadfast in the Catholic faith: "We have renounced definitively all of the errors and idolatries in which our ancestors believed up until now. We have learned that our Lord Jesus Christ, human and divine, descended from heaven to earth to be made incarnate in the womb of the glorious Virgin Mary, his mother. For the well being of all mankind . . . he was killed upon a wooden cross in the city of Jerusalem, was buried and risen from the dead on the third day." [13]

Afonso believed that his own adherence to the Christian faith had placed him in conflict with his father and members of the Kongo elite, noting that "because we remained firm in the true faith . . . we were hated by the king (João I) and by the nobility of the kingdom." [14] The king had sent his son to oversee the governance of Nsundi, one of Kongo's provincial regions, and for the prince, the office at Nsundi represented an exile, distancing him from the more important matters occurring at central court. But rather than encouraging Afonso to fall more in line with the beliefs and rituals of the monarch, which by the turn of the century had moved well away from Catholic practice, this semi-exile only strengthened Afonso's resolve and faith. In fact, he suffered his position with great contentment and satisfaction because he saw it as a service to the Lord.

In 1509 Afonso learned that his father was very near death and that his brother, Mpanzu a Nzinga, had seized the throne with the blessings of the nobility and provincial lords. [15] Despite the distance, both political and religious, that separated Afonso from his father, the exiled prince still felt himself to be the only rightful heir to the throne. He felt that his brother had occupied the throne "in a manner indignant and against all justice." [16] Certain that he was the proper heir, Afonso left Nsundi for the capital city to "take possession of the kingdom according to the old customs," that is, through battle. [17] Afonso had determined that only Christians could join him on his trek to the capital, so when he arrived at the Mbanza Kongo his total force numbered only thirty-seven men. [18]

Afonso's difficulty in amassing a large army suggests the relative weakness of the Christian faith in Kongo at the turn of the sixteenth century. Still, his willingness to march to the capital and engage in battle, to pit thirty-odd Christians against a well-manned and well-armed force, suggests the power of his own personal faith in Christianity. When he arrived at the capital he found himself considerably outnumbered, facing an army of massive force. For Afonso, the ensuing battle had both political and religious implications. He knew full well that the people of Kongo, whom he described as "almost all infidels and idolaters," wanted to see his brother installed as king. Still, he found comfort in the certainty that "power does not reside in a large number of men, but in the will of the Lord. That's why we had confidence." [19] Afonso was sure that with the grace of God, "it was not necessary to have a large number of men."[20] He was convinced that God would grant him the victory against the infidels who had received the Gospel but turned away from God's good graces. So began the battle.

The soldiers exchanged arrows and swords until, suddenly and without warning, Afonso's opponents turned around and began to retreat desperately, though Afonso did not know the cause of their withdrawal.[21] He gave chase only to find that many in his brother's company had fallen dead. Afonso subsequently won the battle and the Kongo throne and determined immediately that the victory had been granted by divine intervention. He soon learned that his opponents had retreated due to the appearance in the sky of a tremendous vision. An image of St. Jacques, to whom Afonso had prayed for divine intervention just before the battle, had appeared in the sky mounted atop a horse and accompanied by a band of armed cavalrymen. In addition, a large white cross could be seen emblazoned in the heavens. These images had so frightened Mpanzu a Nzinga and his men that they forfeited the throne and retreated as quickly as possible. Afonso interpreted the victory as a miracle granted by God, and after the victory, he imprisoned Mpanzu a Nzinga and sentenced him to death.[22] Such an unlikely victory confirmed in Afonso the ultimate truth of the Christian faith.

Whether this story of divine intervention is apocryphal or not, Afonso certainly embraced it as a none-too-subtle warning to any would-be competitors of his divinely inspired mission. In this, Afonso's legitimation included the familiar trope of Christian victory over "heathens" used by rulers and soldiers alike in contexts as varied as the Crusades, the Boer War's Battle of Blood River in South Africa, or American Indian relocation policy. With Christianity as the new reigning political cult, Afonso found little difficulty in convincing his subordinates to adopt the religion, which they did in great numbers during the early years of the sixteenth century.

Although Afonso's victory had been confirmed by divine intervention, his position atop Kongo's throne was yet less than stable. As an outcast prince zealous in his adherence to an already discarded faith, who claimed neither manpower nor arms, his leadership would likely have been challenged by rivals. And yet Afonso (1506–43) enjoyed the longest and certainly one of the most important reigns in Kongo's history.[23] He devoted his initial energies to shoring up support for his rule. He made a deliberate effort to connect political power and influence with religious faith, and over his long reign he developed an impressive Christian state infrastructure that operated primarily among the royal court and provincial nobility. To begin the process, Afonso sent his son Henrique to Portugal to be educated in the Portuguese language, the classics, and the humanities. Henrique learned to speak Latin fluently, received training as a cleric, and eventually enjoyed promotion to the bishopric. In addition, Afonso constructed schools in the capital of the country devoted to the education of the nobility's children. These schools instructed students in the classics and trained them in the Christian faith. The success of these schools, which hundreds of students regularly attended, is well documented.[24] Afonso wrote persistently to papal authorities requesting building materials for the erection of new churches and schools, and he continued to ask that more missionaries be sent to Kongo to perform the sacraments.

Just as Afonso fomented an infrastructure of royal Catholic practice, he also engaged in an equally zealous program to rid the country of "infidels" and "idolaters." He actively "burned numerous idols" and waged a year-long campaign against a "fetish house" he desperately wanted to destroy.[25] Christianity, as practiced by Alfonso, may be understood as something of a ruling doctrine, a set of practices, rituals, and beliefs mobilized as a way of ensuring power and granting favor in direct opposition to competing practices. For Afonso, Christianity served as both a faith and a political campaign. By eliminating infidels, that is, would-be competitors for the throne, he ensured his own power base and developed that manner of support that had escaped him in his initial installation. For members of the royal elite, conversion to Christianity made clear political sense, especially at a time when the king was not only denouncing but also violently eradicating other practices. By the end of his reign in 1543, Afonso had effectively instituted Christianity as part of the body politic in the country, supported by a newly strengthened Christian church. His efforts to educate Kongo's young, his tireless attempts to suppress other ritual practices and his undying faith in Catholicism combined to establish Christianity in Kongo from the sixteenth century onward. Even fifty years after Afonso's death, the royal court continued to support Christianity. At his own installation, Alvaro II (1587–1614) announced himself: "Alvaro II, by the grace of God, augmenter of conversion to the faith of Jesus Christ."[26]

The Kongolese elite, however, did not accept the faith as presented by European missionaries at face value. Even as Christianity assumed increasing importance at court, Kongolese officials practiced it through their own cultural lens. Kongolese converts regarded Christian missionaries in much the same way as they did indigenous Kongolese ritual experts (*nganga*; pl. *banganga*) and demanded that they act accordingly. Just as *banganga* secured plentiful rains and bountiful harvests, so were Catholic priests expected to perform similar functions. When droughts struck Kongo in 1674, Kongo officials blamed Capuchin missionaries, arguing that while the converted regions of the country suffered, the so-called pagan districts enjoyed plentiful rains and harvests. This, the officials argued, was the direct result of several excommunications that the clergy had recently performed, and the officials demanded that the relevant parties be absolved. When the missionaries refused, they were summarily expelled from the area.[27] King Garcia II (1641–61) argued similarly in 1645 that several military defeats were God's way of punishing the kingdom for the sins of early leaders who had not been Christian. Fearful that the sins of the father were being visited upon the sons, Garcia II appealed to Rome in hopes that Kongo might be shielded from past iniquities. The pope fulfilled Garcia II's request, offering the kingdom an absolution and benediction for past transgressions.[28] These events suggest that ritual practice in Kongo, though under a Christian idiom, continued to respond to the immediacy of everyday life.

From its earliest introduction until the mid-seventeenth century, Christianity remained a faith closely associated with the royal court and provincial nobility. Kongo elite developed literacies in European languages, and Kongolese heads of state maintained regular correspondence with papal authorities and European monarchs. The nobility dispatched ambassadors to European metropoles to discuss matters of state and sent their children to be educated in the manners of Christianity. For their part, European missionaries arrived in Kongo, always woefully undermanned, to perform holy sacraments, install royal officers, and conduct Christian rituals.

Christianity in Kongo, 1645–1704

In the mid-seventeenth century Capuchin missionaries established churches and schools in the provincial areas that served primarily families of the nobility and the retinues of provincial lords. Though they operated in the rural sector, these schools and churches had little effect on the local populations, who remained largely illiterate well into the eighteenth century. Moreover, most ordained priests in Kongo came from the noble class.[29] Even during the eighteenth century, when the missionary establishment in Kongo was greatly decreased, Catholic informed ritual practice never entirely disappeared at court.[30]

While Christianity developed as a ritual cult closely connected to and controlled by the court, spiritual practice in the village sector operated differently. Kongolese monarchs enjoyed special access to the spiritual realm, which they used to justify their authority and empower other members of the ruling class. In the outlying village sectors, local religious leaders, called *kitome* (pl. *itome*), governed the spiritual life and well-being of the community. The *itome,* a network of community religious leaders that extended from the capital to the outlying areas, validated noble governance through ritual installation and ensured the safety and prosperity of each village community through the resolution of disputes and the maintenance of prosperity, community health, and rains. Other individuals, called *banganga* (sing. *nganga*), assured the individual health of any member who sought luck or protection from hardship. In effect, the king, *kitome,* and *nganga* all laid claim to spiritual access to the otherworld, and although their relationship was not explicitly contentious, the *kitome* and *nganga* could pose a potential threat to the king's ritual status.

It is in this context that missionaries introduced Christianity into the village sector during the mid-seventeenth century. For much of the sixteenth century, and well into the seventeenth, Kongo nobility opposed the practice of indigenous religion. As a result, villagers often regarded the arrival of Christianity as an intrusion upon local religious practice. Afonso regularly destroyed fetish houses and idols throughout the country. For Afonso, Christianity represented a type of royal doctrine that opposed other forms of ritual practice, and villagers often perceived of Christian missionaries as extensions of the central authority of the king. In fact, Catholic missionaries and adherents to indigenous belief often clashed. One missionary, Luca da Caltanisetta, suggested as much when he wrote, "At one point some men and women told my interpreter that my mission was evil because I showed myself to be an enemy of the 'feticheurs' and burned their idols; they added that they were unable to forsake the practices of their country. . . . They turned to the 'feticheurs' in order to get healing from the devil, honored in these idols. This response demonstrates the profound disposition of all inhabitants of this unfortunate kingdom of Kongo."[31]

Caltanisetta's statements highlight the contentious relationship between village inhabitants and the Christian clergy who acted as a new arm of the politico-religious power residing at central court. The burning of idols was important not only for Christian missionaries, bent on removing all traces of the devil from the Kongo countryside, but also for the Kongo court, intent on removing the potential for spiritual and religious competition from outlying areas. This state-sponsored campaign to rid the country of "feticheurs" further cemented the position of the king at the apex of Kongo's religious establishment, vested with special access to the spirit realm. When Capuchin missionaries arrived in Kongo in 1645, they sought actively to convert in the rural and outlying regions. The Kongolese regarded Capuchins and the Jesuits who preceded them as ritual experts on the order of an *nganga* and thus as representing a real threat, sanctioned by the king and ruling elite, against rural religious leaders.[32] Whereas the king encouraged the establishment of a priestly order over which he exerted considerable control, villagers often rebelled against the intrusion.[33]

Still, Capuchin missionaries proved themselves exceptionally successful with respect to the distribution of certain Christian sacraments, especially baptism. Unlike the Kongo nobility, whose introduction to the faith included instruction at school or attendance at mass, the village faithful experienced Christianity first and foremost in receiving baptism, which principally involved the conferring of salt sacrament.[34] Catholic baptismal ritual called for the priest to place a small amount of salt on the tongue, followed by holy water.[35] Though priests proved terribly unsuccessful in the conferring of other rites—marriage, confession, the last rites—they were successful with baptism, or the eating of salt, *yadia mungwa*, as it was called locally.[36] Caltanisetta acknowledged that the Kongolese referred to salt as the central aspect of the baptism and recounted the following story: "I was in the process of distributing salt to several people when heavy showers came; I told them to take shelter in some neighboring hut until the rain stopped, and afterwards to return for the rest of the ceremony. . . . They promised me that they would return, but, thinking themselves baptized, they did not reappear."[37] After having learned from that experience, Caltanisetta thought it necessary to administer the salt at the end of the ritual.

This is not to suggest, however, that the Kongolese attached no spiritual importance to water. To the contrary, a critical component of Kongolese perceptions of the otherworld included reverence for Simbi water spirits. These spirits, common especially in the relatively dry coastal zone, inhabited local rivers, streams, ponds, and other bodies of water. In fact, many Kongolese regarded them as pervasive and "made offerings to them whenever they approached water, crossed a ford with a strong current, [or] fished."[38] Notably, these spirits demanded obeisance, which they rewarded with fecundity, and deplored disobedience, which they punished with disease and death.[39] These spirits caused certain fatal diseases, often contracted in the rain, the victims of which would be ceremonially thrown into bodies of water, rather than being buried according to normal custom, for fear that failure to sacrifice them to the water would result in a cessation of the rains. Anne Hilton relates that in the seventeenth century, missionaries began insisting on burying the victims of these rain-borne afflictions, but if the rains subsequently failed, "the people dug them up and took them to the water."[40] The Simbi spirits could take human form but were easily detected due to certain physical abnormalities. Indeed, the Kongolese venerated albinos, dwarfs, twins, and cripples as Simbi spirits incarnate. Or Simbi spirits might attach themselves to healers, aiding them in their work to cure the sick.[41]

While the Kongolese had preexisting notions of the spiritual powers of water, no evidence suggests that they transferred their reverence for Simbi spirits onto the sprinkled water featured in the Catholic baptism, and European missionaries made no effort to encourage among their would-be converts any such connection. As a result, Kongolese villagers referred not to the cleansing power of water when describing baptism but to the power of the salt. In line with the general belief that evil people and spirits detested salt and would thus avoid a baptized person, they conceived of the salt and not the water as conferring the blessing of baptism.[42] When Capuchin priests recognized that villagers thought of baptism as a rite of protection from evil spirits, they attempted to break the association between salt and salvation. Their efforts failed miserably, as few were persuaded to accept the rite without the requisite salt.[43] During the last decades of the seventeenth century missionaries baptized as many as 340,000 in Kongo, with certain missionaries conducting upward of 50,000.[44] Bernardo da Gallo, a Capuchin missionary writing in 1710, noted that in the rural regions, people were baptized in great numbers, without having a true knowledge of the faith.[45] Da Gallo acknowledged that many among the village sector had a "true awareness" of the Christian faith and were, in fact, "*bons chretiens.*" He maintained that many others, even after having been baptized, never developed a true understanding of the faith and never "abandon[ed] their pagan customs"; as a result, "the evangelical seed" was "suffocated by diabolic discord, and never fully formed."[46]

Capuchin missionaries who traveled throughout the countryside conducted annual baptisms en masse, and local liaisons translated key Christian concepts—such as the Holy Bible, priest, God, excommunication, and the meanings of the cross—not only into local tongues but also into local cosmologies. In the translation of key Christian terms, the Kongolese developed iconographies and sacraments with multiple meanings, thereby molding Christianity toward Kongolese belief, ritual, and rite.[47] When translated into kiKongo, key Christian concepts took on a complexity of meaning not always understood by Christian missionaries. Itinerant Kongolese Christians, accompanied by European missionaries, traveled the countryside, translating key terms, spreading the gospel, and administering sacraments. This raises the very real possibility that communications occurred between the translator and the congregation without the knowledge of priests.[48]

European Christians adopted the kiKongo term for God, *nzambi*, to denote the Christian God.[49] The Kongolese term *nzambi* could mean "soul" or be used generally to refer to an ancestor or other deity.[50] In this way, the term *nzambi a mpungu*, meant to denote "God Almighty," connoted the first, highest, or greatest ancestor, deity, or spirit.[51] *Nzambi a mpungu* took much of its meaning from the context within which it operated. In the family the term referred to a maternal uncle or father; when used in an otherworldly sense, the term connoted the founder of the land of the dead—or an ultimate creative power. *Nzambi a mpungu* only carried meaning contextually, allowing the Kongolese faithful to interpret it variously.[52]

Moreover, Christian priests adopted the title *nganga*, thus using the term for indigenous Kongolese ritual experts, a group missionaries roundly dismissed as "fetishers." In that capacity they performed all of the rituals expected of that office, including providing individual charms for protection as well as consecrating and coronating kings. The activities over which Christian priests presided resembled analogous Kongolese rituals that shared the same essential vocabulary.[53] Missionaries translated the term *nkisi*, the indigenous term Europeans used to denote Kongolese "fetish cults," to mean "holy." As a result, there was no linguistic distinction between Christian religious practice and other indigenous rituals. One missionary, for example, described the experience he had as he approached a large group of people while walking along the road: "Big and small, man and woman, everyone yelled: *en ganga anquissi zambi ampong* [*nganga a nkisi nzambi a mpungu*] which means in their language 'holy priests of God.'"[54]

Similar difficulties attended the translation of other words. Missionaries translated "church" as *nzo a nkisi* or *nkisi* house, "Holy Bible" as *mukanda nkisi,* and "excommunicate" as *loka* (curse, conjure, bewitch).[55]

The villagers' desire for baptism and their concomitant opposition to a state-sanctioned Christianity may seem curious. The apparent paradox may be resolved, however, through an examination of the state of the Kongo kingdom during the latter seventeenth century. The era that began with the rule of Garcia II in 1641 and ended with the death of Pedro IV in 1718 marks a crucial period in the history of Kongo, when peasants and villagers found themselves in the midst of near-constant civil war, succession disputes, and Kongo's increasing involvement in the slave trade. The Battle of Mbwila in 1665, the most crucial conflict of the period, pitted the Kongo kingdom against Portuguese forces at Angola in a bitter boundary dispute in which Kongo's King Antonio I was killed along with other high-ranking nobles. The country subsequently fell into an extended period of bloody yet indecisive succession battles that rapidly deteriorated into decades of civil war. Most Kongolese, including the nobility, fled the capital city during this period as the highly centralized Kongo state all but dissolved. In the absence of centralized political authority, nobles and provincial lords established new allegiances in the latter part of the seventeenth century. The influence and power of these provincial warlords grew, as did internecine warfare and slaving activities and many of the nobles and ruling elite established commercial relationships with European traders on the coast vis-à-vis the slave trade. Through clientage networks and precarious alliances, these nobles waged intermittent and bloody battles throughout the outlying regions in hopes of supplying European traders on the coast with slaves. As a result, thousands of Kongo's villagers found themselves in the crossfire. Slaves were valuable commodities during this period for several reasons. Slaveholders could force bondsmen into agricultural labors, helping to provision warlords and soldiers or press them into military service, thereby increasing the fighting capabilities of warring factions. And increasingly, slave traders sent these captives into ever-growing transatlantic slaving networks in exchange for munitions and money.[56]

In this context, the villagers' widespread demand for baptism makes sense as a salt sacrament conceived as a protection against evil people and spirits. With baptism as its central rite, Christian conversion in Kongo clearly spoke to real and immediate concerns regarding the power and reprisals not only of evil witches, neglected deceased, and vengeful neighbors but also of powerful nobles and slave traders. More than ritual ablution, baptism, via the spiritual power of salt, protected the convert. And Christianity, the vehicle through which baptism was administered, served as the site for the adaptation of new spiritual information to very real and immediate conditions. Considering the political situation in Kongo from the mid-seventeenth century through the first quarter of the eighteenth century, the widespread popularity of baptism resonated for the many people who participated in the rite.

Many among Kongo's rural population perceived of the baptismal rite as something of a social leveler. Some sources contend that many Kongolese underwent the rite simply to win the prestige of being called "Dom," a title of respect afforded to the converted. If, as is true, the primary victims of the transatlantic trade came from the outlying rural regions, then some of the participants might have sought advantage in the assumption of a moniker of social prestige, hoping that it would afford some protection from the slave trade. Luca da Caltanisetta made the point quite strongly in 1697, when he wrote, "If it is true that the inhabitants of this kingdom want to be baptized, it is only for the power to be called Dom and not to be taken for pagans."[57] The connection that Caltanisetta made between baptism and power suggests that some Kongolese co-opted a ritual practice to achieve a deeply personal yet political end: protection from the slave trade through the social status afforded by baptism. The rural population certainly would have contrasted their own poverty and vulnerability against the relative prestige and power of Kongo's lords and provincial nobility, who raised armies and profited by capturing slaves and delivering them to Western traders along the Atlantic Coast. In the mid-seventeenth century, another priest, Giovanni Francesco da Roma, recounted his own experiences: "Everyone of them, no matter how poor, wants to be called by the title Dom."[58] For da Roma and other missionaries, the very idea that there were presumed titleholders among Kongo's poor and rural population was a matter ripe for ridicule and consternation. When a godfather requested of da Roma that he baptize a young boy under the title Dom Julien, the priest responded with a mixture of anger and hilarity and reprimanded the godfather for a request that he found utterly ridiculous.[59]

The village sector interacted with Christianity primarily in the conferring of baptism, a ritual that for them assured safety from witches and slave traders and freedom from the reprisals of evil spirits. The theology of the religion was translated into Kongolese spiritual notions in ways that significantly altered its meaning.[60] Moreover, the baptismal rite itself was conducted through a translator and performed for large groups of people at a time. The numbers of priests in Kongo remained woefully small, especially in the seventeenth and eighteenth centuries, and this situation was only exacerbated in outlying regions. Indeed, da Gallo maintained that there were some regions where "due to the small number of missionaries, many people pass their entire lives without hardly ever seeing a priest."[61] The adoption of some of Christianity's rituals by Kongolese in the rural sector—including baptism and the taking of social titles—must be regarded as markedly different from the experience of members of the Christian urban elite. As mentioned earlier, education in schools, training in seminaries, travel to European metropoles, and more regular contact with clergy characterized Christian conversion at court.

In this way, one notes the establishment of two rather distinct negotiations with the Christian faith in Kongo between the sixteenth and eighteenth centuries: one headquartered at central court and radiating outward through provincial lords and nobles and a second that operated in the rural and outlying regions of the state and was practiced by those who, as a response to the exigencies of the transatlantic slave trade, saw opportunities for protection and status in the ritual of baptism. In both instances, Christianity was, at best, a faith highly mediated by Kongolese notions of spirit and cosmos—so much so that conversion, such as it occurred in the country, "rarely involved any fundamental religious change."[62]

What did it mean, then, to be a Christian or a convert in such a complicated religious (not to mention political) landscape? Being baptized, especially in the village sector, did not preclude one from engaging in indigenous rituals, observing prior practices, or holding fast to other beliefs. Baptism in no way entailed the surrender of one form of ritual practice for another. Kongolese converts continually negotiated and tested Christian precepts and tenets against other ritual forms. Some of the elite may very well have studied Christian theology in Europe (one thinks here of Henrique, Kongo's first bishop), whereas others saw it as little more than a ritual protection.

Despite the varied complexities and subtleties associated with Christian conversion in Kongo, John K. Thornton contends "with confidence that a form of Christianity, practicing its local variations but recognized in Rome as orthodox and accepted by European priests operating in the country, had become the national religion of Kongo."[63] Notwithstanding the great degree of what he terms "syncretism" in the faith, Thornton maintains that because Catholicism did not arrive in Kongo through colonial agents (as was the case in most other African locales), Africans themselves determined the main contours of religious and theological translation and adaptation.[64] And so they did, transferring their own vocabularies of faith unto Christian ritual and rite. Thornton maintains that "Christianity 'conquered' Kongo peacefully—but at the cost of adapting itself almost wholly to Kongolese conceptions of religion and cosmology."[65]

But if this is so, then Thornton may have stretched the definition of "conversion" beyond its limit. The fact that Christianity in Kongo "adapted itself almost wholly" to Kongolese religious precepts and that Kongolese Christians rarely underwent any fundamental religious change raises several concerns. May a person who, after having been baptized in an outlying region of the country, be rightly regarded as a Christian even though he has not experienced any religious change and understands the primary rites and agents of the religion in terms of previous Kongolese rituals? The answers to this question raise other, equally compelling matters. Thornton notes that church leaders regarded much of Christian practice throughout Europe during the sixteenth and seventeenth centuries as highly unorthodox. The correlation of festivals of ancestor worship and Christian holidays as observed in Medieval Spain, for example, never oppugned the Spanish as valid Christians. In this sense, Thornton argues that to regard the Kongolese as anything less than Christian is to establish Europe, perhaps unwittingly, as the sole province of valid Christian expression, even when that expression controverts orthodox Roman Catholicism. However, to magnify the role, extent, and depth of Christianity in Kongo is to give short shrift to the persistence of traditional African religious expression, which continued to play a central role in the lives and belief systems of the Kongolese throughout the period for which Thornton regards Kongo as a Christian country.

Notably, Thornton argues for the validity of Kongolese Christianity by virtue of the fact that European missionaries considered it so. Even as they decried the persistence of Kongolese traditional religion in the expression of the faith, Thornton maintains that missionaries rarely argued that the presence of so-called fetishistic practice disqualified the Kongolese as Christians.[66] Because they were severely undermanned, European missionaries regularly wrote from Kongo to church authorities to request that additional priests be sent to the region to help with the massive work entailed in the conversion of the country. In this light, missionaries may have emphasized or even exaggerated the successes won in the numbers of baptisms or the degree to which the country was being converted.[67] Catholic missionaries in Kongo might even have overlooked the persistent "transgressions" of the Kongolese in the conversion process in official reports in order to give the overall impression that Christian conversion in the country was proceeding well enough, if only the work might be further supported by sufficient reinforcement.

Bernardo da Gallo's general assessment of the state of Christianity in Kongo during the early eighteenth century is, for example, quite dismal. He decried mass baptisms because many of the presumably converted had little or no true knowledge of the faith and as a result either continued to practice their own religion with some inflection of Catholic faith or abandoned Christian practice altogether. In a rather pointed passage, da Gallo expressed great concern for the veritable absence of European missionaries in some of Kongo's rural regions and for the Church of Kongo in general.[68] Blaming failed missionary efforts, da Gallo conceives of European missionaries as errant fathers to the nascent Kongo church: "The father who leads the church, instead of securing the child in the Catholic faith, turned his eyes to the left and so the church . . . began to fall back into ancient superstitions. The little children . . . due to a lack of evangelical sustenance were left to fall prey to all vices . . . and became the miserable slaves of the devil and the hell-fire." [69] Despite this rather dark portrayal, da Gallo still maintained that the Christianity of Kongo was a "true Roman Catholic Christianity, albeit seriously weakened" by a lack of sufficient numbers of missionaries to do the job.[70]

Notwithstanding the degree to which European missionaries may have exaggerated the prevalence of Christian conversion in Kongo, Thornton's assessment raises concerns for another reason. To regard European missionaries as the primary judges of valid conversion establishes them as the principle arbiters of the basic threshold of Christian conversion in Kongo. That some European missionaries accepted Kongolese religious expression as sufficiently Christian is a matter of great import, the merits of which must be weighed against Kongolese assessments of the same. This is true all the more in the face of evidence that the Kongolese themselves developed not only their own understandings of what constituted valid Christian conversion and ritual practice but also their own Christian theologies. In the life and significance of Dona Beatriz, treated below, one notes a particularly Kongolese interpretation of Christianity, its missionaries, and of baptism as its central conversion ritual.

The Kongolese Saint Anthony

Perhaps the most notable example of Kongolese Christianity was the eighteenth-century campaign of Kimpa Vita, baptized Dona Beatriz.[71] In August 1704 Kimpa Vita lay upon her bed, deathly ill. After seven days of violent sweats and wild visions, she resigned herself to imminent death. Then, as if by miracle, her sickness abated and calm was restored to the young girl through the image of St. Anthony, dressed like a Capuchin monk. Transfixed, the twenty-year-old woman listened and became possessed by the saint.

The tale of the young woman and her possession by St. Anthony soon spread to surrounding areas. She reported that St. Anthony had entered her head and replaced her own soul, thereby describing an experience consistent with Kongo cosmology, where those with special otherworldly sight often experienced visions and possession.[72] Indeed, the Kongolese often regarded illness as a spiritual summons such that a person afflicted with a particular disease might be initiated as an *nganga* specially suited to address that very sickness.[73] Dona Beatriz had already established herself as gifted when, as a child, she had a vision of two children, white in color, who came to play with her and give her gifts.[74]

Dona Beatriz further established her special gifts when she underwent initiation as an *nganga*, a process that formally invested her with the power to communicate with the other world. As an *nganga*, Beatriz could practice as a diviner or interpreter of dreams; she might see visions, hear voices, or experience possession while in trance, during which time beings from the other world might enter her head. In this way, the *nganga* traversed the parturition of otherworldly waters and entered the realm of the dead. In fact, Beatriz reported the repeated experience of death on Fridays and subsequent resurrection on Mondays, when she returned with special insights derived from the spirit world regarding Kongo.[75] As she experienced death and resurrection during this period, she consulted God during her absences from this world.[76]

Perhaps most striking, Dona Beatriz challenged the theology espoused by European missionaries. God had revealed to her a more accurate and thoroughly revised version of Christianity. Jesus was not born in Bethlehem but in the Kongo capital, Mbanza Kongo; Nazareth, the location of his baptism, was actually the northern Kongolese province of Nsundi. Moreover, Beatriz maintained that takula wood, whose bark produced a red dye used often in marriage and rites of passage ceremonies, was the blood of Jesus Christ. The color red in Kongo cosmology marked the interstitial space between the land of the living and the land of the dead. This association with the color red reflected the sunrise and sunset, the moments when the sun emerged from the land of the dead in the morning and returned there each evening.[77] St. Francis, Jesus, and Mary were all Kongolese according to Dona Beatriz, who maintained further that Mary, mother of Jesus, was descended from slaves. In a country embittered by decades of civil war and slave raiding, the notion that the Son of God was also of slave lineage must be seen as a veritable ideological and theological revolution for Dona Beatriz and her followers, and as a despicable blasphemy for European missionaries.

Dona Beatriz expressed deep concern for race relations and decried the Catholic Church for the lack of black saints in the church's pantheon. At the same time, however, she imagined a world without race. During an interview with Bernardo da Gallo, Dona Beatriz revealed herself as St. Anthony, to which da Gallo replied caustically, "So, what news do you bring from on high? . . . Tell me about heaven, are there any blacks from Kongo[?]"[78] Dona Beatriz responded that, in fact, there were blacks from Kongo in heaven, but that there is no color, neither black nor white in heaven, presumably portending an afterlife free of racism.[79]

In addition, St. Anthony revealed truer versions of the Ave Maria and Salve Regina to Dona Beatriz, the text of which she recited as follows:[80] "*Salve* you say and you do not know why. *Salve* you recite and you do not know why. *Salve* you beat and you do not know why. God wants the intention, it is the intention that God takes. Baptism serves nothing, it is the intention that God takes. Confession serves nothing, it is the intention that God takes. Prayer serves nothing, it is the intention that God wants."[81] Intention in the act of worship was, for Dona Beatriz, the critical marker of its validity. Without intention there was no prayer, baptism, cross, or sacrament. This had tremendous implications for European missionaries who, in the face of Beatriz's new theology, could no longer argue that the thousands of baptized Kongolese in the rural regions were valid Christians.

Indeed, in the midst of Dona Beatriz's movement, Christian missionaries discovered that scores of Kongolese now refused to accept the once popular baptismal rite, in line with Beatriz's claim that the sacraments serve nothing. Laurent de Lucques was surprised to learn that parents were no longer bringing their children to him to be baptized because of the teachings of Dona Beatriz. Incensed at this turn of events, de Lucques reported that the "ministers of Satan had so suppressed baptism that between Bamba and Soyo, we had not baptized anyone."[82]

Moreover, Dona Beatriz engaged in a sustained program of burning so-called fetishes, including the cross, which, she argued, had itself become mixed with superstitious practice.[83] Well before the arrival of European missionaries, the Kongolese revered the cross icon as a visual representation of one's relationship to the world, denoting the cycle of life that leads man from birth to death, through the other world and into rebirth.[84] In burning the Christian cross as a fetish, Dona Beatriz suggested that both inside and outside the context of Christian worship, the cross carried simultaneous and multiple meanings for the Kongolese faithful such that its presence could invoke Christianity even as it marked the intersection of this world and the next common to the whole kiKongo speaking world, both Christian and non-Christian.[85] Beatriz argued that the cross, as an icon, had failed to distinguish itself as a ritual symbol markedly different from other ritual symbols.[86] Dona Beatriz's revised Christian theology makes clear that European missionaries were not the only arbiters of valid Christian practice and that the Kongolese had erected their own definitions of valid Christian practice.

Although a religious and spiritual movement, Beatriz's campaign contained clear political overtones as well. St. Anthony had warned Beatriz that "God would punish the people if they did not return to the then abandoned capital."[87] For most of her life, incessant civil wars had seriously compromised Kongo's stability, making life at the capital city tenuous at best. Her demand for the reoccupation of Mbanza Kongo harkened back to a golden age, a previous period of peace and stability that had eluded the country for several decades. At the same time, however, this ostensibly political aim included clear social and religious overtones. The Kongolese viewed Mbanza Kongo as something more than the political seat of government. Indeed, the capital city served as a ritual and common ancestral site with which outlying regions and tributary states identified.[88] The disruption at

Mbanza Kongo reflected a political as well as a ritual crisis in the country, and Dona Beatriz's call must be seen in this light.

Still, Dona Beatriz was not the first Kongolese prophet to have sounded such alarms. As early as 1703, a prophet emerged announcing that God would punish the people of Kongo unless they reoccupied the capital city.[89] One year later, Mafuta, another prophetess and associate of Dona Beatriz, had similar premonitions. Mafuta claimed to have seen an image of the Virgin Mary, who, having lain prostrate at the feet of Christ, begged that mercy be shown to the people of Kongo. The people of Kongo, and especially the king, had angered Christ, Mafuta reported, by their reluctance to reoccupy the capital city. As evidence of her prophecy, Mafuta produced an oddly shaped rock she had found in the Ambriz River. The stone resembled the battered head of a man, and Mafuta described it as an image of Christ, his face beaten by the hoes and knives of women and men who worked on religious holidays. Defiant in the face of da Gallo, Mafuta refused the priests' demand that she confess her blasphemous sin— pitting her powers of prophecy above their authority. Instead, Mafuta spread her message further, attracting many adherents who were amazed by the miracles that the old prophetess performed. In one instance, she healed a gravely ill woman who had been struck by a poisonous snake using only the sign of the cross and the name of the Trinity. Mafuta became so powerful that King Pedro granted her an interview and, against the objections of da Gallo, refused to punish the prophetess for having proffered her presumably blasphemous message. King Pedro's wife seems to have been among her most devoted adherents.[90] In addition to miracles, Mafuta offered as a remedy to Christ's anger a new form of prayer whereby believers recited the Ave Maria three times and invoked divine mercy three times at nightfall.[91] Like Beatriz, Mafuta opposed the use of all Kongolese ritual objects and implements, including Christian crosses, in line with the belief that they had been diverted away from their proper use in favor of evil ends.

In effect, Mafuta played the role of John the Baptist, preparing the way for what would become a much more extensive movement. Even more, the dual campaign of Mafuta and Beatriz suggests that political opposition and spiritual insight could take on undeniably gendered forms. Though the followers of both Mafuta and Beatriz were both men and women, their leadership may point to a particular provenance that women may have had over spiritual matters of national sovereignty and unity.

The life and work of Dona Beatriz illustrates conversion as a continual negotiation between different realms of belief. Her mediation of Christianity along with her initiation as *nganga* complicate notions of conversion. Dona Beatriz embraced a faith and developed a theology that responded to the immediacy of Kongolese conditions reflected in civil strife, war, and an increasing slave trade. Social disruption plagued Kongo throughout much of her life, and the war captives taken from these battles served to satiate the ravenous appetites of New World plantation communities for labor.[92] Dona Beatriz saw the slave trade as a moral evil based on greed and a relentless desire for goods.[93] Her campaign attempted to rid Kongo of the evil that plagued it, and her voice remains critically important as a statement in opposition to the impending tragedy of the slave trade. Though state authorities eventually captured and executed her in 1706, her movement persisted. For years after her death, thousands of "little anthonys" devoted their lives to the movement, remaining staunch in their opposition to civil war and the slave trade.[94]

By the beginning of the eighteenth century, then, Christian missionaries had exposed an unspecified number of Kongolese to Christianity. While some, especially those close to central court, converted to the faith, many others in the outlying regions adopted some of the tenets of the religion as part of their larger engagement with other preexisting religious practices. When residents of the rural region did adopt Christianity, they typically did so in an attempt to address the social and political disruptions wreaking havoc throughout the country. Some were certainly aware, to varying degrees, of basic Christian precepts, though that knowledge had little or no effect on their everyday lives or on their spiritual understandings.

The Slave Trade and Conversion during the Middle Passage

In theory, all captives destined for the transatlantic slave trade had to be certified Christian in preparation for their passage from Africa to the New World. Established by King Phillip III of Spain in 1607 and confirmed in 1619, this certification implied religious instruction followed by baptism.[95] Religious instruction justified the claim made by many Europeans that the slave trade represented an essential good for Africans because it brought them into contact with the Christian God. In practice, however, the exigencies of slave trading and concomitant desires for the maximization of profit all but stifled any rituals of repentance and purification. Owners wished to avoid excessive and extraneous expenses, especially for slaves particularly weakened and dying, whose physical condition made no pretense or promise of return on further investments. Many owners delayed religious instruction, baptism, and taxes until the very last moment.[96]

Catholic priests conducted religious instruction at points of embarkation along the Kongo coast with the aid of African translators. Some scholars argue that the degree to which this instruction would have been understood by a multilingual body of captured Africans is "an open question," that the instruction given most slaves and the baptism itself was in fact little more than a caricature whereby "cynical and careless priests fulfilled their duties by last minute sprinklings from a hog trough filled with holy water rigged hastily aboard ships ready to leave."[97] Such callousness obviously stemmed from the owners' desire not to waste the cost of saving souls that death would soon release.[98] John Thornton contends that catechists might spend an hour with a whole group of captives, rewarding those who showed themselves particularly adept at learning with tobacco while the others "received some knock on the head as a penance."[99] As the slave trade increased along West-Central African ports of embarkation, captives were procured from further and further in the interior of the country, far from the Christianity of the Kongolese central court or outlying country. Some captives may have been merely passing through Kongo on their way to the Atlantic Coast, rendering virtually meaningless missionaries' attempts at shipboard conversion.

As noted above, many Kongolese captives believed salt, rather than water, conferred the ritual baptismal blessing, so their engagement with water baptism at slave ports would not have been perceived by them as a proper baptism. Remembering their own prior experience with the faith, Kongolese captives would have maintained counternarratives to Christianity than that experienced during the Middle Passage. Many followers of the Antonian movement were enslaved after the execution of Dona Beatriz in 1706, and they would certainly have had their own notions of Christianity that remained contrary to the religious instruction they received during the Middle Passage. For many of them, Christianity was a religion with Kongolese roots that asserted millenarian aims toward a reunification at Mbanza Kongo. The hasty and inadequate attempts to convert them during the Middle Passage would have done little to rupture their own belief. Still, the Kongolese experience with and exposure to Christianity in Kongo did establish a certain ritual lexicon that they could utilize throughout the Americas to help them mediate their interactions with Protestant missionaries in the New World.

Missionaries conducted the conversion of captured Africans in an atmosphere of extreme violence. Contextually linked with the horrors of capture and sale, baptism could not have connoted spiritual cleansing and rebirth for would-be converts who were so imminently at the threshold of death. The violence of enslavement certainly would have affected would-be converts' engagement with the catechists and priests that they met at points of embarkation and disembarkation. Notwithstanding the lack of missionaries in Kongo, the halfhearted attempts of many missionaries, and the disparity between the religious experiences of the town and countryside, conversion to Christianity among Kongolese, such as it was, remained willful. That is, the faithful, both in town and in the country, accepted Christianity on their own terms, adapting it to suit their own conditions and their own notions of spirit and cosmos. No such intent can be deciphered through the baptisms performed along Kongo's ports or at varied New World ports of disembarkation. The efforts to baptize slaves reflect slaving interests' need to justify coercion and their desire to veil violence behind the promise of eternal salvation rather than the spiritual rebirth of would-be converts.

When Laurent de Lucques, a missionary in Kongo, came face to face with the violence of slavery and the Middle Passage, he justified the pain and suffering that he witnessed by suggesting that the victims would enjoy otherworldly redemption. In 1708, after having completed his missionary service in Kongo, de Lucques returned from Kongo to Europe via Brazil aboard a slave ship that departed from Luanda. De Lucques recalled that the ship soon assumed the appearance of a hospital. Confusion reigned on board as some slaves cried and moaned while others, at the edge of sanity, laughed. Space was so constricted in the hold of the ship that the captives could scarcely move or bring food from hand to mouth. In fact, de Lucques himself fell ill with fever during the trip and believed that his life would end at sea. He wondered whether the pains suffered by the captives would be compared best to hell or purgatory and finally settled on the latter because the many sufferings aboard ship were temporary and hell is eternal. And yet, even in the midst of such horror, de Lucques comforted himself and justified his faith in the notion that those who "endure these sufferings with patience, would find the means to extirpate their sins and acquire great merits for their soul." [100]

Eighteenth-Century Missionary Activity in
South Carolina and Georgia

Two years after de Lucques's voyage aboard a slave ship, Francis Le Jau, an
Anglican missionary to St. James Parish in South Carolina, encountered a
small group of enslaved Africans who requested that he admit them into
holy communion. Although the congregants were regular churchgoers, Le
Jau did not eagerly welcome them. He wrote, "I have in this parish a few
Negroe Slaves and were born and baptized among the Portuguese. . . . They
come to Church and are well instructed so as to express a great desire to
receive the H. communion *amongst us,* I proposed to them to declare openly
their Abjuring the Errors of the Romish Church without which declaration
I cou'd not receive them."[101] In noting that the would-be converts desired
communion "*amongst us,*" that is, among Anglicans, Le Jau acknowledged
that both priest and parishioner understood full well the significant differences between Kongolese Christian theology and the practices of Anglican
Protestants in South Carolina.[102] After an eighteen-month term of religious
instruction, two of the men were still interested in taking communion and
Le Jau finally welcomed them. But before administering baptism to the
converts, he required that they take an oath, to wit: "You declare in the presence of God and before this congregation that you do not ask for the holy
baptism out of any design to ffree (sic) yourself from the duty and obedience you owe to your Master while you live, but merely for the good of your
soul and to partake of the graces and blessings promised to the members
of the church of Jesus Christ."[103]

Despite his best efforts, Le Jau still found himself confounded by the degree to which slave converts managed and manipulated the doctrine to suit
their own spiritual and temporal needs. Considering the ability of the black
faithful to render freedom and resistance from a doctrine that presumably
ensured docility and submission, Le Jau wondered if "it had been better if
persons of a melancholy constitution . . . had never seen a book."[104]

In colonial South Carolina, Anglican ministers saw it as their duty to
uphold secular authority. In this sense, colonial preachers spread a doctrine
of civil obedience to all of their followers, both white and black, free and
enslaved.[105] But the question of slave obedience was especially important
to Anglican ministers in colonial South Carolina. Indeed, most ministers
joined the ranks of slaveholders shortly after their arrival in the colony
because parsonages and glebe lands often included slaves.[106] In order to

convince members of the colonial elite (and themselves) that the conversion of slaves served a positive good, missionaries assured masters that slaves would be more tractable and docile as Christians. Indeed, Le Jau attacked aspects of slave culture deemed inconsistent with the productive interests of the plantation. Rather than allowing slaves to engage in the feasts and dances they typically enjoyed on their day of rest, Le Jau required slaves interested in baptism to "promise they'l [sic] spend no more the Lord's day in idleness, and if they do I'l cut them off from Comunion." Le Jau made the case rather plainly, assuring planters that Christian slaves "do better for their Master's profit than formerly."[107]

To be sure, the actual numbers of slave converts during the eighteenth century remained small. A 1724 report sponsored by the bishop of London revealed the low rate at which missionaries had spread the faith among slaves. Missionaries blamed the failure to convert slaves on several factors, including the "planters' reluctance and outright resistance, the great size of the parishes, the scarcity of the clergy, linguistic and cultural difficulties with African-born slaves, the absence of legal support, and the sheer size of the task."[108]

Enslaved West-Central Africans, some of whom had been exposed to the tenets of Catholicism, played a crucial role in the early development of the colony. Writing in "African Dimensions of the Stono Rebellion," John Thornton argues convincingly that the leadership as well as many of the participants in the South Carolina Stono uprising of 1739 consisted of slaves from the kingdom of Kongo. The military tactics employed by the rebels, their expertise with weapons, their use of military banners, flags, drums, and their reported dancing all point to their prior experience as soldiers in eighteenth-century wars in Kongo.[109] More recently, Mark Smith has built on Thornton's work to argue not only that the Stono rebels were from West-Central Africa but also that the very date of the rebellion, September 8–9, 1739, held portentous religious (Catholic) meaning for the captives. That is, the Stono rebels "revolted when they did because of their specific veneration of the Virgin Mary, [and] their general commitment to and understanding of the Catholic calendar developed in Kongo," which held September 8 to be the day of Nativity of the Virgin Mary.[110] Smith argues that Stono rebels summoned Mary "because of her Kongolese historical significance and her protective and revolutionary power."[111]

The Stono rebels cut a path southward during the uprising, hoping to reach Spanish Florida and thus secure sanctuary in the Catholic outposts of St. Augustine. In this, the rebels followed a course first established in the late seventeenth century, when, in 1687, a group of Carolina slaves fled their masters, stole a canoe, and made their way to St. Augustine, requesting that Spanish authorities there baptize them in the "true faith." Spanish officials not only performed the sacrament but also protected the runaways from Carolina slaveholders who traveled to Florida in search of the fugitives. More fugitives from Carolina followed suit, and in 1693 Spanish officials in Florida adopted a general policy of manumission for all escaped slaves from the British North American colonies.

Between 1693 and the Stono Rebellion waves of fugitives arrived in Florida from South Carolina and neighboring Georgia, eventually establishing a black town called Garcia Real de Santa Teresa de Mose.[112] In this light we better understand the aims and ultimate motives of the Stono rebels, who were as interested in sanctuary as they were in open revolt. Indeed, some argue that the Stono Rebellion was "less an insurrection than an attempt by slaves to fight their way to St. Augustine."[113] Catholic missionaries interviewed the newly arrived runaways, who informed the clergymen that they were familiar with Catholicism due to their exposure to the faith in their homeland. Still, parish priests in colonial Florida remarked in horror that some presumably Catholic refugees could not understand Catholic doctrine and "still prayed in their native tongue."[114] As a result, even when fugitives acknowledged familiarity with the faith, parish priests still required them to be baptized anew and subjected them to additional religious instruction. This was the case for two Kongolese slaves in Florida, Miguel and Francisco, who received provisional baptisms administered by parish priest Francisco Arturo because, though nominally Catholic, the two had been baptized in their home country and prayed in their own language.[115] This example illustrates further that even if some Catholic priests acknowledged the Christianity of Kongolese converts as valid—even if wrought with heathen practices, as Thornton argues for Kongo—priests in other regions of the African Atlantic clearly regarded the Christianity of some Kongolese as a thoroughly unacceptable expression of the faith. Notwithstanding the perception of Catholic clergy, the very exposure that some Kongolese had with the faith colored the manner in which they dealt with slavery and freedom in the Americas. The Stono rebels mobilized their exposure to Christianity as a means to restore their freedom, a practice that is inherently resistant. Of the Kongolese who dared to escape from Georgia and South Carolina to venture southward to Spanish colonial Florida, surely some regarded themselves as devout Catholics. Still others may very well have seen in the invitation to freedom an opportunity to parlay their former exposure to Catholic precepts into a promise of manumission.

With Protestant power firmly entrenched in the Lowcountry, it is highly unlikely that a viable community of black Catholics would ever have developed in South Carolina or Georgia. While some fugitives made their way south to Spanish Florida to seek sanctuary with Catholics, the vast majority remained in the Lowcountry, casting their lot with the Anglicans who attempted, though at times only halfheartedly, to proselytize slaves. In this sense Lowcountry slaves, whether or not originally born in Kongo, whether or not Christian, had to make certain conciliations to Anglican missionaries.

Indeed, coincident with the flight of Lowcountry slaves southward toward Florida was another movement that also set its sights on the souls of South Carolina slaves. In 1738, one year before the Stono Rebellion, a singular religious zeal, embodied in the person of George Whitefield, captivated South Carolina. Whitefield, upon his arrival in South Carolina immediately criticized the brutality and violence of slavery and the slave trade and excoriated planters for their failure to adequately convert bondsmen. His theology ostensibly espoused the equality of all human souls, regardless of race. And indeed, the Great Awakening marked the first significant conversion of slaves to Christianity. Whitefield's theology of equality attracted slaves who, though relatively small in number, attended his revivals faithfully.

But Whitefield was no Moses, so rather than shepherding his flock away from slavery's chains, he acquiesced to the power of Pharaoh's slaveholding plantocracy, eventually becoming one of their number. Only five years after attacking southern slaveholders, Whitefield acquired a slave plantation in the mid-1740s. He remained an opponent of the slave trade, though he enjoyed its bounty, arguing that the trade "will be carried on whether we will [it] or not; I should think myself highly favored if I could purchase a good number of them." [116]

A generation later, slaves looked, once again, to the church as a possible guarantor of freedom. In the midst of revolutionary rhetoric regarding natural rights, some churches took bold stances against slavery. In 1784 a Methodist conference took up the issue of slavery and established the Emancipation Laws, requiring all members to emancipate their slaves and resolving that slavery was "contrary to the laws of God, man, and nature—hurtful to society; contrary to the dictates of conscience and pure religion."[117] Baptists followed suit five years later, condemning slavery as a "violent deprivation of the rights of nature."[118] But the reactions of slaveholders were so swift and severe that Methodists suspended the Emancipation Laws just six months after they were initially adopted. Baptists again followed suit by distancing themselves from their earlier antislavery positions. Because evangelicals proved unwilling to adopt a firm antislavery stance, independent black churches took shape throughout the South and in the urban areas of the North as the eighteenth century drew to a close. In 1790 Andrew Bryan, a former slave who had converted during the Great Awakening, established the First African Baptist Church of Savannah, Georgia, the oldest independent black church in the country. It was not until the antebellum period, however, that slaves would be attracted to the Christian faith in large numbers.[119]

Antebellum Missionary Activities, 1831–1845

The increase in the number of enslaved Africans captured in and around Kongo's several ports and arriving at points of disembarkation in the Americas between the last decade of the eighteenth century and the early decades of the nineteenth century coincided with increased Methodist and Baptist missionary efforts in the Lowcountry directed at the enslaved population.[120] During the first 150 years of slavery in the United States, only a small minority of slaves received any instruction in the Christian faith. The objections and indifference of slaveholders along with the paucity of missionaries served as serious obstacles to any sustained program for the religious instruction of slaves during the seventeenth and eighteenth centuries.[121] As late as the 1840s, C. C. Jones, a prominent missionary and proponent of the religious instruction of slaves, lamented that "the systematic religious instruction [of the slaves] has never received in the churches, at any time, that general attention and effort which it demanded; and a people have consequently been left, in great numbers, in moral darkness, and destitution of the means of grace."[122]

Missionaries found themselves in the precarious position of attending to the religious instruction of slaves while assuaging planters' fears that this instruction "be exhorted in a safe and salutary manner, 'qui ne leur donnnerait point d'idées.'"[123] James Andrew, a Methodist missionary and slaveholder from Georgia, acknowledged as much in 1831 before an audience of the South Carolina Agricultural Society when he maintained that "any attempt on the part of [missionaries], to pay anything like marked attention to the religious instruction of the slaves was met on the part of the owners [particularly those of the Lowcountry] by a decided refusal. . . . Not only did [the religious instruction of the slaves] hold out no inducements of honor or ease, but, in addition to its hardships and privations, it required so much prudence and delicacy of management, that most were afraid to enter upon it."[124]

In order to gain access to would-be slave converts, missionaries espoused a doctrine that pleased southern planters in its emphasis on slave obedience and temperance. Many southern planters opposed the religious instruction of slaves on the grounds that it was "the cloak assumed to cover the nefarious designs of insurrection."[125] On one South Carolina plantation the religious instruction of slaves was "done [only] in the daytime and confined to that part of the Bible which shows the duties of servants and masters."[126] Missionaries responded to planter demands for a theology of obedience and deference as evidenced by the 1852 publication of William Capers's *Catechism for the Use of the Methodist Mission,* which emphasized the role and obligations of the dutiful servant: "Let as many servants as are under your yoke count their own masters worthy of all honor . . . and they that have believing masters, let them not despise them because they are brethren, but rather do them service because they are faithful and beloved."[127] Slaveholder John Tucker of All Saint's Parish, South Carolina, provided religious instruction to his slaves once every fortnight between the months of November and May and three times during the summer, each service consisting of a catechism emphasizing honesty, faithfulness, chastity, and discipline.[128]

Many abolitionists vehemently opposed the missionaries' emphasis on slave obedience. In 1829 David Walker highlighted the hypocrisy of many missionaries: "I have known pretended preachers of the gospel of my master, who not only held us as their natural inheritance, but treated us . . . as though they were intent only on taking our blood and groans to glorify the Lord . . . and told us that slaves must be obedient to their masters or be whipped. They chain us . . . and go into the house of God of justice to return him thanks for having aided them in their infernal cruelties."[129]

Abolitionists increasingly pressured slaveholders throughout the antebellum period and in 1836 and 1837 drafted petitions to Congress for the abolition of slavery. Moreover, they distributed abolitionist literature widely throughout the slave South.[130] Under these conditions, slaveholders watched any movement that looked to the improvement of the slave—as in religious instruction—with great suspicion.[131] In fact, the abolitionist movement revealed a striking ambiguity with respect to the religious instruction of slaves. On the one hand, abolitionist agitation provoked a clear reluctance on the part of planters to instruct slaves in the Christian faith for fear of potential rebellion.[132] On the other hand, planters relied on the presumed religious instruction of slaves as the centerpiece in their arguments regarding slavery as a positive good.[133] Reverend William Barnwell, minister to slaves in Beaufort, South Carolina, wrote in 1831, "I have thought sometimes when surrounded by upwards of an [sic] hundred of them singing and praying together that I would be glad if some of my Northern Brethren could take a peep at us. Surely they would not revile me for keeping as bondsmen in the flesh, those who I am striving to make free in the Spirit."[134] When in 1833 outbreaks of cholera reached Charleston, Reverend Barnwell's attentions turned, at length, to the country's enslaved population:

I assure you that in our neighborhood here, there is at present a far greater concern for the souls of the negroes, than for their value. And though should [sic] the Cholera be permitted by the Almighty to take off many of them, some persons amongst us would be reduced to poverty, yet I believe this would be nothing in their sight to the loss of their Negroes' souls. . . . The true way of doing the Lord's will respecting them is to labor for the conversion of their souls, for without this, they cannot be happy . . . not even if they exchange places with their Owners. . . . Those of us who are leading them into the Glorious liberty of the Sons of God . . . have powerful prejudices to overcome in the minds of those . . . [who are] disposed to associate Religious instruction of the blacks, with Insurrection. If therefore our Northern brethren would let us alone in this matter . . . they may be assured that Religion would prevail. . . . Otherwise they may provoke our legislatures to rash Enactments on the subject, and thus subject the Blacks to hardships and even more deplorable ignorance, and expose those of us here who are on the Lord's side to persecution and odium.[135]

Despite the pressures of abolitionists and the strictures of southern planters, South Carolina Methodists established in 1831 a special department designed specifically to minister to the slave population.[136] Although some measure of religious instruction reached the slave population in the eighteenth century, due in large part to the work of George Whitefield and the Great Awakening, by 1830 only a very small percentage of slaves in the region attended church regularly or even heard a sermon.[137] Andrew Bryan admitted as much in 1831, when he wrote, "That the various denominations of Christians have done *something* we thankfully admit. But alas! *Much, very much* yet remains to be done. . . . The Negro, through whose sweat and labour we have derived this substance, has too often been suffered to languish in ignorance the most imbruted."[138]

After fifteen years of missionary work in the region, a symposium on the religious instruction of the slaves was held at Charleston in 1845, attended by ministers and planters from South Carolina and surrounding states.[139] In preparation for the meeting, conference organizers sent a pamphlet to planters requesting information regarding slave conversion, piety, and baptisms. The forty-four responses that they received for the May 13 conference served as the basis of discussion for the three-day meeting. While the published proceedings of the meeting proposed the utility of religious instruction to the slaves as a catalyst for slave obedience and deference, the report makes clear the persistent and imposing barriers to the religious instruction of the slaves. The prevailing perceptions of slave conversion based on the 1845 meeting at Charleston highlight the efforts made by some missionaries to instruct slaves, but a lack of widespread conversion of slaves to any of the main evangelical denominations.[140] Participants at the meeting noted the distance of many plantations from churches and the insufficiency of accommodation (were it practical to attend), the lack of missionaries devoted to the service, the general inability of slaves to understand the gospel, the exorbitant costs involved, and the poor state of religious devotion on the part of the planters themselves as impediments to the effective instruction of slaves.[141] No less an authority than C. C. Jones observed that the "numbers of professors of religion, in proportion to the whole, is not large, that can present a correct view of the plan of salvation. . . . *True religion* they are inclined to place in *profession . . . and in excited states of feeling. And true conversion, in dreams, visions, trances, voices.*"[142]

Notably, missionaries also pointed to the influence of the Catholic Church as a barrier to Protestant missionary efforts. That a significant number of African captives had prior experience with Catholicism was a point not lost on several Protestant missionaries. South Carolina authorities and clergy expressed concern that the Catholics in Spanish Florida presented a real threat to the slave holding population by encouraging slaves to escape. An anonymous English reporter in South Carolina remarked in the mid-eighteenth century that "amongst the Negroe slaves there are a people brought from the Kingdom of Angola in Africa, many of these speak Portugueze [sic] . . . by reason that the Portugueze have considerable settlement, and the Jesuits have a mission and school in that Kingdom and many thousands of the Negroes there profess the Roman Catholic religion."[143] In the mid-1830s Thomas Turpin, a prominent missionary who spread the gospel on several Sea Island plantations, maintained that although a third of the slaves under his charge were affiliated with the local Baptist church, Baptist preachers rarely visited the churches to which the slaves ostensibly belonged. As noted earlier, Turpin suggested that some Sea Island slaves had organized what appeared to him to be Roman Catholic societies.[144] C. C. Jones maintained that some slaves had "grown up in a Christian land and in the vicinity of the house of God, [and] have *heard* of Jesus Christ."[145] During the antebellum period at least some of South Carolina's slaves attended one of several Catholic churches in the coastal region. Both St. Mary's as well as St. Finbar's churches in Charleston, South Carolina, held mass regularly attended by slaves.[146]

Massive numbers of Kongolese arrived in the Sea Island region during the final period of the legal slave trade and as many as 40 percent of slaves in the region were of Kongolese origin.[147] The persistence of "Roman Catholic principles" in the spiritual lives of coastal slaves suggests that some of the enslaved Africans in the Sea Islands continued to hold at least some appearance of a prior exposure to Catholicism in Kongo. The distinctions between the town-orientated Catholicism and the rural-based Christianity in Kongo continued to carry significant import for Kongolese captives in several areas of the New World. As noted earlier, Christian Oldendorp, the Moravian clergyman and poet who interviewed hundreds of West Indian slaves during the late eighteenth century, noted that Kongolese captives enslaved in the West Indies had, for the most part, a recognition of the true God and of Jesus Christ due to the role played by Portuguese and Italian missionaries in Kongo. Oldendorp qualified that statement further by acknowledging that the greatest evangelical success was achieved for those Kongolese who lived in urban areas, closest to the missionary establishment. Those who lived "far from them [the Portuguese] deep in the inland had a religion that was a combination of Christian ceremonies and heathen superstition." [148] Even the presence of Roman Catholic principles among some of Carolina's slaves did not qualify them as valid Christians in the eyes of Protestant missionaries. Turpin, though noting the influence that Catholicism had on some Sea Island slaves, still characterized slave religion in the region as superstitious. "I observed," he wrote, "having to contend with all this superstition and ignorance, together with their prejudice against Methodism, that I had added very few to the Church; and I had, moreover strived very little to do this, but rather strived to beat down their prejudices and to establish a better principle of religion among them." [149]

That some slaves resident in the Sea Islands had some previous experience with Catholicism through the work of missionaries in Kongo does not mean that Kongo slaves in Carolina were necessarily Christian upon arrival in the New World. But Catholicism and its attendant missionaries, churches, and schools had been a part of the Kongolese body politic, social, and religious since the end of the fifteenth century. A certain familiarity with Christian dogma and doctrine would have emerged among Kongolese of all classes—whether Christian or not—in the three centuries between the arrival of Christianity in Kongo and the end of the legal slave trade in the United States. While this familiarity would not, in itself, constitute conversion, the prior experience that some Lowcountry slaves had with Christianity shaped the manner in which they responded to Protestant missionaries. As noted above, the Kongolese developed a vocabulary and language of ritual practice that enabled them to respond to Christianity on their own terms. Enslaved Africans carried this tradition of religious mediation and adaptation with them as they were dispersed throughout the African Atlantic, providing their contemporaries and progeny with the tools to negotiate the mandate of Christian conversion in the plantation Americas. The shift that some slaves made from a Catholic ritual milieu toward a Protestant one—though informed by a larger African Atlantic vocabulary of Christian conversion—would not have been simple or assumed. The differences between the two religious experiences, especially the differences between rituals of conversion in the two cases, must be addressed. But in both cases, either salt sacrament among Catholics in Kongo or total body immersion for Baptists in the Sea Islands, converts mediated the faith and its rituals to respond to the immediacy of their lives and the specificity of their own symbolic and cosmological constructions.

Slave Responses to Christianity

Although both the Methodist and Baptist denominations led the antebellum revival movement that gradually brought modest numbers of slaves into the Christian fold, by the dawn of the Civil War most Christian slaves had converted to the Baptist faith. Although the actual numbers of converted slaves remained small throughout the antebellum period, certain Christian rituals assumed great importance. In fact, "de biggest meetin' house crowds was when dey had baptizing,' and dat was right often," one slave remarked. "Dey damned up de crick on Sadday so as it would be deep enough."[150] Baptismals were social events and the community gathered to support them.

The Baptist denomination appealed to slaves for a variety of reasons. Baptists maintained an open organizational structure that allowed for mixed, though segregated, congregations, and they sanctioned independent black religious associations that operated outside the direct purview of the master class. Baptists facilitated the relationship between the missionary and would-be convert by allowing religious leaders from within the slave population to become exhorters of the faith. Moreover, Baptists emphasized the conversion experience over catechistic instruction, thus allowing for greater latitude in slave religious expression. Baptists also accepted, in greater measure than other denominations, enthusiastic and highly charged emotional expression of the faith, including the ring shout. All of these factors are generally agreed by scholars to be significant as regards the religious conversion of slaves to the Baptist denomination.[151]

Other theories, however, look to Africa in an attempt to explain the popularity of the Baptists among slaves. Noting the varied rituals of water immersion in Africa and the deep reverence for river priests on the continent, Melville Herskovits argued that slaves came to the Americas with strong traditions of water immersion rites that they transmuted onto Christian baptism in the New World.[152] Certain Christian symbols, as in the river Jordan, for example, were symbolic representations of both an ostensibly Christian, yet deeply African spiritual meaning. The prevalence of the imagery of the river Jordan in the musical traditions of slaves further emphasized this connection. That is, the River Jordan reflected a multitude of African rituals of water immersion in the Americas.[153]

Given the great significance of baptism rituals among Lowcountry slaves, it is certainly reasonable to assume—as do Herskovits and others—that water immersion rites in Africa informed the Christian conversion experience of slaves in the plantation Americas. But these immersion rites would not have initially resonated with West-Central African captives, for whom salt was the sine qua non of Christian conversion. And yet West-Central Africans did gravitate toward Protestant baptismal rituals, a matter that likely reflects the results of the cultural and religious interactions that occurred between Africans of varied backgrounds, commencing on the slave ship during the Middle Passage and continuing on the plantations of the American South. That is to say that in their interactions with West Africans, West-Central African captives may very well have applied spiritual meaning to baptismal waters. They would certainly be predisposed to do so, as water baptism conformed perfectly with the cycles of death-burial-resurrection featured in *nganga* ritualism as reflected, for example, in the life of Dona Beatriz. In effect, water baptism as mediated by West Africans served as the mechanism through which West-Central Africans transferred their beliefs across the Atlantic.

This highlights a view of slave culture as a composite, the product of separate elements that, through interaction and exchange, produce slave cultural practices. Far from being either indecipherable or individually soluble, these cultural elements reflect the particular and ongoing relationships that existed between enslaved Africans of varied origins. In this view not only West-Central Africans but also West Africans contributed the necessary memories and materials for the transposition of African water rites to Christian baptism.

Where Herskovits's treatment generalized African ritual experiences, more recently, scholars have investigated the specific relationships between African rituals and slave conversion. Margaret Washington, for example, links slave conversion in the Lowcountry with initiation rituals found among Africans of varied ethnicities throughout West Africa's Windward Coast, including Sierra Leone, Liberia, and Senegambia. In particular, Washington focuses on the role that secret societies played as the primary organizing units for a multitude of social, cultural, religious, and governmental enterprises. Operating much like their Western analogues, as in social organizations, political parties, and federal agencies, these societies managed diplomatic affairs, established generally recognized standards of behavior, provided education for youth, and acted as agencies of socialization.[154]

Washington's treatment of initiation societies in Sierra Leone, including the Sande for women and the Poro for men, reveals a ubiquitous social and political institution that operated throughout precolonial Sierra Leone and Senegambia. Washington argues that some "adaptive concepts of community (and aspects of spirituality) inherited from secret societies fused with Gullah interpretations of Christianity, becoming part of the folk religion in the slave quarters."[155] In particular, the initiation into Poro and Sande was regarded as a spiritual death and rebirth that culminated in dramatic displays and celebrations much on the order of slave baptismal rituals. Moreover, the leaders of these societies were responsible for the temporal as well as the spiritual well being of the societies' members, serving as the primary mediators between this world and the otherworld. According to Washington, these leaders performed a role similar to that of the Gullah elders—spiritual and religious leaders chosen from among the slave community as guides and interpreters of Christianity. In both cases, the leaders served as spiritual ushers, shepherding their followers from a state of symbolic death toward spiritual rebirth and reintegration into the larger community. For enslaved Africans, this reintegration was symbolized in the conversion experience and the baptismal ritual.

Washington argues moreover that the stamp of West African secret societies can be discerned at each stage of the Christian conversion ritual. Indeed, in the slave South, the black faithful organized themselves into "black societies" resembling the Poro and Sande initiation societies of Sierra Leone. These black societies were, like their African counterparts, "units of organization that regulated conduct and served to integrate individuals into the plantation community." Within those societies, "Gullahs practiced their own version of Christianity, and created their religious folk-culture."[156]

Notably, initiation societies were common not only in Sierra Leone but also in various parts of West and West-Central Africa. In Kongo, for example, Kimpasi societies constituted one of the most important ritual and religious institutions in the country. Kimpasi groups comprised a loose federation of acephalic, though closely related, societies located throughout the country. Based in uninhabited areas, especially densely wooded or secluded regions, Kimpasi societies were situated around large open enclosures hidden by trees, logs, and thorny underbrush. Members of these societies concerned themselves principally with alleviating societal suffering and hardship and thereby invested its initiates with the regenerative healing and protective powers of the otherworld.[157]

Dona Beatriz's initiation into a Kimpasi society sheds light on several of the central themes treated in this chapter. At her initiation, Beatriz was brought to the Kimpasi enclosure and, through a series of rituals, fell into a symbolic death characterized by a deep catatonia. She was then brought to the initiation altar, which included a large earthen mound in the middle of which stood a large wooden cross, symbolizing, at one and the same time, Christianity and the junction of this world and the next world common throughout kiKongo-speaking regions. On either side of the cross lay other ecclesiastical goods, including censers and aspirators. In addition, several *kitekes*—human shaped sculptures ritually invested with the power to seek out malfeasance, jealousy, and greed—guarded the altar. Other items, such as the claws of a predator meant to "capture" wrongdoers, served metonymically to heighten the sense of ritual potency. Once inside the enclosure, Beatriz was ceremonially revived, though, after her ritual foray into the land of the dead, she returned possessed of a new, otherworldly soul. In the subsequent weeks and months, she, like other new initiates, met secretly at the Kimpasi enclosure and learned a new language that symbolized her passage. Novitiates into the society also enjoyed exemption from several taboos and social restrictions that applied to other people.[158]

Because of their newly earned powers, Kimpasi initiates were both revered and feared by others in the community and Catholic clergy roundly denounced them. In the late seventeenth and early eighteenth century, Kimpasi societies actively opposed the theology of Catholic priests (Dona Beatriz being a prime example). One Capuchin described Kimpasi as "an extremely secret and redoubtable society; more redoubtable even than the Ministers of the Holy Inquisition are amongst us. . . . No chief, however great, has power over them. They are convinced that if they mark their opposition to them they will die from magical influences."[159]

In all likelihood, the social and ritual organization and operation of African initiation societies from various West and West-Central African societies played crucial roles in the subsequent development of slave culture and society in the New World. If, as is true, Washington's treatment of West African secret societies along the Windward Coast illuminates slave ritual practice in the Lowcountry, then the same is true all the more of enslaved Kongolese, who enjoyed both a demographic majority in the region and whose initiation societies had already been engaged in a century's long conflict with Christian theology in West-Central Africa. The response of enslaved Africans to the mandate of Protestant conversion in the eighteenth and nineteenth centuries merely reflects a continuation of this transatlantic interaction.

That the following discussion focuses on the relationship between slave Christianity and Kongo ritual practice does not discount the crucial role that Africans from other regions played. Indeed, Washington's central contention—that West African secret societies affected the manner and course of religious conversion and cultural formation in the Lowcountry—is convincing, shedding light on both the long arm of Africa in the cultural formation of blacks enslaved in the New World and the great adaptability and versatility of slaves, who so elegantly managed and manipulated certain cultural elements in a new ritual and social context. Her conclusions run parallel to my own formulations.

Significant numbers of enslaved Kongolese developed strong tendencies toward the Baptist faith. Even where rituals of water immersion in Kongo (performed after the Catholic fashion, without total body immersion) and Christian baptism in the slave South differed quite markedly, certain cosmological and symbolic notions, first developed in Kongo, made slaves more amenable to Christian conversion. Even absent the formal similarities between African water immersion rituals and Christian baptism, certain theoretical and symbolic connections persisted.[160] This informs studies of cultural continuity between Africa and the Americas by demonstrating that these links need not be identified solely in the formal affinities that connect ritual practices in two locales but might also be the offspring of intellectual processes. Moreover, this draws our attention, once again, to the discussion first raised in chapter 1 regarding tradition. Enslaved Africans not only received a cultural and religious inheritance from Africa but also actively engaged in the process of putting Africa to use in their own lives.

Slave conversion and Christian baptism for the slaves of coastal South Carolina and Georgia reveal the very conscious and deliberate efforts made by captive Africans and their descendants to maintain and transmit meaning for themselves even in a context of violence and coercion. Christianity in the Sea Islands was refracted through the lens of slaves' own memories of Africa and the immediacy of their condition as bondspersons on the plantation. At least one scholar suggests that "there is very little mention of the cardinal dogmas of the church. . . . The antebellum Negro was not converted to God. He converted god to himself."[161] Writing of her own experience as a missionary and teacher in the Sea Islands in 1865, Mary Ames was surprised to find "they [slaves] know so little of the life Christ; not knowing even of his birth."[162] Other observers noted that many slaves "almost completely reconstructed the most important events of the Bible," chronicling them in such a way as to defy imitation.[163]

As a ritual of community import, the conversion experience in the slave South took on a rather formalized pattern, generally acknowledged by the community as valid.[164] The following example is typical:

> I was chopping in the field. I began to feel faint and sick. It seemed that I was going to die. . . . I fell to the ground and said, "goodbye and farewell; I am going to die.". . . The next thing I knew I was in a helpless condition. My body lay on the brink of a great and dark pit. . . . I realized my helplessness and surrendered. . . . I didn't see anything but myself and the other white images like me. . . . It seemed as if a great burden were lifted from me, and my soul took a leap and left the old body. . . . My soul took the air, and having wings like a bird I flew away into a world of light with thousands of other images like myself.[165]

The conversion began with a life-threatening fever or illness. But this affliction was no mere physical ailment, it was a sin sickness, a malaise of the soul.[166] So serious were its symptoms that the convert felt herself in the presence of Death. Soon after, she was released from her body to view the shell of the woman she once was. Now released from the burdens of the body, the convert was transported to the fires of hell, witnessed its flames, knowing it full well to be the final resting place for those whose lives continued on the path of sin. And then, as if by miracle, God delivered the poor sinner, snatching her from the bowels of hell to be transported into the bosom of heaven: "The darkest hour of the night is just before the break of day. The darkest hours of my life as a slave came just before freedom, and in the same way, in my trials with sin, when everything seemed lost I was delivered."[167]

New converts saw heaven, Jesus, the angels, and even themselves as symbolically white, a feature peculiar to the conversion experiences of former slaves. Black converts often had visions during and after the baptism of being carried on a white chariot or a white horse to the glowing heavens and God. One convert remembers, "I saw myself a little body, pure white."[168] During these visions, converts saw also God and Jesus as white as well as the walls of the Heavenly City, the robes of the angels, and the Holy Mother.[169]

In the Lowcountry, slaves understood the baptismal waters to be a boundary between this world and the next that could be crossed at the moment of baptism. When one resident of the Georgia coastal region was baptized, she came up smiling: "Oh Jedus . . . uh see Gawd onduhneet' de water! Uh fin' me Gawd. 'E look 'puntop me!"[170] This revelation corresponds with the notion that true religion can only be found in the underwater spaces, the murky swamps or in any number of otherworldly places. So one spiritual encourages would-be converts to search the darkened and hidden away corners for true religion:

> O where d'ye tink I fin' 'em?
> I fin' 'em, Lord, in de graveyard.
> I fin' 'em in de boggy mire.[171]

The perception of water as a spiritual boundary was not merely metaphoric or symbolic. Instead, the black faithful experienced it as real, such that God and other spiritual beings could be seen under the water's murky surface. Edmund Ruffin suggested as much when, on an agricultural survey in South Carolina in 1843, he came across a series of natural springs and fountains the local blacks deemed inhabited by special water spirits. These Cymbee spirits resembled sprites or nymphs and lived below the surface of certain springs, lakes, or fountains. One elderly South Carolina slave described the Cymbee that he had seen as a boy: "She was seated on a plank which was laid across the water, & . . . the long brown hair of her head hung down so low, & so covered her face & whole body & limbs" that no other feature of her visage could be seen.[172] Ruffin reported that though descriptions of the Cymbee are few in number, "they are nevertheless believed by the negroes to be frequent & numerous."[173]

The springs and fountains in which the Cymbee spirits lived commonly disappeared entirely only to reappear in a nearby locale. For this, Ruffin offered an explanation: "As mentioned previously in regard to *matters of fact* of these fountains . . . , and which facts are in strict accordance with the cavernous foundation which I suppose, these fountains sometimes suddenly disappear entirely, & in other places, new springs burst out."[174] Blacks explained these phenomena differently, arguing that the disappearance of a spring denoted that the Cymbee "has died, or has been offended & abandoned her residence." So when one plantation owner enclosed his spring "with masonry & raised & confined its water, an old half breed Indian of the neighborhood, who was half negro in blood, & wholly in habits & superstition, remonstrated with him, upon the ground that the cymbee might be made angry & leave her haunt, & that then the spring would be dried." [175]

Ruffin's Cymbee correlates with the Simbi water spirits mentioned earlier, emphasizing the close similarities between notions of the spiritual powers of water in both Kongo and the Lowcountry. That some of the slaves drew not only on their African heritage but also on Indian spiritual beliefs suggests the role that cultural interaction played in the creation of slave culture, a point to which Ruffin makes reference, noting that "in Indian folklore dwarves, water babies, and old women variously inhabit springs and other wet places." [176]

Water acted as both barrier and passage connecting two opposing yet complimentary realms. [177] Indeed, one South Carolina folktale reminds the Christian faithful that if you want to find Jesus, you have to go down below: "Yes, Buddy, dat is de way I fine him I went down below." [178] The newly converted dies so as to enter a new world: "I knew at that time that I was in another world, and I knew that I had left my earthly body behind." [179] Slaves did not necessarily perceive death as a negative. Rather, some thought of it as a relief from the drudgeries of slave life, an avenue toward freedom:

> See the Christian lyin on his deathbed,
> An' a death come a-steppin in;
> You heah dat Christian say to death,
> O death, you are welcome. [180]

Elizabeth Roberts recalls of a baptism she witnessed, "One by one he dip em in duh watuh an dey is buried in baptism." [181] The connections between baptism and death are highlighted also by the practice in Kongo of burying men "in the marshy bank of a river . . . and then allowing the waters to flood the site," which had been dammed for the purpose of creating a watery grave. [182] In the Lowcountry, blacks further cemented the notion of baptism as a symbolic death by carefully preserving the long white robes worn during the ritual "to serve as their [burial] shrouds one day." [183] The image of death and rebirth in river baptisms coincides with the practice of denying church membership to anyone who had not first died and been reborn. In regarding baptism as but a spiritual death, slaves looked to the Bible: "We are buried with Him [Christ] by Baptism into death: that like as Christ was raised up from the dead by the glory of the Father, even so we also should walk in the newness of life; except a man be born of water and the spirit he cannot enter the Kingdom of God."[184] During her baptism, Easter Lockhart of South Carolina "seemed to walk real light. . . . [She] looked down and [her] gown was floating on top the water." She knew full well that the ritual conferred upon her a new life, that the "Lord done reached down from Heaven and created a new soul."[185]

Taken together, then, several cultural elements largely explain the attraction of West-Central Africans to Protestantism. A centuries-long experience with the mandate of Christian conversion by Catholic missionaries in Kongo and its environs prepared much of the groundwork for eventual conversion. But Kongolese captives held in the slave South had yet to overcome the largest obstacle to their large-scale conversion, namely, the transition from regarding baptism as principally a ritual of salt protection toward a belief in the spiritual capacities of water. This task was likely aided not only by their own experience with death and rebirth as embodied in Kongolese *nganga* but also by their own conceptions of Simbi/Cymbee spirits. Crucial also were the cultural interactions between West-Central Africans and West Africans, whose rituals of total water immersion served as the basis for the spread of new ideas about the spiritual uses of water. This interaction led ultimately to a notion of baptism as a ritual of death and rebirth in which water signified the line of demarcation between the realm of the living and that of the dead.

In addition to these factors, one recognizes also a set of striking affinities that attend slave conversion experiences with those of Dona Beatriz mentioned earlier. In both instances one notes the oncoming of a great distress. For Beatriz this stress resulted in a morbid fever; and in fact, only after Dona Beatriz found herself "at the moment of death, in agony" did Saint Anthony finally descend to enter the spirit and heal her afflicted body. Lowcountry slaves understood this as a sin sickness, attended by the very real knowledge that the punishments of hell are real. In both instances one notes the transmigration of the soul and an acknowledgment of the body as a vessel, a mere shell within which inhabits the substance of the soul. A return to health follows, and with it the burdens of a new insight, a new understanding of life and its consequences, in effect, a conversion of the spirit from one realm of being to another.

This is not to say that the conversion experiences of slaves harkened back simply onto the possession ordeal exhibited by Dona Beatriz. Antebellum slaves did not simply replicate a ritual practice that appeared in Kongo nearly one and a half centuries earlier. Instead, Lowcountry slaves drew on the cultural and spiritual vocabularies of faith and conversion that spread throughout the African Atlantic during the era of slavery and the slave trade. One must not understand the experiences of Dona Beatriz, or of antebellum slaves, for that matter, as individualized, as localized in the body of the convert. In fact, individual spiritual expressions indicate much larger spiritual understandings and reflect the cultural and social milieu that conspire to support, produce, and interpret them. Thus Dona Beatriz as prophet is less an anomaly—some oddity to be studied in its peculiarity—than an embodiment of early-eighteenth-century Kongolese notions of life, death, conversion, and prophethood. So, too, the rather formalized conversion experiences of slaves in the Lowcountry region comprise the elaboration of certain theories of ritual experiences and understandings. The similarities between Kongolese spiritual experience and New World slave conversion suggest a certain connection between the peoples involved or, as I am arguing, a certain vocabulary of ritual expression that existed in varied African Atlantic sites throughout the period of slavery and the slave trade.

This vocabulary of ritual expression could be found, for example, in Brazil, where in 1666, Dionigio de Carli, an Italian Capuchin missionary came across "a black woman, who kneeled, beat her breast, and clapt [*sic*] her hands upon the ground." De Carli inquired as to "what the good woman meant by all those motions with her hands; and a Portuguese answered . . . 'Father, the meaning of it is, that she is of the kingdom of Congo, and was baptized by a Capuchin; and being informed you are going thither to baptize, she rejoices, and expresses her joy by those outward tokens.'"[186] Notwithstanding the deep devotion displayed by that woman, Catholic priests in Brazil encountered much the same frustration as their colleagues in Kongo, noting the paucity of priests in the country along with a significant language barrier between clergy and would-be converts. One Brazilian priest expressed sentiments that echoed around the African Atlantic:

> Even if they were baptized in Angola . . . rarely or never does one find that one knows what he received in the baptism and to what he is obligated to God, and they are totally ignorant of everything that pertains to the substance of the mysteries of Our Holy Faith; and thus with this blindness they persevere after coming from Angola among the Christians, and in the face of the Church for a space of many years, after being 4,

5, and 6 years in the house of their masters, without knowing what is necessary for them for their salvation.[187]

Much like missionaries in other American locales, Brazilian priests found irksome self professed Christian slaves who continued to engage in divination, conjure, witchcraft, and ritual medicine. Slaves of West-Central African provenance presented Brazilian priests with special challenges, principally because many of them regarded themselves as Christian, though their practice stood in direct opposition to crucial aspects of Catholic liturgy. Some priests in Brazil expressed great irritation because they were obliged to correct what they regarded as a multitude of errors and misconceptions, "principally in the Angolan slaves in which predominated, in some, so much ignorance that they did not have anything more than the name of Christians."[188]

In other regions as well Kongolese slaves continued to assert their own independent vision and interpretation of Christianity. Catholic priests in Saint-Domingue (Haiti) noted that enslaved Africans from Kongo were familiar with Christianity, though they continued to indulge in so-called heathen practice. At least one missionary in Saint-Domingue, Father Moreau de Saint-Méry, acknowledged that there were many Congos who had some idea of Catholicism, though their religion was very much mixed with various idolatries and reflected a "monstrous assemblage" of Christianity and paganism.[189] In Venezuela, black Christians, if not the Vatican, canonized San Juan Congo, a public hero, whose image "combines the colour and wavy hair of the mulatto with the semi-erect phallus of many Koongo *nkisi* figures (ritual objects)."[190] Monica Schuler recorded hymns in Jamaica directed to the power and presence of *nzambi a mpungu*.[191] Writing in the late nineteenth century, L. Crookall, a Protestant missionary in British Guiana, recounted his confusion at being addressed by a deferent Christian by the title "Gorgonzambe." Upon inquiring into the meaning of that title, a local resident replied, "In Africa de medicine man am de doctah for a' we body, but you am de doctah for a' we soul; and de African name for de minister am Gorgonzambe [*Nganga a Nzambi*], which mean God-doctor. When de soul am sick you mus' gib us medicine." To this, Crookall pointed the patient "to the Great Physician, who alone can heal the maladies of the soul."[192]

In the Lowcountry, slaves mediated the Christian faith and its meanings not only in conversion and baptism but also in the very symbols of the faith. For example, Sterling Stuckey argues that the prevalence of the cross in the baptismal ritual "recall[ed] Bakongo religious mythology."[193] Building on the work of Robert Farris Thompson, Stuckey argues that the cross represented specific Kongolese notions of life, death, and rebirth.[194] For Stuckey, "Christianity provided a protective exterior beneath which more complex, less familiar (to outsiders) religious principles and practices were operative." Stuckey argues further that some of those aspects of Christian practice deemed peculiar to slaves were actually "outward manifestations of deeper African religious concerns."[195] In this sense, enslaved Africans knew what members of the master class did not know, namely, that their veneration of the cross was not Christian but African in nature. Stuckey's position raises the thorny question of cultural and religious authenticity. To regard slaves' engagement with baptism primarily as a protective cloak for African ritual is to forestall the possibility that some, even if only few in number, engaged in the ritual as veritable Christians. To be sure, Stuckey is correct to suggest that Christian missionaries, not to mention most slaveholders, exerted only little effort toward proselytizing slaves. In light of the small numbers of enslaved Christians on the plantation, the communal acknowledgment and popularity of baptisms suggests that other meanings and interpretations were at work. Water baptism, as Michael Gomez suggests, "allowed for varying religious perspectives to engage in the ceremony simultaneously."[196] In all likelihood, African interpretations of the ritual predominated until well into the antebellum period.

My own view, though not radically different from that espoused by Stuckey and others, is that the cross likely stood as a symbol of dual significance from which participants could draw a variety of meanings, both Christian and non-Christian. This certainly seems to have been the case in Kongo, where the cross was mobilized by various people in different ways. If members of the Kongo elite adopted Christianity and the cross as a politico-religious tool to enhance their power over potential religious and political competitors, then Dona Beatriz saw the same icon as merely another "idol," subject to eradication. Africans of Kongolese descent, even if they did not think of themselves as Christian, would likely recall the varied uses to which the cross had been put in Kongo in both Christian and non-Christian arenas. In this way, the cross carried simultaneous if also alternate meanings for the black faithful whether inside or outside a context of Christian worship. Its presence could act as both an invocation of Christianity and a marker that symbolized the junction of this world and the next. In areas where slave populations of Kongo descent were largely represented—as in Charleston, Savannah, or cloistered within Sea Island communities—these multiple understandings would have been readily recognized and likely shared with slaves from other regions of Africa.[197]

Archaeologist Leland Ferguson has analyzed bowls made by slaves in South Carolina that were decorated with cross-marked cosmograms. The bowls were found under water, suggesting ritual submersion or baptism, and were inscribed with counterclockwise arrows at the end of the cross marks, indicating probable resonances not only with the Kongo cosmogram but also with the counterclockwise movements of slaves during the ring shout.[198] The bowls are part of a much larger network throughout the African Atlantic religious complex, linking the emblazoned cross seen by Afonso in the sixteenth century and the crosses burned as fetishes by Dona Beatriz. Crosses carried multiple interpretations and may be interpreted variously, signifying at one and the same time Kongolese notions of the cycles of life and death, the ring shout, and Christianity.

The quilts of Harriet Powers, an artist born into slavery in Georgia and renowned for her appliquéd Bible textiles, contain multivalent symbols, including Kongo cross motifs, situated within otherwise Christian contexts, highlighted by the depiction of Jesus' crucifixion in the lower right panel (fig. 1). The small sun, located directly below Jesus, suggests the continued counterclockwise movement of the sun and rests at "high noon" for the underworld. This high noon positioning implies Jesus' transition into the otherworld and reflects his eventual rebirth (resurrection), a notion consistent not only with Kongo cosmology but also with slaves' notion of baptism as a movement from a worldly life to spiritual death and rebirth. Powers renders the relationship of mirrored opposition and movement between this world and the next, so central to Kongo cosmology, through the two sets of mirrored bodies, figured around a central sun in the upper left panel. These mirrored bodies, and indeed many of the bodies figured on the quilt are set with one arm akimbo, the other raised in the air, a gestural posture that acts as the physical embodiment of the crossroads marking the junction between the land of the living and that of the dead.[199] In the quilt, the Kongo cosmogram and the cross appear side by side in the upper left panel, suggesting the multiplicity of potential understandings. The cross in this instance belies simple interpretation and stands as neither a strictly Christian symbol nor a mere replica of a Kongo cosmogram.[200]

The cross represented a variously marked point where different geographies, iconographies, and belief systems merged: the Kongo with the Americas,

Pictorial quilt by Harriet Powers
Museum of Fine Arts, Boston. Bequest of Maxim Karolik. Photograph © 2007 Museum of Fine Arts, Boston.

the Christian with the non-Christian, this world with the other world. We can think of the cross, then, as a graphic emblem of African Atlantic religiosity that remained amenable to interpretation and reinterpretation for the faithful.[201] The invocation of the baptismal at the water's edge coincided with Kongolese notions of the otherworld, of spiritual cleansing, and rebirth.

A baptism required careful planning so as to correspond to optimal conditions. The faithful might have to "wait till a Sunday wen a ebb tide come at a good time."[202] Liza Basden of Harris Neck remembered that "they always hole em [baptisms] on the ebb tide; that's so the sins be washed away."[203] Rosa Sallins, also of Harris Neck, maintained that "we alluz baptize on duh ebb tide [because] duh watuh washes duh sin away."[204] Slaves outside of Harris Neck also adhered to the same practice. On Possum Point "dey alluz baptize on duh ebb tide cuz duh ribbuh is spose tuh wash duh sins away."[205] When Samuel Lawton conducted research on the religious lives of Lowcountry blacks in 1939, he found the practice still prevalent: "Dey baptizes de candidate in de outgoin' tide so de tide kin carry de sins on out to de deeps ob de sea. Effen you baptize in de incoming tide, de water will wash de sins right back up on 'em." [206] In effect, the spiritual power of water washes sins away, even absent the name of Jesus.

While the condition of the tide might affect the date and time of a baptismal, adverse weather conditions were not likely to cause a rescheduling of the ritual. In *Folk Beliefs of the Southern Negro* Newbell Niles Puckett notes that "no matter how bitter the weather may be when a person is baptized he can never catch cold." [207] God so protected the convert that they "ain mine gittin wet in duh ribbuh." [208] Writing in *Slave Songs of the Georgia Sea Islands,* Lydia Parrish, upon observing a river baptism, notes similarly that "although the water was bitterly cold, the young people behaved very well, and only one squealed a little—which was considered very bad form." The faithful knew full well that they and the officiating minister "ran no small risk of catching cold, but to this penance they most cheerfully submit[ted]." [209] If you did not come up like a lamb, the congregation suspected that your conversion had not been authentic and the baptism needed to be performed again.[210] Perhaps the black faithful drew on an old Negro spiritual to help them withstand the cold:

> Chilly water, chilly water
> Hallelujah to that Lamb.
> I know that water is chilly and cold,
> Hallelujah to that Lamb.
> But I have Jesus in my soul,
> Hallelujah to that Lamb.
> Satan's just like a snake in the grass
> Hallelujah to that Lamb.
> He's watching for to bite you as you pass
> Hallelujah to that Lamb.[211]

Because baptism transformed the soul, the material conditions of the water were irrelevant. In fact, converts might think of the freezing water of a baptism as a test of sorts, for if the soul was pure, the water would do the convert no harm. So goes the spiritual, sung frequently at baptisms:

> Sister, if your heart is warm
> snow and ice will do you no harm. . . .
> You must mind how you step on the cross
> your foot might slip and your soul get lost.[212]

The cooling of the body had other resonant meanings for slaves. In spirituals related to death and dying, slaves commented on the cooling of the body and the subsequent onset of the afterlife: "When-a my blood runs chilly an' col', Ize got to go, ize got to go, ize got to go." [213] Slaves along the coastal region of Georgia and South Carolina observed a spiritual reverence for the water that rinses the sins away and prepares the convert for a new life. Acknowledging this power, the preacher often made a prayer in its honor: "Duh preacher he make a great prayuh tuh duh ribbuh." [214] Though traditional Christian figures and symbols were not completely absent, the preacher and the congregation that accompanied him exhibited a parallel reverence for the river such that "fo heah baptize each ub um, he say a prayuh tuh duh ribbuh an ax fuh all duh sins tuh be wash away." [215]

The baptismal ritual in the slave South operated as a complex and variously marked ritual. These multiple understandings would have been both implicit and explicit. This layering of meaning upon meaning would have been both spoken and unspoken to the various participants and onlookers at the baptismal ritual such that any given member of the congregation would have variable access to the ritual. We need not contend that each and every participant was fully aware of the resonances between slave baptismal and Kongolese rituals. Certainly, some were fully aware of the signs and symbols. Others, however, may not have recognized the conjunction of the cross as a symbol, both Christian and non-Christian, or the relationship between river baptism and the Kongolese conception of a watery otherworld. [216] Cultural resonance between different Atlantic locales, as in Kongo and the Lowcountry, was held in the ritual's symbolism (the living water, the cross) and not necessarily in the body of each and every adherent. In the baptismal itself one finds all of the signs, symbols, and allusions that connected it with Christian sacrament and with other (and for our purposes here, Kongolese) notions of spirit and cosmos. We are suggesting here a notion of culture that is collective, a social dynamic that is, at any given point, larger than the individuals who come together to create it.

The revelatory experience of southern slaves—the experience of soul sickness, death, travels through a fiery hell followed by heavenly redemption, and a return to earthly realms—relates to the revelatory experiences of Christians in Kongo. A specific historical trajectory linked Christian conversion in Kongo with that experienced in the slave South. The conversions of Lowcountry Sea Island slaves connect historically, conceptually, and cosmologically to those cavalrymen and that white cross emblazoned in the sky that marked Afonso's conversion, to Dona Beatriz's travels through death, heaven, rebirth, and takula wood, and through an African Atlantic ritual vocabulary of revelation, iconography, death, and rebirth.

Trance and Spiritual Ecstasy

As a ritual of corporate importance, slave baptism reveals slave agency and resistance in the antebellum period. In response to a planter-sponsored theology that demanded duty, compliance, and restraint, slaves developed a theology that highlighted free will and the improvisation of the slave body. Some slaves noted, "When white folks go to meetin', they never crack a smile, but when colored folks in church, you'll hear um laugh er mile."[217] The slaveholder, under the aegis of drivers and overseers, compelled the slave body to conform to a set labor regime and ignore daily abuses and oppressions. But the same may not be said of the praise-house meeting or the baptismal rite in which slaves laid bare the pains of this world in ritual prayer, trance, song, and dance.

Margaret Washington detailed the critical role that praise houses played in the development of black religious societies in the antebellum South.[218] First built in the slave South during the antebellum years as mechanisms of social control, these modest structures were erected by planters determined to proscribe the mobility of bondsmen by depriving slaves from different plantations the opportunity of gathering and worshiping together. In theory, the proscription of slave mobility ensured an obedient slave population, more easily monitored and controlled. In practice, the praise house became the center of the slaves' religious life, and one of the primary locales for ritual practice and ecstasy. Slaves assembled at the praise house on several nights throughout the week and on Sunday afternoon to worship. Song and dance accompanied prayer as the faithful formed a circle, performing the ring shout.[219] The manner of worship in the praise house often struck deep emotional chords in the hearts of observers. So Charlotte Forten offers a portrait of slave ritual practice rendered in shadow and light:

> The large, gloomy room, with its blackened walls,—the wild, whirl-ing dance of the shouters,—the crowd of dark, eager faces gathered around,—the figure of the old blind man, whose excitement could hardly be controlled, and whose attitude and gestures while singing were very

fine,—and over all, the red glare of burning pine-knot, which shed a circle of light around it, but only seemed to deepen and darken the shadows in the other parts of the room,—these all formed a wild, strange, and deeply impressive picture, not soon to be forgotten.[220]

Even when slaves were constrained to attend church services under the watchful eye of members of the master class, they continued to attach their primary religious loyalties to the praise-house congregation. Indeed, slaves remained critical of the hypocrisy they saw in the Christianity of slaveholding whites. Perhaps Frederick Douglass articulated this hypocrisy best. Writing in *The Narrative of the Life of Frederick Douglass,* the author expressed concern that, in view of his critical statements about Christianity, readers might question his faith. To clarify his position, Douglass set himself the task of differentiating the Christianity of Christ from that of the slaveholder:

> Between the Christianity of this land, and the Christianity of Christ, I recognize the widest possible difference—so wide, that to receive the one as good, pure, and holy, is of necessity to reject the other as bad, corrupt, and wicked. . . . We have men-stealers for ministers, women-whippers for missionaries, and cradle-plunderers for church members. The man who wields the blood-clotted cow skin during the week fills the pulpit on Sunday, and claims to be a minister of the meek and lowly Jesus. . . . He who sells my sister, for purposes of prostitution, stands forth as the pious advocate of purity. . . . We have men sold to build churches, women sold to support the gospel, and babes sold to purchase Bibles for the *poor heathen! All for the glory of God and the good of souls!* . . . The dealer gives his blood-stained gold to support the pulpit, and the pulpit, in return, covers his infernal business with the garb of Christianity. Here we have religion and robbery the allies of each other—devils dressed in angels' robes, and hell presenting the semblance of paradise.[221]

Douglass, and no doubt many of his comrades similarly bound under the threat of the lash, saw too much hypocrisy in the religion of the master class and readily acknowledged that the Christianity of the master was not the Christianity of the slave. Instead, the religion of slaves, hidden away under the cover of darkness or amid wooded areas, was a self-contained ritual practice. The spirit moved in the praise house, where slaves knew and felt God in very personal ways, as a seeing, listening God. While whites laid their primary religious loyalties with the church, slaves experienced religion in the praise house. Indeed, the slave faithful had first to obtain permission from the praise-house congregation before petitioning the master and the church for official membership.[222]

Much like the hidden enclosures of Kimpasi rituals, praise houses were deeply recessed in wooded areas or otherwise nestled in swampy nether spaces, often overlooking slave cemeteries that stood as a constant reminder of the imminence of death, the close proximity of the grave. To be sure, there were practical reasons for slaves' preference for worship in wooded areas. The seclusion of the praise house offered a measure of autonomy and a moment's reprieve from the purview of the master class. On the close relationship between the praise house and the cemetery, Harriet Jacobs, a fugitive slave, wrote:

> His grave was marked by a small wooden board, bearing his name, the letters of which were nearly obliterated. I knelt down and . . . poured forth a prayer to God for guidance and support in the perilous step I was about to take. As I passed the wreck of the old meeting house, where, before Nat Turner's time, the slaves had been allowed to meet for worship, I seemed to hear my father's voice come from it, bidding me not to tarry till I reached freedom or the grave. I rushed on with renovated hopes. My trust in God had been strengthened by the prayer among the graves.[223]

Slaves developed their own geography of spiritual power in the world represented in the very structure of the praise house, which conformed to slaves' particular forms of worship. In this, the praise house afforded a manner of worship that emphasized a particular liberality of movement, a point of no small importance for a people held in bondage. The location of the praise house in wooded areas ensured yet another type of freedom, that is, the freedom from the purview of whites. On another level, the construction of the buildings in spiritually specific spaces—connected both to cemeteries and the spirits generally resident in outlying areas—allowed slaves to establish praise houses as loci of power and communication between this world and the next.

To all outward appearances, the buildings were anything but impressive; they were small, dilapidated structures located on the outskirts of the plantation. As northern missionaries arrived at Port Royal Island during the Civil War, they often described the houses as rather humble structures, often "merely a larger and nicer negro hut than the others."[224] Harriet Ware, a northern missionary and teacher who traveled to the Sea Islands describes the frame of the praise house as "made very roughly of boards whitewashed, inside an earth floor covered with straw, rough wooden benches, the pulpit and altar made in the same way, but covered entirely with grey moss."[225] Given its unimpressive structure and its location in the outer reaches of the plantation, the praise house often failed to attract much attention from outsider observers. By overlooking these structures, most whites completely missed the spiritual practices that took place inside. Indeed, Harriet Ware, finding the structures "rough and ordinary," opted not to venture inside.[226] And former slave Simon Brown recalled that "slaves never said a word to . . . white folks" about their particular brand of worship.[227]

Though unadorned, the praise house cloaked within its walls the heart of slave spiritual and religious practice. Frederick Law Olmsted notes that the owner of one house "told me that having furnished the prayer-house with seats having a back-rail, his Negroes petitioned him to remove it, because it did not leave them *room enough to pray.* . . . It was their custom, in social worship, to work themselves up to a great pitch of excitement, in which they yell and cry aloud, and, finally shriek and leap up, clapping their hands and dancing, as it is done in heathen festivals. The back rail they found to seriously impede this exercise."[228] Of particular note, slaves made demands regarding the construction of the praise house. For them, the very architecture of the cabins need be made amenable to their particular form of worship. Above all, there remained a paramount concern for the space and mobility afforded in the praise house. Writing of St. Helena Island, T. J. Woofter reports that "there is no doubt as to the antiquity of the building, for it nestles beneath a great oak half-hidden by a screen of cassina bushes such as only time can erect. It is built of log framing, with rough clapboards on the sides and roofed with hand-split shingles. Inside the oil lamp yellows the small pine pulpit of the leader, but leaves the faces of the audiences almost in the dark. The floor is uneven and the hand-made benches have no backs."[229]

Notwithstanding their presumed "antiquity," praise houses first appeared during the late antebellum period, when white missionaries began to make some headway in convincing planters of the importance of the religious instruction of slaves. They proliferated quickly, however, and were common features of the southern landscape into the early twentieth century. One writer notes that "on every one of the old plantations you will come across a tiny building furnished with rude backless benches and a leader's stand in front."[230] In some cases the benches were not only without backs but displaced entirely, having been pushed against the walls of the praise house so as to effect better the space necessary for worship.

W. E. B. Du Bois describes this manner of worship and maintains that the "frenzy" was an essential element of black religion, "more devoutly believed in than all the rest. . . . Many generations firmly believe that without this visible manifestation of God there could be no true communion with the invisible."[231] This worship, he continues, "varied in expression and form from the silent rapt countenance or the low murmur and moan to the mad abandon of physical fervor,—the stamping, shrieking, and shouting, the rushing to and fro . . . the weeping and laughing, the vision and the trance."[232] James Smith, a black preacher, described slave religion in this way: "The way in which we worshipped is almost indescribable. The singing was accompanied by a certain ecstasy of motion, clapping of hands, tossing of heads. . . . The old house [itself] partook of the ecstasy; it rang with their jubilant shouts, and shook in all its joints."[233] That the old house itself partook of the ecstasy suggests that the very structure itself participated in the ritual, that it, too, mere mud, wood, and dust, engaged in the religious fervor experienced by the slaves inside. No small number of observers described the praise house in terms that highlight its being, its very real presence. As Mrs. William R. Wister, a teacher in South Carolina's Penn School for newly freed men, recalled, the "Praise House filled slowly. It was a small one-roomed cabin that looked weirdly alive as you approached it through the darkness."[234] The buildings enjoyed only so much light as might be provided by an open door or by a flickering candle or oil lamp, the shadowy effects of which contributed to the sanctity of the structure.[235] Because the buildings were roughly built, any light emanating from inside shone through the many cracks and crevices of the building, much as a beacon welcoming would-be worshipers.[236]

Of course, the rituals performed within the praise houses, as in the ring shout, contributed to the life of these houses: "The faithful begin first walking and by-and-by shuffling round, one after the other, in a ring. The foot is hardly taken from the floor, and the progression is mainly due to a jerking, hitching motion, which agitates the entire shouter, and soon brings out streams of perspiration. . . . Song and dance are alike energetic, and often, when the shout lasts into the middle of the night, the monotonous thud, thud, thud of the feet prevents sleep within half a mile of the praisehouse." [237] In dancing the ring shout, with its slow, sedimented steps inscribed around an ever-revolving circle, slaves marked off an autonomous sphere of spiritual practice. Taken together, praise-house worship—in its seeping light, backless benches, song, sound, and dance—comprised an invaluable space over which slaves maintained ultimate control.

The record of the master class as it related to worship at the praise house is mixed. Whereas some perceived it as a mechanism for social control, others saw in its communal expression the very real possibility of rebellion. For their part, Christian missionaries were largely appalled by praise-house worship. One observer writes, "We cannot determine whether it has a religious character or not . . . but it is probable that they are the barbarous expression of religion handed down to them from their African ancestors." [238] Others were not so kind, linking the religious experience of slaves to lascivious frolic, savagery, and "idol worship." Still, some slaves went to extraordinary lengths in order to participate in praise-house worship. Peter Randolph, a former slave from Prince Henry County, Virginia, notes the manner in which slaves might arrive at these ceremonies: "The slaves assemble in the swamps, outside the reach of the patrols. They have an understanding among themselves as to the time and place of getting together. This is often done by the first one arriving breaking boughs from the trees, and bending them in the direction of the spot." [239]

Despite their slight stature, humble constitution, and early establishment as mechanisms for social control, planters came soon to understand the rebellious potential of praise-house worship. After Nat Turner's slave rebellion, for example, many slaveholders in Virginia forbade worship in the praise house, opting instead to appropriate the nether reaches of their own church balconies and galleries for slaves' use. Previously mentioned runaway slave Harriet Jacobs recalled that "slaves begged the privilege of again meeting at their little church in the woods, with their burying ground around it. It was built by the colored people, and they had no higher happiness than to meet there . . . and pour out their hearts in spontaneous prayer. Their request was denied, and the church was demolished." [240]

Even after the antebellum period praise-house worship continued in black churches throughout the country. One reverend reports in the early twentieth century, "When the ole spirit hit you, honey, I'm gonna tell you the truth, you're not of yourself. . . . I 'member one time old Deacon Jones got to shoutin' so that he actually flew around the altar, not a hand or foot touchin'.[241] So recalled John Bivens, a former slave from Sandfly, Georgia: "Wen we git tuh duh ribbuh some uh duh folks is so happy an dey scream an jump roun so much dat some uh duh udduhs hab tuh hole um."[242] Simon Brown reports that for slaves, this manner of spiritual zeal was common. Sometimes the candidate would come "up from the water so happy that he'd begin to shout right out in the pond, and it would take both deacons to bring him safe to shore."[243]

Indeed, this manner of religious practice continues to inform contemporary African American religious life. Writing in *Quicksand,* Nella Larsen describes the experience of Helga Crane:

> It was a relief to cry unrestrainedly, and she gave herself freely to soothing tears, not noticing that the groaning and sobbing of those about her had increased, unaware that the grotesque ebony figure at her side had begun gently to pat her arm to the rhythm of the singing and to croon softly: "yes, chile, yes chile." . . . She did notice, though, that the tempo, the atmosphere of the place, had changed. . . . Men and women were swaying and clapping their hands, shouting and stamping their feet to the frankly irreverent melody of the song. Without warning the woman at her side threw off her hat, leaped to her feet, waved her long arms, and shouted shrilly . . . and then, in wild, ecstatic fury jumped up and down. . . . Little by little the performance took on an almost Bacchic vehemence. Behind her, before her, beside her, frenzied women gesticulated, screamed, wept, and tottered to the praying of the preacher, which had become gradually a cadenced chant. . . . It went on and on without pause with the persistence of some unconquerable faith exalted beyond time and reality . . . and as Helga watched and listened, gradually a curious influence penetrated her; she felt an echo of the weird orgy resound in her own heart; she felt herself possessed by the same madness; she too felt a brutal desire to shout and to sling herself about . . . and in that moment she was lost—or saved.[244]

In their particular brand of worship, slaves redirected their bodies and their behavior away from the dominance of the master class.[245] In place of master class imperatives toward submission, the praise meeting and the baptism imparted a resistant improvisation and free will. This reading differs from the treatment traditionally afforded slave religious expression. Frantz Fanon, in *The Wretched of the Earth,* argues that

> the native's relaxation takes precisely the form of a muscular orgy in which the most acute aggressivity and the most impelling violence are canalized, transformed, and conjured away. At certain times, on certain days, men and women come together ... fling themselves into a seemingly unorganized pantomime, which is in reality extremely systematic. ... Shakes of the head, bending of the spinal column, throwing of the whole body backward. ... The river bank down which you slip as if to show the connection between the dance and ablutions, cleansing and purification—these are sacred places. ... In reality your purpose in coming together is to allow the accumulated libido, the hampered aggressivity, to dissolve as in a volcanic eruption. Symbolic killings, fantastic rides, imaginary mass murders—all must be brought out. The evil humors are undamned, and flow away with a din as of molten lava. ... When they set out, the men and women were impatient, stamping their feet in a state of nervous excitement; when they return, peace has been restored ... it is once more calm and unmoved.[246]

Eugene Genovese suggests that slave religious practice inspired docility and submission because, while it enabled the slaves to do battle against the slaveholder's ideology, it did so defensively within the system it opposed; offensively it proved a poor instrument. In short, Christianity "softened the slaves by drawing the hatred from their souls, and without hatred there could be no revolt."[247]

Most observers discuss spiritual ecstasy as an individual experience, something that, in a given ritual context, occurs to a certain person: a particular flailing and flinging of the body to and fro. But this is clearly not the case. For indeed, the faithful regarded religious excitement and ecstasy as community events. The community produces the ecstasy, and the trance only emerges once the community of believers conspires to create the necessary conditions—a particular percussive rhythm, a certain hymn, a special ritual practice (i.e., baptism). In this way, ecstasy does not belong to the individual as much as it belongs to the entire community. God does not speak to the person in trance as much as through the person in trance, the body in ecstasy being little more than a vessel, a line of communication through which the community comes into closer contact with God.

In the moment of ecstasy, the body in trance is not controlled (or even controllable for that matter). Rather, the spirit that moves through the body and, by extension, the body itself is communally shared and protected. If, as suggested above, the congregation communicates with and knows God through the body in trance, then that body, and the messages it conveys are directed at all members of the community and are not the exclusive property of the individual in trance. That is, the body in trance is harbinger of community. Because it is not controlled, or controllable, the body in ecstasy is neither subject to the plantation labor regime, nor to notions of ownership. It is in the moment of religious ecstasy that the slave body ceases to be controlled or owned by members of the master class. By extension, the slave body ceases to be a commodity. The body and the spirit that moves through it are transcendent at that moment, unbridled, governed from on high. Without ownership there is no slavery, and so in that moment, the believer briefly enjoys freedom. So suggested one antebellum commenter regarding slaves' particular brand of worship, noting that "in religion he finds also an element of freedom which he does not find in his hard life. And in these wild bursts of melody he seems to be giving utterance to that exultant liberty of soul which no chains can bind, and no oppression subdue."[248] In this way, the resistant body rejects the ideology of slavery in an attack aimed at the very system of commodity exchange that would have bodies bought and sold.

This chapter represents the first of several investigations into an African Atlantic religious complex that developed during the period of the Atlantic slave trade and included West and West-Central Africa along with the slave populations of the New World. Specifically, this chapter describes this religious complex as a site for the accommodation and interpretation of the rituals of Christian conversion, namely, baptism, in two locales: the Kongo kingdom of West-Central Africa and the coastal region of South Carolina and Georgia. Africans and their enslaved counterparts in the New World negotiated the signs, symbols, and meanings associated with Christianity through the development of complex vocabularies and iconographies of conversion and baptism. In this way, the meanings associated with Christianity were characterized by a notable fluidity and adaptability of belief in ways that challenge simple notions of conversion.

Like the chapters that follow, this chapter focuses on both the aesthetic and theoretical aspects of cultural continuity. In fact, I argue in this chapter that even in the absence of formal cultural affinities (i.e., different

rituals of conversion), the cultures of the Atlantic are linked philosophi-
cally and theoretically in the ways in which African diasporic peoples
think of themselves, their beliefs, and their environments. These cultural
continuities are not the result of some passive inheritance of an African
past; they reflect the willful efforts made by people determined to maintain
and construct meaning for their lives, even in dire circumstances. As a
result, this investigation emphasizes the Kongolese and their counterparts
in the New World as historical agents and subjects.

In both Kongo and coastal Georgia and South Carolina, the recently
converted interpreted Christianity as a tool of resistance. Many Kongolese
converts adopted baptism as a protection against the evils of the slave
trade, and Dona Beatriz developed a movement that was both religious and
deeply political in its aims. Enslaved Africans in the Lowcountry utilized
the baptismal ritual to resist the brutalities of the master class.

Most studies of slave resistance highlight slaves' persistent opposition
to the formal institutions of slavery, focusing on forms of resistance such
as theft, work slowdowns, feigned illness and injury, arson, self-mutilation,
running away, and poison.[249] But slaves opposed more than the systems
of slavery that oppressed them; they opposed the very theoretical and
religious underpinnings that supported and justified the enslavement of
Africans in the first place. Missionaries and some planters justified the
oppressions of the slave in this world with the promise of eternal salvation in the next world. That is, they sought to bring the "heathen" souls
of Africa into the light of Christian salvation through the propagation of
the Christian faith. Such was the case for Capuchin missionary Laurent de
Lucques, who rationalized the brutalities of the slave trade by noting that
those who endured their sufferings with patience "would find the means to
extirpate their sins and acquire great merits for their soul." [250] He deemed
the pains and oppressions of slavery a necessary evil and viewed the slave
trade as part of a larger civilizing mission that promised the austerity,
sobriety, and (most important) the obedience of the slave.

But many slaves defied this theology of submission and, in the face of
the demands of austerity, sobriety, obedience, and the promise of salvation in the next world, engaged in the rituals of Christian conversion as a
means to resist the condition of slavery, assert their free will, and articulate
their own theologies of resistance.[251] Slaves' own notions of baptism—the
reverence for water, particular notions about the nature of death and the
cycle of life, and the "shout"—all undermine the authority and theologies

***Baptismal Scene* by Doris Ulmann**
Museum of Fine Arts, Boston. Gift of William Clift in memory of Otelia Barnes
and Dora Zeigler. Photograph © 2007 Museum of Fine Arts, Boston.

upon which slavery is based. Along with this, slaves opposed the com-
modification of their bodies, the notion that they were only valuable in
their capacity to work. Slave rituals of conversion attest to the slave body
as a vessel for the expression of spirit, ritual, and rite. In this way, the resocialization of the slave body during the rituals of conversion—as in the
ring shout, the praise-house meeting, and spirit possession—challenge
the very underpinnings of slavery itself.

Coda

Few have captured southern black ritual life as well as photographer Doris Ulmann. On Lang Syne Plantation, South Carolina, located on a peninsula at the junction of the Congaree and Wateree Rivers, Ulmann conducted photographic investigations into the lives of the four hundred Lowcountry men and women who labored there. Many of them had lived on the plantation since the antebellum period.

Ulmann's photographs of the baptismal ritual on the plantation are marked by soft opposition: white gowns against a murky water's surface, the tense stillness of the bodies of the faithful juxtaposed against the rippling motion of those same bodies reflected in the water, and the intense focus of the foreground against a hazy and undifferentiated backdrop. The candidate stands eyes averted, head bowed low, surrounded by the deacon to her right and the preacher to the left. Ulmann's photos of black baptisms imply a vast majesty in the natural landscape as against the meekness of the faithful. Ulmann's attitude toward her subjects on Lang Syne was "reflected in her delicate use of natural light and the soft focus lens . . . designed to induce spherical aberration—that is, a lack of sharpness at the edges of the image."[252] In this, the observer notices a sense both of that which is to be seen, marked by sharp focus, and that which is to remain unseen, marked by shadow and haze.

In fact, Ulmann's photographs are perhaps most telling in that which we do not see. We do not see the immersed body or the wetness of the newly born as she returns from the other side. Ulmann remains silent on that which is most sacred and, perhaps, in that way speaks volumes regarding the sacredness of the rite.

3

Minkisi, Conjure Bags, and the African Atlantic Religious Complex

The idea of the fetish derives from the medieval Portuguese term *feitiço,* which referred to sorcery or magical arts. In its earliest use, the term articulated clerical denunciations of witchcraft and other illicit popular rites. The Catholic priesthood used the term to deride the varied charms and ritual arts of their parishioners. In this way, clerical authorities used the idea of the fetish in their efforts to maintain religious authority. In applying the label "fetish" to religious activities that they derided as pagan, priests defined the limits of acceptable religious practices.[1]

In the fifteenth and sixteenth centuries notions of the fetish coalesced around Western imperialism as Portuguese traders used the term *feitiço* to refer to the varied charms, amulets, and ritual objects they found along the western coast of Africa. From *feitiço* the hybrid *fetisso* developed, and when naval dominance shifted to England, so did the "fetish," entering the English language in 1625.[2] Eventually, the fetish came to stand as a category of thought, belief, and practice against which the West understood itself. At a time when the Western Enlightenment project proclaimed the necessity of reason and rationality, the fetish stood as an example of the horrors of superstition and bestial irrationality, "the very image of the truth of unenlightenment."[3] The fetish was all the West was not.

But European notions of the fetish, rather than telling us about the African societies and belief systems they purport to describe, represented Western European cultural propaganda, which extended ideas of European sovereignty and dominance.[4] Western thinkers used the fetish as proof positive of presumed European superiority, progress, and evolution and regarded the fetish as an appendage of primitive times. These notions reinforced the sense that the West was not only technologically and intellectually superior but also temporally more developed than societies still connected with the fetish. The West presumed itself to occupy a higher place on the "timeline of human development." Father Laurent de Lucques, an eighteenth-century missionary in Kongo, suggested as much when he noted that Kongo's inhabitants "put their confidence in these idols because they have a *poorly developed* intelligence."[5] In creating a fictive Africa presumably populated by the fetish and its corollary monsters and goblins, in describing its unbridled barbarity and ritual orgies, European travelers, clerics, and government agents played the part of what Edward Said terms the "secular creator, a man who made new worlds as God had once made the old."[6] This echoes the sentiments of famed essayist Caryl Phillips, who in *The European Tribe* argues, in reference to European chauvinism, that "she still looks askance at 'strangers' as they alone reinforce a sense of self. Ultimately, the one certainty for Europe is that she knows a 'nigger' when she sees one: she should—they were a figment of her imagination, a product of her creative mind."[7] Indeed, European expansion around the globe was a central component in the construction of Western ethnocentrism. The widening of Europe's horizons maintained "Europe firmly in the privileged center, as main observer."[8] Rooted, as it was, in European clerical denunciations of illicit rites practiced by its own parishioners, the mobilization of the fetish *outre-mer*—in the newly explored regions of Africa, Asia, and the Americas—entailed the transposition of certain Western tensions throughout the colonial world. European travelers, missionaries, and colonial agents identified the fetish in Africa even as they refused "to face and think the implicit, the unthought . . . negated in their own cultural experience."[9] In this sense, the discovery of the fetish and all of its corollaries reflect, in the words of V. Y. Mudimbe, "an ambiguous invention of a history incapable of facing its own double."[10]

So powerful, in fact, was the idea of the fetish that it became common in popular literature and cultural discourse. In *Moby-Dick,* for example, Herman Melville describes the carved wooden figure carried by Queequeg as a "Congo Idol," a "curious little deformed image with a hunch on its back, and exactly the color of a three days' old Congo baby." Queequeg placed the "little hunchbacked image" in front of a makeshift shrine in front of a fireplace and offered the image a bit of sacrificial bread, an act that, for Melville's protagonist, Ishmael, confirmed Queequeg's status as a heathen.[11] The fetish represented a temporal, theological, and intellectual barrier between the West and others and reflected a Western presumption that if "backwards peoples" (read: people living in the past) were ever to enjoy the fruits of civilization and enlightenment—if they were ever to become "modern"—they must first do away with the ritual remnants of the past.

Olfert Dapper provided one of the earliest descriptions of the fetish in Kongo when he reported in 1686 that "these Ethiopiens call Moquisie or Mokisses everything in which resides, in their opinion, a secret and incomprehensible virtue to do them good or ill, and to discover the past and the future."[12] For Dapper, Kongo remained a "kingdom still immersed in a great blindness:"[13] "Most of the inhabitants . . . are still idolaters, they have moquisies [*minkisi*] or false wooden gods . . . [and] strongly believe that all of the sicknesses that afflict them are caused by the anger of the moquisies. The Gangas [*nganga*] who are the priests of these idols are respected themselves as gods."[14]

Wyatt MacGaffey has written extensively on *minkisi* (sing. *nkisi*) and their construction and use in Kongo. His writings on the subject detail the critical importance of *minkisi* in state construction in West-Central Africa and delve into the role they played regarding intercultural communication between Africans and Europeans.[15] The idea of the fetish originated in a mercantile intercultural space created by ongoing trade relations between dissimilar cultures that defined value in very different ways.[16] European traders on the African coast valued objects as commodities to be sold for profit. Their African counterparts, however, held objects dear not only as transferable commodities but also as sites for the articulation of certain religious and spiritual beliefs. European traders adopted the idea of the fetish as a means of characterizing "the strangeness of African societies and the special problems they themselves encountered in trying to conduct rational market activities" with a people whose notions of value were so different.[17]

Much of what we know about *minkisi* in Kongo during the era of the slave trade comes from European explorers and Christian missionaries, who scarcely shielded their disdain in describing the objects. They found little or no value in *minkisi* themselves and relegated them to that class of objects and beliefs that characterized so-called primitive peoples. European observers included in their descriptions of the fetish heavy doses of ethnocentrism, which tell us more about European notions of cultural superiority than about the ritual objects themselves or the beliefs that attended them. As Wyatt MacGaffey writes, the "fetish is an entirely European term, a measure of persistent European failure to understand Africa

[and] . . . we are still trying to disabuse ourselves of this condescending misrepresentation."[18] Despite their ethnocentrism, European descriptions of Kongolese ritual objects are valuable as they illustrate the ubiquity of *minkisi* in Kongo and offer some information regarding their construction, use, and maintenance.[19] This chapter moves away from notions of the fetish as the anachronistic ritual objects of backward peoples to investigate the historical and cross-cultural creation and operation of these objects in Kongo during the era of the transatlantic slave trade. It discusses the relationship between *minkisi* in Kongo and the use of conjure in the Georgia and South Carolina Lowcountry, highlighting the historical dynamics that link these objects theoretically, symbolically, and aesthetically.

Moreover, in this chapter I investigate the manner in which ritual practitioners on both sides of the Atlantic challenged modernity or, at least, claimed their own space in the modern world by proclaiming their own theories of the nature of power, the notion of value, the limits of agency, and the importance of ritual resistance. Emblematic of this form of resistance is the life and death of Father Georges de Geel, a Catholic missionary in seventeenth-century Kongo.

Father de Geel, much like his clerical colleagues, traveled throughout the Kongo countryside in an effort to preach the gospel and rid the country of its many idols and fetishes. Arriving at a small village in 1652, he witnessed a ritual ceremony, directed by an *nganga* and complemented by the use of several *minkisi* and other ritual objects. De Geel implored the participants not to worship wooden objects or revere the local *nganga* and proceeded to "gather all wooden objects and statues and put them into the fire."[20] The villagers demanded to know why de Geel had burned their *minkisi,* and after receiving no satisfactory response, they beat him so severely that he died several days later.

Upon hearing the news of Father de Geel's murder, the Kongo king Garcia II (1641-1661) reacted forcefully. He condemned to death the chief of the village and its resident *nganga* and ordered the capture of all of the villagers involved in the incident, eventually selling them to Portuguese traders as slaves.[21] In addition, he issued an edict to be distributed throughout the kingdom in which he vowed to punish harshly anyone who disrupted Christian priests engaged in the destruction of idols or the pursuit of "false priests and sorcerers." If by chance there were numerous villagers in the guilty party, Garcia II vowed to burn their entire village and kill its leaders for failing to prevent their subjects from disobeying his orders. Such was the fate of the *nganga* and chief involved in the de Geel incident, who, Garcia II assured his countrymen, were presently burning in hell. As they traveled throughout the kingdom, Christian missionaries carried a copy of the edict to be read by interpreters.

Garcia II's brutal response in this case reveals a significant uncertainty that the monarch felt regarding the extent of his authority in the kingdom. Much like other Kongolese monarchs, Garcia II justified his power through his status at the apex of a spiritual and religious redistributive network that guaranteed good fortune, rains, and bountiful harvests. As Kongo became increasingly decentralized during the seventeenth and eighteenth century—due in no small part to the increase in slaving activities in the country—the king's influence over the spiritual realm waned while the provincial *nganga* became increasingly important. Indeed, the *nganga* had become a central figure in the country's outlying provinces. Father Raimondo da Dicomano, a Capuchin missionary who worked in the provincial region, noted that the Kongolese had the custom of "attributing to the fetishers all sickness and death."[22] The king recognized the *nganga* as a serious threat to royal power and sought to eradicate their presence and rid the nation of their influence. Kongo's king utilized Catholic missionaries as appendages to royal authority to be deployed in the provincial regions. In this way, Garcia II desired the eradication of *minkisi* and waged a religious campaign in the provinces, aided by missionaries. Garcia II's brutality in the de Geel case highlights the ubiquity of rural-based forms of ritual practice in Kongo as a significant threat to the authority of the kingdom. Garcia II directed his edict toward the *nganga* and their *minkisi,* thereby establishing the boundaries between the state-sanctioned Christianity of the court, urban and centralized, against the religion of the countryside, decentralized and resistant.[23]

Sources and Kongo *Minkisi* Defined

European officials in the newly colonized Belgian Congo consolidated their power during the late nineteenth and early twentieth centuries not only through the establishment of political and economic structures but also through the development of social and religious networks, highlighted by the work of Protestant missionaries. In order to better proselytize the local population, missionaries studied indigenous religious practice and amassed a large body of ethnographic and anthropological knowledge concerning Kongo and its people. Most notably, missionary Karl Edward Laman directed a vast program that collected information regarding varied aspects of Kongo culture, especially religion and ritual practice.[24] Laman's studies of *minkisi* include extensive descriptions, detailing their contents and creation along with explanations concerning the theories and symbolisms that attended them.

Although these ethnographic texts contain a massive amount of useful information, they cannot simply be read backward into cultural practice in Kongo during the era of the slave trade. Indeed, *minkisi* are dynamic objects that responded to the immediacy of everyday life and changed significantly over time. Much changed in the time separating the reports of Catholic Capuchin missionaries in the late eighteenth century and the ethnographic projects of the late nineteenth and early twentieth centuries. Some of the *minkisi* used during the earlier period likely fell into disuse, whereas others sprung up to deal with new challenges and concerns. Still, the nineteenth- and twentieth-century ethnographic texts do reveal a remarkable amount of stability with respect to *minkisi* and may be used, with care, to help understand their operation during the era of the slave trade. The following discussion relies first and foremost on the reports of seventeenth- and eighteenth-century missionaries, observers, and travelers. The ethnographic sources of the late nineteenth and early twentieth centuries are consulted only for the manner in which they clarify or enhance the earlier texts. Such an approach reveals both the dynamism of the *nkisi* tradition as well as its relative stability over time.

Defined simply, the *nkisi* is a ritual object invested with otherworldly power, allowing it to affect special spiritual and material functions in the world. In 1643 Father Capelle, a Capuchin missionary, offered a useful introduction into their construction and contents: "They have their moquisis in which they believe. . . . [They] were made by their fetishers and consist of small rocks, little bones, feathers, herbs and other useless rubbish, with which . . . they practice magic and speak with the devil, as if they were insane and possessed. . . . The moquisis are wrapped in the skins of certain small animals. They keep them on their person, or suspend them in their homes. . . . Others wear bracelets with which the fetishers transmit their magical forces."[25]

At the turn of the twentieth century, the following description collected by Nsemi Isaki under the aegis of Karl Laman emphasized the *nkisi* as a container for medicines:

The *nkisi* is the name of the thing we use to help a man when he is sick and from which we obtain health; the name refers to the leaves and medicines combined together. . . . An *nkisi* is also something which hunts down illness and chases it away from the body. It is a hiding place for people's souls, to keep and compose in order to preserve life. . . . Some people keep them in large bags. The medicines are the ingredients [of the *minkisi*]; their strength comes from each individually and from their being joined together.[26]

Minkisi existed at all levels of Kongo society, and although some of the more common *minkisi* might be created by a general practitioner and used to ensure personal protection, healing, or good fortune, others, being more complicated, required the expertise of a properly initiated *nganga.* They might be utilized in myriad ways and were, in fact, as diverse as the many diseases that afflicted people. Some *minkisi* healed, others caused illness, and still others helped determine the innocence or guilt of accused criminals.

Because the *nkisi* spirit itself has no physical form, the *nkisi* object—either raffia bag or wooden sculpture—harnessed the animating spirit.[27] The *nkisi* object maintained a symbiotic relationship with its animating spirit. Without the inhabiting spirit, the object was no different from other mundane objects. Likewise, the animating spirit, though powerful, would be difficult to access by ritual experts were it not confined within the body of the object. And yet *minkisi* were more than ritual objects or the medicines held therein; they comprised all of the rules, regulations, songs, and recitations required to invoke the emanating spirit.[28] Although they were the focal object for particular ritual practices, the *nkisi* reflected a much larger set of broad theological and cosmological concerns. These included a particular understanding of human agency that challenges the distinction in Western thought between persons and objects, a point to which we shall return below. In addition, the *nkisi* tradition assumed its own notions of causality. This is especially important in terms of how the Kongolese thought of human illness, the mastery of which was determined by special access to the spiritual realm. Lastly, *minkisi* tell us much about how the Kongolese conceived of power and its operation in both the physical and spiritual worlds.

The Kongolese drew distinctions not between the operation of good and evil in the world but between the uses to which people put otherwise neutral power. They regarded as evil any spiritual power mobilized to increase one's own status or prestige or used to inflict harm. These selfsame powers could be mobilized for community benefit or in the interests of health and healing. In this sense, the Kongolese presumed that chiefs (who assumed a role of personal power and advantage) used their powers aggressively, while priests who adjudicated conflicts and healed sickness, used their powers more positively.[29] Notably, the Kongolese recognized that the mobilization of all spiritual power, whether for good or evil ends, entailed a certain measure of force and violence. This force they defined as *kindoki,* which characterized the exercise of all ritual powers in social relations. While *kindoki* is commonly translated as "evil" or "witchcraft," the Kongolese regarded it as a necessary element in the exchange and transfer of spiritual power and in the administration of leadership. But like ambition, too much *kindoki* concentrated in a single individual would become, almost certainly, an instrument of evil.[30]

For the Kongolese, power resided in the land of the dead but could be harnessed through the use of *minkisi* under the expertise of an *nganga.* The Kongolese understood most human illnesses as the effects of the retributive powers of the other world, harnessed by ritual experts. Wyatt MacGaffey has detailed the basic structure and operation of what he calls the "*minkisi* complex," a nexus of forces that constrain, control, and direct otherworldly spirits, making them useful in the material world.[31] That the *minkisi* in the preceding descriptions were said to be "wrapped in animal skins" and kept in "large bags" suggests the importance of containment. An *nkisi* is, in large part, a container for the medicines/powers/spirits that are bound up tightly inside. This theory of containment reflects a Kongolese perception of the human body as a mere shell or container for an animating spirit that operates below the surface. Ritual experts adopted several conventions to emphasize containment including the tying, binding, and knotting of *minkisi* to illustrate the control or submission of the inhabiting spirit. The *nganga* contained powerful *nkisi* spirits by wrapping medicines and other ritual materials into bags they, in turn, confined inside large calabashes or pots. In the case of wooden *minkisi*—which often took the shape of men or animals—the *nganga* carved abscesses in the belly or atop the head into which he placed (contained) certain medicines and the inhabiting spirit. Once the abiding spirits had been effectively invited or induced, the *nkisi* acted as a portal for communication with the dead.[32]

The nganga used medicines in *minkisi* for their metaphorical or metonymic importance rather than for their pharmacological properties. For this reason, color symbolism was important and could communicate certain symbolic functions. The color white, signifying the land of the dead, recurred regularly through the use of kaolin, whereas red connoted that interstitial space between this world and the next.[33] Color symbolism could extend beyond the *minkisi* to the ritual experts who used them. Dapper noted that during one ritual, the *nganga,* with the aid of red and white pigments, painted cross figures on his entire body.[34] In this context the cross stands as an icon denoting the supreme access that the *nganga* had to both this world and the otherworld. Thus color coding could be used in concert with iconographic symbolism to enhance further the role of the *nganga.*

In addition to color symbolism, the use of metonyms was also widespread. The nganga might place a small stone inside an *nkisi* meant to remove a tumor or use a feather to connote flight for an *nkisi* meant to seek out a wrongdoer. The feathers, herbs, and bones mentioned in Father Capelle's description operated as metonyms in this manner. In addition to these visual elements, verbal metaphors, in the form of punning, were also important. The *tonda* (a mushroom) may be included as a pun on the kiKongo term *tondwa* (to desire) such that the *nkisi* invested with *tonda* evoked desire.[35] When combined, these varied symbolisms, metaphors, metonyms, and puns entailed a complicated richness, allowing for multiple interpretations of a single *nkisi.* A single object (a small, white river rock, for example) might operate, at one and the same time, as a color symbol (connoting a connection with the other world) and a metonym (noting its relationship to a tumor). In addition to materials included for their metaphorical, metonymic, and symbolic significances, some medicines were included in the *nkisi* because they elicited a sense of awe.[36] Hair and fingernails in the *nkisi* identified the intended victim while claws and horns contributed to the visual power of the objects and to their overall complexity as evidenced in the following example: "All of the little rarities that one can find, several sorts of shells, stones and bells, dried plants, herbs, feathers, rock crystals, gum, tree bark, roots, grains, pieces of fabric, claws and horns, teeth, hair and fingernails . . . sewn up and crowned with the feathers of parakeets, chickens, or some other bird, with cords and pieces of fabric and woolen cloth and canvas of divers colors hanging all about."[37]

Minkisi and the Subtleties of Agency

Central to an understanding of the *minkisi* complex is the recognition of *minkisi* as living entities. Although *minkisi* are fabricated objects, they have a will of their own that they exert in the world. Indeed, they could be very jealous and so temperamental that one attributed both success and failure in an endeavor to the proper observance or regrettable neglect of their demands.[38] As living entities, they might be considered superior to human beings in that they regularly moved between this world and the land of the dead and were active in both worlds in ways that exceed human capabilities.[39] Moreover, the *minkisi* took their animating spirit from the land of the dead and continued to maintain very immediate connections to that world throughout the duration of their lives. Minkisi existed in a state of ambiguity: "For if they are of the nature of a person—which is what behavior toward them argues—they are also of the nature of a thing."[40] While they are created much like other, mundane objects, they are treated as human subjects and accorded a sort of deference and reverence ordinarily reserved for persons." The *nkisi* acted as both object and person, a matter clarified by kiKongo grammar in which the word *nkisi* belongs not to the class of nouns used to denote things but to the class of "semi-persons."[41]

Writing in *The Powers of Presence*, Robert Armstrong suggests that the nkisi "sometimes *is* and at other times *is not* with power." That is, at times it is merely a thing, whereas at other times it is more like a person.[42] Yet even when the *nkisi* was without power—when it was just a thing—it still harbored a certain ritual potential not commonly accorded other things or objects in Western thought. Even without the requisite medicines, the *nkisi* was always imminently with medicine and always on the verge of power. In this way, *minkisi* challenged the commonly held assumption in Enlightenment thinking that things are categorically different from persons and thereby created something of a crisis for European observers who first described them in the sixteenth and seventeenth centuries. In response, some chroniclers decried the so-called fetishes they encountered, charging "anything upon which an African's eye happened to fall might be taken up by him and made into a 'fetish,' absurdly endowed with imaginary powers."[43]

Rather than regard the *nkisi* object as proof of the presumed irrationality and ignorance of Africans, one might acknowledge the fact that Kongolese ritual objects blur the distinction between things and persons and alter the way we commonly conceive of agency such that some "objects" (namely, *minkisi*) could be conceived as agents. The converse is also true: Human agents may be deemed mere objects or vessels, animated by resident spiritual forces.

Nailing and the Invocation of *Minkisi*

Even after having constructed the *minkisi* and investing it with proper medicines, there remained the task of invoking it to action. One of the more common methods for invoking an *nkisi* was burial, especially in cases in which the *nkisi* was not a wooden figure but a container of some other sort, as in a raffia bag or an animal skin. In these cases the *nganga* might bury the *nkisi* in a strategic place to reflect a symbolic connection between it and the graves of the dead. Luca da Caltanisetta, a Capuchin missionary in Kongo, recounted the burial of spiritual elements that enabled the *nganga* to establish a connection through which "he had demons come as witnesses."[44] Burial suggested a connection to ancestral spirits whom the *nganga* might call upon to effect good fortune, seek out a criminal, or cause harm.

Yet the arousal or awakening of *minkisi* could be achieved in a number of ways. One of the more common and most spectacular methods of invocation consisted of the driving of nails into the body of the *nkisi,* especially the wooden objects of the *nkondi* type, the primary purpose of which was to seek out wrongdoers. In fact, the Kongolese sometimes spoke of nailing as the "burying" of an issue in the body of the *nkisi.*[45] These nails aroused the *minkisi* to action and contributed to their spectacular appearance. Interestingly enough, nailing had not always been the manner of invocation in Kongo and appears to be a convention dating back to the late seventeenth and early eighteenth centuries. Before that time, ritual experts used striking or banging to arouse the *nkisi.* Writing in 1698 Caltanisetta observed, "She, herself, was a feticheuse, called *nganga* zagi, that is to say, priestess of the devil having power over thunder and lightning. . . . In the name of these idols, she was cursing her enemy, invoking strikes of lightning upon him . . . [as] she knocked the idols together, one against the other."[46] Caltanisetta was obviously shaken by the *nganga's* demonstrative exhibition and he clearly acknowledged the efficacy and validity of her ability to harness the powers of thunder and lightning. He admitted fear and refused to challenge, instruct, or even engage the *nganga.* Instead, he excused himself by saying that a confrontation with the woman might provoke a tumult and hinder him from completing more urgent work that awaited him. He resigned himself to the notion that "in order not to lose all of the good, I tolerated a little of the bad."[47]

Decades earlier Father Pero Tavares recounted his own experience of having been struck by a bolt of lightning in the dead of night as he lay asleep in bed. Tavares had been searching for a local man, Francisco Casolla, who, despite being a converted Catholic, continued to practice as an *nganga,* having built a reputation as a great healer. Tavares had gathered a posse intent on arresting the man when he was struck, which convinced his party to end the manhunt and thereby avoid harm. Though Tavares had planned to have the offender excommunicated, he later decided that Casolla, having fled his home, likely never to return, had excommunicated himself, effectively terminating the need to seek him out further.[48]

The practice of banging, as described by Caltanisetta, was replaced by driving nails into the figures to produce the desired effect. The Kongolese began producing nails at the turn of the eighteenth century and the association between driving nails into *minkisi* seems to correlate with a very particular interpretation of the Christian crucifix. The image of the crucifix and the symbolism of Christ nailed upon a wooden cross resonated with Kongolese notions of an *nkisi* being aroused to action. Many Kongolese recognized Christ as the greatest or highest *nkisi,* and his death on the cross and ultimate resurrection evoked a symbolic and theoretical connection between Kongolese *nkisi* and the Christian crucifix. Both were objects of power that were aroused/resurrected after being nailed and evidence suggests that many Kongolese understood the crucifix as yet another powerful *nkisi.*[49] Dona Beatriz actively encouraged the destruction of crosses and crucifixes and regularly burned them because she maintained that they were being revered by the Kongolese as "idols" and "fetishes."[50] Hence the first references to "nail-fetishes" date from the late seventeenth and early eighteenth centuries and reflect a practice based on a novel interpretation of Christian iconography.[51]

Dapper offers an interesting report regarding the relationship between nailing and the invocation of an *nkisi* called Kikokoo, a wooden statue carved in the shape of a seated man. Kikokoo stood near the community cemetery at Loango in the village of Kinga, highlighting its role as guardian and keeper of the dead. Loango was a coastal port city, and accordingly, Kikokoo governed the seas, prevented thunderstorms, ensured the safe arrival of ships at port, and, notably, protected the dead in the cemetery from witches who might steal their souls in order to bind them in perpetual slavery in the other world. Under the cover of night several Portuguese traders stole Kikokoo and brought him back to their ship, where they accidentally broke his head and arm. They dared not return him in such a state and decided to reattach the arm and head with a large nail. In that somewhat compromised condition, they replaced Kikokoo in his proper post, once again under the cover of night. The next day, a Portuguese ship ran aground and the *nganga* cried out that it was due to Kikokoo's vengeance for those who had invoked him by driving nails into his head that the ship failed to arrive safely at port.[52]

Minkisi and the Context of the Slave Trade

The growing intensity associated with the slave trade had tremendous effects on Kongolese society. Father Dicomano noted that intragroup jealousies and hatreds could be manipulated so as to feed the growing desire for slave labor. He observed that if any one fell sick or died, the community invariably accused someone of harming him through witchcraft. A trial by ordeal ensued and if convicted, local authorities confiscated all of the goods owned by the accused. Moreover, if the presumed victim of witchcraft were a child or a village lord, the convicted was put to death and his whole family was sold to traders and shipped to the Americas. Such was the case for one *nganga,* who, being accused before the Portuguese governor at Luanda, pleaded his case: "If I have caused the clouds to rain, was this a crime? If at a time when there was no boat to be found in the river, I out of pure compassion called the crocodiles to carry us over, must this be accounted a sin?"[53] In the end his eloquence did not serve him and he was sent as a slave to Brazil.

So extensive was the sale in slaves during this period that Dicomano concluded that slaving was the only commerce to speak of in Kongo.[54] Kongolese in the Bamba region transported the largest quantity of slaves to the English who traded guns, powder, fabrics, and pots. As the volume of the trade increased, so did the number and size of slave caravans intent on capture. Led by guides, these caravans were well armed with guns "but even more by carrying special caravan *nkisi,* or charms, which were feared by local people inland far and wide."[55] Indeed, the Mubiri, an infamous band of caravan traders, were "feared and respected since people believed they were great sorcerers."[56] The Mubiri sold captives at various ports, including Cabinda, Soyo, and other areas where they "obtained copper with which they constructed their idols."[57]

Even the fiercest slave caravans required the cooperation of inland communities so they could pass freely from place to place. As a result they were careful not to raise the ire of any local communities by "unwittingly offending a [local] fetish."[58] Moreover, customs barriers stood guard along the route where armed men and religious shrines protected border checkpoints.[59] Caravan leaders had to be ever aware of the areas through which they passed and had to be knowledgeable about local customs and ritual practices to avoid conflict. Knowledge of the varied *minkisi* that operated along the caravan route helped greatly. In this way aspects of Kongo indigenous belief had not only religious but also economic implications for traders who desired to travel through the interior regions without incident and arrive safely at the coast to turn a healthy profit.

The *minkisi* complex operated at all levels of the Atlantic slave trade in Kongo extending from the inland areas where slaves were procured to the coastal trading towns. Through the dynamics of the slave trade, captive Africans dispersed an *nkisi* tradition throughout the Americas that became a crucial component in the religious expression of enslaved communities in a number of New World locales. Still, *minkisi* did not simply reappear in the New World. Instead one notes that New World slaves utilized a series of ritual objects that resonate, in construction, symbolism, and use, with the *minkisi* tradition of West-Central Africa. When they appeared, these objects were characterized by innovation and creativity and, for that reason, should not be read as some form of diminished memory. Rather, these objects continued to respond to the immediacy of everyday life.[60]

Ritual Objects in the New World Context

Robert Farris Thompson defines the *nkisi* as a strategic object used throughout the African Atlantic to encourage healing and other related phenomena. In Cuba, enslaved Africans recast these objects as *prenda,* figures created by a ritual expert who filled a kettle or pot with "all manner of spiritualizing forces: there he keeps the cemetery and the forest, there he keeps the river and the sea, the lighting bolt, the whirlwind, the sun, the moon, the stars."[61] In addition to the *prenda,* nineteenth-century Cubans also created carved figurines used to attack enemies and slaveholders. In Haiti, ritual experts created *pacquets-congo* by wrapping sacred medicines in silk, cotton, or raffia cloth secured with pins and ribbons and invested with the Simbi spirits first mentioned in chapter 2. In Brazil *ponto de segurar* (securing points) were yet another set of ritual objects wrapped in cloth and tied tightly with cords.[62]

Ritual objects were ubiquitous in the antebellum South, known variously as conjure bags, tricks, hands, charms, and tobys. C. C. Jones describes a conjure bag commonly used along the Georgia coast: "The ordinary fetich consisted of a bunch of rusty nails, bits of red flannel, and pieces of brier-root tied together with a cotton string. A toad's foot, a snake's tooth, a rabbit's tail, or a snail's shell was sometimes added . . . to insure the efficacy of the desired spell, it was necessary that the charm should be secretly deposited under the pillow of the party to be affected, placed upon the post of a gate through which he would pass, or buried beneath the doorsteps of his cabin."[63]

Enslaved Africans used conjure bags to heal the sick, harm enemies, reveal the unknown, protect themselves from the brutalities of slavery, and achieve countless other aims. They resembled Kongo *minkisi* in that they served as focal objects for a rather large network of ritual beliefs and practices. W. E. B. Du Bois suggests the complexity and multiplicity of this ritual network when he described the conjure doctor as "the healer of the sick, the interpreter of the unknown, the comforter of the sorrowing, the supernatural avenger of wrong, and the one who rudely but picturesquely expressed the longing, disappointment, and resentment of a stolen and oppressed people."[64]

By the end of the nineteenth century the collection and documentation of the arts of slave conjure had established the operation and persistence of a coherent system of ritual practice and belief. Much of what we know of slave conjure practices in the antebellum South comes from travelers, missionaries, and planters who acknowledged a widespread belief in slave conjure along the coastal regions of Georgia and South Carolina. Much like European reports of the Kongo *minkisi* tradition, these sources are marred by a marked ethnocentrism and cultural arrogance. Leonora Herron, one of the earliest investigators of slave conjure, described it as a "curious conglomerate of fetishism, divination, quackery, incantation, and demonology."[65] Others maintained that the widespread practice of conjure reflected an obtuseness and narrowness of intellect on the part of slaves.[66]

Many early reporters presumed that slave conjure represented a rather hazy and undifferentiated set of beliefs that originated in Africa and survived through the period of enslavement. C. C. Jones noted that "they believe in second-sight, in apparitions, charms, witchcraft, and in a kind of irresistible Satanic influence. The superstitions brought from Africa have not been wholly laid aside. Ignorance and superstition render them easy dupes to . . . conjurers; to artful and designing men." [67] Julien Hall, one of the first scholars to look systematically at the arts of slave conjure, echoed this sentiment, concluding that conjure was "brought here from Africa by the first comers and continue[s] in full force." [68] Virginia historian Philip Bruce writes similarly: "Their superstition is the same as that of Congo blacks." [69]

In asserting a generalized African influence on the ritual beliefs and practices of antebellum slaves, these commenters equated slave ritual practice with what they termed the dark and idolatrous beliefs of an African past. But their comments do not represent any actual attempt to understand the history and operation of slave conjure; instead they reflect a reduction of slave conjure to that set of ritual practices and beliefs thought contemptible and, therefore, subject to eradication. Their perspective corresponds closely to ideas regarding fetishism and idolatry that first developed during the fifteenth century but continued to enjoy significant currency throughout the period of slavery and the slave trade. In the end their comments obscure not only the ritual practice of American slaves but also the religions of West and West-Central Africa by conflating a broad and varied vocabulary of ritual practice into a flat and monolithic rubric dominated by the idea of the fetish and other related notions. C. C. Jones, for example, thought it necessary to "restrain the practice of Fetichism by positive inhibition, or by labored persuasion of its utter absurdity." [70] He decried the "fabrication of fetiches, and their sale to those who desired to utilize the powers of the deities which they were supposed to represent" and hoped that a "plain and faithful presentation of the Gospel" would weaken and destroy those aspects of slave ritual practice deemed offensive. [71] Interestingly enough, in acknowledging the "powers of [those] deities," Christian missionaries and slaveholders, perhaps unwittingly, asserted the efficacy of the ritual practices in question.

Conjure Bags, Containment, and Astonishing Invocations

As in Kongo *minkisi,* the notion of containment carried significant import for the conjure bags of the slave South. To that extent root doctors often wrapped or bound their powerful medicines inside a conjure bag or sealed their concoctions tightly inside glass bottles. Lowcountry slaves often made use of dark-colored bottles that they filled with mysterious aqueous solutions along with pins and needles to be "secreted in some corner of the room in which the victim lives or placed along the road" where the target is known to travel.[72] Rattlesnake master was a root "pulled at a certain angle of the moon. It [was] put in a bottle, told what to do, corked tightly, and put in a secret place."[73] Moreover, conjurors often placed "ground-dogs," a certain type of salamander, inside wide-mouth bottles that they then buried under the threshold of a person targeted for conjure. The conjure doctor then made cross marks above the burial site and, after a time, the "ground-dogs" burst from the bottle and, finding their way into the stomach of the victim, effected an immediate and painful death.[74] In 1899 a student at Hampton Institute in Virginia recounted her own childhood experiences with the religious and ritual practices of blacks in her community. Referring to conjure bottles, the student recalled, "these medicine bottles, often called 'walking boys,' typically featured string tied tightly about the neck. The bottles are generally dark in color, that one may not see what the doctor puts in it—something alive, you may know, which enables it to move or even flutter briskly—and this makes you certain of whatever fact the doctor is trying to impress."[75] Indeed, Lowcountry residents commonly used these walking boys as a form of protective decoration. Blacks in the Lowcountry decorated trees using brightly colored shiny glass bottles with the understanding that evil spirits would be attracted to the bottles and, in an effort to satisfy their curiosity, would venture inside and thus be trapped.[76]

The National Museum of Ethnography in Stockholm is home to *Nkisi Nkondi Mungundu* (before ca. 1907), which takes as its body a dark green wine bottle, the neck of which is decorated by a collar of fibers and a pack of medicine. The bottle itself is stopped with a cork, out of which emerges a plume of raffia strips, cloth, and red leather. The strips, raffia cloth, and leather "flutter when the *nkisi* is made to dance in the course of the ritual," evoking signs of spirit possession.[77] *Nkisi Nkondi Mungundu* is not a mere replica of seventeenth- and eighteenth-century *minkisi.* Kongolese ritual experts constructed *minkisi* out of a whole range of materials, both old and new, including items that originated in Kongo (raffia and ritual medicines) and in Europe (wine bottles and corks). The *nganga* creatively adapted *nkisi* construction, assimilating new elements and methods into their practice, yet a certain set of core principles—as in theories of containment, color symbolism, and astonishment—connect *minkisi* found during the seventeenth and eighteenth centuries with those of a later period.

Likewise, the temporal relationship between *Nkisi Nkondi Mungundu* and the "walking boy"—only eight years separating their construction—suggests that even as the *minkisi* complex is dynamic and flexible, a certain vocabulary of ritual construction persists so that both objects may be considered together.

The temporal link between *Nkisi Nkondi Mungundu* and the walking boy is crucial in this formulation of the African Atlantic religious complex. Most treatments of African cultural continuities in the Americas posit Africa as a source, an original point from which springs cultural practice in any number of African diasporic locales. This formulation presumes a certain linear progression between the cultures of West Africa and their counterparts in the Americas, whereby Africa inhabits a cultural space that is ever prior to the space occupied by the Americas. Related to this, these studies tend not to treat the ongoing dynamism that characterize West African cultures and tend not to delve into the ongoing relationships that attended the cultures of West Africa and their counterparts in the Americas. The fact that ritual experts on both sides of the Atlantic utilized *Nkisi Nkondi Mungundu* and the "walking boy" during the same period of time suggests that not only were certain *minkisi* brought to the Americas and embellished by African captives and their progeny but also that the objects existed, in a temporal sense, side by side and together contributed to an ever-developing African Atlantic religious complex that extended, in this case, from Kongo to the Americas and throughout the African Atlantic. Thus Africa need not always precede ritual belief or practice in the New World but may also stand along side the slave cultures of the Americas.

Neither were conjure bottles peculiar to Kongo or the Carolinas; they existed throughout the African Atlantic complex. Domingos, an enslaved African in eighteenth-century Brazil used bottles to perform divination. It was said he had the ability to make his divination bottles dance and could suspend them in midair. Just as blacks in the Lowcountry fashioned bottle trees as a way of trapping evil spirits, so Domingos used the bottles to ensnare suspected criminals and evildoers, causing their images to appear inside his divination bottles. Domingos's special form of divination and its relationship to bottle trees, walking boys, and Kongo *minkisi* reveal the African Atlantic to be a wonderfully rich constellation of practices and rituals, with each site connected and conversant with the others.[78]

Just as nailing characterized the construction and use of *minkisi* in Kongo, so enslaved Africans adapted their own ideas about the importance of nailing, slashing, and cutting in Lowcountry conjure bags.[79] C. C. Jones highlights the use of "rusty nails" as a key component in the construction of conjure bags in the Lowcountry. The presence of pins and needles in the conjure bag described by Jones establishes its connection to Kongo practice. Even when nails were not used, a set of metaphorically equivalent items—needles, razors, and blades—served similar purposes and were common. Examples taken from Georgia describe conjure bags made "with snake-root, needles and pins, tied up with pieces of hair of the person to be conjured in a bag of red flannel." [80] These metaphors related also to certain visual puns, so that a hoe, plow point, or axe could be placed under a bed in order to "cut" the pains of childbirth.[81]

Although the use of rusty nails, pins, and needles recalls the driving of nails into Kongo *minkisi,* the conjure bag in antebellum America did not replicate a prior African archetype. Nails, pins, and needles were put to a variety of uses in the conjure bag, representing a creative elaboration of Kongo *minkisi.* Newbell Niles Puckett reports that slaves made rude images of prospective conjure victims modeled of wax or of mud and pierced with pins and thorns.[82] In addition, blacks in Louisiana created small human effigies, covered with blood and pierced through the heart.[83] Indeed, some Lowcountry conjure doctors sold "small doll like figures called "sufferin' roots," which when named for an enemy could cause a complete loss of health as pins were repeatedly stuck in various parts of the doll's anatomy." [84] In addition, slaves recast notions of nailing by including pins and needles inside ritual objects as in the example of a conjure bag containing a "rusty nail, finger and toe nails, hair and pins sewed up in a piece of red flannel" that had been buried in the yard of a victim.[85] Moreover, antebellum slaves fashioned a rather large set of colloquial remedies, cures, and conjures that connoted nailing, cutting, and slashing. For example, in order to "pin bad luck" on a person, one need only drive a rusty nail in the front doorstep of the victim; a hair wrapped tightly around a nail could be buried with the tip pointing upward under the doorstep of an enemy to induce insanity.[86] Enslaved Africans in the Lowcountry adapted the prevailing theories of nailing that had operated in Kongo to create a dynamic ritual practice in the Americas, which, though based on earlier forms was neither static nor formulaic.

In addition to nails and needles, hair was commonly used in conjure bags intended to bring harm or even death upon an enemy. One Sea Island resident asserted that hair is one of the most "powful tings yuh enemy kin hit hole ub" because it grows near the brain and, therefore, a conjure made from hair can affect the brain.[87] Writing in *Folk Beliefs of the Southern Negro*, Newbell Niles Puckett reports that in order to ensure death or sickness, all an enemy has to do is get some of the victim's hair, toenails, or fingernails and have a special concoction made that is then buried in front of the victim's door or secretly hung in his room.[88] Hair and nail clippings identified the victim to be conjured, thus ensuring that the effects of the conjure would be properly directed. Without the requisite hair or nail clippings, the conjure might miss its mark completely or injure an innocent. In order to avoid the effects of this harmful conjure, many antebellum blacks burned hair and nail clippings and regularly removed hair from their combs.

As is the case with Kongo *minkisi,* a certain set of implements and medicines were included in the conjure bag because they elicited a sense of astonishment. Included in this set of items was the infamous black cat bone crucial to so many conjure recipes. So powerful was the bone of a black cat that it could ward off conjure, cure disease, or even give its possessor the power to fly. The manner of securing the bone was gruesome and required that one capture the requisite cat and boil it alive until the powerful bone could be recovered.[89] In lieu of this, the hairs from the right hind leg of a black cat produced a powerful, though less potent, conjure.[90] In addition to the black cat bone, ritual experts invested conjure bags with the power of "snake's heads, lizards, and scorpions, dried and beat into a powder."[91]

Color was another important factor in the construction of conjure bags, especially red, the color of choice for the vast majority of conjure bags. One notes repeated references to "red flannel," such as in the reference to "a small red flannel bag filled with pins, small tacks, and other things . . . buried under a gate-sill."[92] Lenora Herron and Alice Bacon recount a similar case in which a man, believing himself the victim of conjure, found a bottle, filled with roots, stones, and an unknown reddish powder under his doorstep. He burned the bottle and its contents and immediately recovered.[93] Lowcountry blacks might further embellish this color symbolism as in the general practice of wearing red flannel underwear as a protection against rheumatism.[94]

Graveyard dirt in conjure bags connoted a relationship between the arts of conjure and the spirits of the dead. If possible, graveyard dirt to be used in conjure was to be collected from the grave of a murdered person and money left in exchange.[95] Similar practices are found in the West Indies, where the idea of working magic "through soil from a grave, and leaving a coin on it" was well known.[96] Although the implements used in conjure bags varied significantly, a certain orthodoxy did develop in the coastal region, such that graveyard dirt, nails, blood, and hair were recognized universally as the basic elements in any conjure recipe.[97] As noted above, Lowcountry slaves further acknowledged the power of the dead by "burying" conjure bags under a pillow, a gatepost, or doorsteps, thereby eliciting this connection to the dead.

All of these embellishments on the *minkisi* complex should not be read as the inability of Lowcountry blacks to replicate West-Central African ritual in a new environment. Indeed, black American conjure traditions were not mimetic; rather, they established a ritual space where Africa was both remembered and (re)imagined. In the end slaves elaborated on the Kongo *minkisi* and created new ritual objects, replete with their own construction and with their own manner of invocation. So we return to the notion of tradition as a practice that involves principally the manner in which enslaved men and women put Africa to use.

Though this chapter focuses on the special relationships between the *minkisi* complex in Kongo and the conjure tradition of the Lowcountry, West-Central Africans did not hold sole provenance over the practice of the conjuring arts in the Lowcountry. Indeed, conjure is best regarded as a ritual practice that featured elements not only from various African regions but also from Native American and European cultures. Slaves learned much from Native Americans regarding the healing properties of North America's pharmacology. One of the more popular medicinal plants employed by Lowcountry blacks was "Cherokee," a root used to ensure good luck.[98] The name of the plant implies a probable connection between black ritual experts and their Native American counterparts. In South Carolina, Boston King, a Methodist minister and former slave, recalled that his mother served as a root doctor, being employed "chiefly in attending upon those that were sick, having some knowledge of the virtue of herbs, which she learned from the Indians."[99] Though quite rare, there were some white conjurors in the Lowcountry whose special talents were highly regarded by blacks. Richard Parkinson, a British agriculturalist touring the United States, reported on a white conjuror who made ritual objects and charms that blacks found exceptionally effective.[100]

Many of the words used by Lowcountry blacks to describe ritual medicine attest to its varied and diverse construction. Several variants of the term "Obeah," used frequently to denote a complex set of African derived ritual practices, constitute part of the religious lexicon of the Lowcountry as in the case of two Carolina slaves, Harry and Cuff, who purchased "a small matter of truck or Ober" from one Quash, called the 'Ober Negro.'"[101] Philip Morgan reports that one Hector, a South Carolina slave and root doctor, claimed, "Let the fire kindle as fast as it will, he will Engage by his Obias to stifle and put it out."[102] W. B. Hodgson, a former slave in Georgia recalled the prevalence and noted the persistence of the "Obi practices and fetish worship of the pagan negroes early imported into this country . . . of which traditional traces may be still be discovered."[103] In addition to variants of the term "Obeah," other words current in antebellum South Carolina attest to the varied influence that Africans from different regions had in the development of the Lowcountry conjure arts. The Hausa word *huduba,* meaning "to arouse resentment in one person against another," may have been a precedent for the hudu (hoodoo) of the Lowcountry, meaning "to cause bad luck." Zora Neale Hurston suggests that both hoodoo and voodoo are derived from the Hausa *juju* for evil spirit. Other words with very similar meanings also emerged, including *kafa* for charm, the Ewe term *wudu* for sorcery, and the Kimbundu (West-Central African) *wanga* for charm or witchcraft.[104]

The latter term, *wanga,* appears not only in the Lowcountry but also in the historical record of colonial Louisiana, where it circulated along with a set of corollary terms, including the Mende-derived *gris-gris* and *zinzin,* which referred to the special ritual objects used as forms of rebellion in that region. Even more, references to a variant of *wanga* can be found in the eighteenth-century slave conspiracy led by Makandal in Saint-Domingue, where slaves produced a charm called *ouanga* used specifically as a poison to be administered to an enemy or a rival. The *ouanga* packets contained roots, cemetery bones, nails, holy water, holy candles, holy incense, holy bread, and crucifixes.[105] The circulation of the term *wanga* through West-Central Africa, South Carolina, Louisiana, and Haiti illustrates the circulation of a certain vocabulary of ritual practice around the African Atlantic. Though slave spiritual practices were certainly not identical in all of these locations, they were connected, one to the other, in a broad network of religious theory and praxis.

Slave conjure, then, was varied and complex in construction and implementation, even as its relationship to particular African Atlantic ritual practices can be discerned. In this sense, slave ritual practice in Lowcountry was far from hermetic. To address the varied components that contributed to slave conjure in the Lowcountry does not minimize the Kongo influence on slave ritual arts. Neither does this attention render slave conjure an undifferentiated ritual practice whose constitutive elements are ultimately unknowable. Tracing the historical trajectory and context by which Kongo ritual came to affect Lowcountry ritual highlights again the composite nature of black culture, thus serving as a corrective to the view that the cultural relationships between Africans and their contemporaries and progeny enslaved in the Americas are either indecipherable or unimportant.

Though slaves employed multiple forms, symbols, allusions, and implements in the operation of slave conjure, the practice was not at all capricious. Wyatt MacGaffey provides special insight on this point when he argues that cultural tradition "is neither a continuously communicated body of lore nor a set of mental habits but an ongoing social practice which relies on, produces, and modifies the knowledge it needs."[106] Such was the case for enslaved Africans along the sea coast of Georgia and South Carolina for whom the theories and symbolisms of *traditional* Kongo ritual practice maintained their importance, even as slaves put these theories to use by adapting their practical applications to respond to the vagaries of plantation life.

Two-Heads, Conjure Doctors, and Root Workers

Known variously as root workers, two-heads, or conjure men, ritual experts held considerable influence and status in the slave community. That they were known by multiple titles illustrates the variety and flexibility of a ritual practice, which included but was not limited to divination, sorcery, and herbal medicine. In this sense, one need not draw too fine a line of distinction between these different realms of ritual action. An expert in herbal medicine might also serve as a conjure doctor; and a fortune teller might be adept at administering spells.

So fluid were these ritual practices that Lowcountry blacks often utilized the conjure arts in concert with other forms of ritual practice. When in the late nineteenth century a preacher arrived at his newly assigned parish, he found himself wholly unwelcome by the congregation. Locked out of his first prayer meeting by shotgun-wielding members of the congregation, the new clergyman was anxious to change the relations with his would-be flock. Week after week he attempted to attract new members, until finally a conjure man approached him, suggesting that he could increase his flock if he simply carried about his person a conjure bag. The preacher consented and immediately enjoyed a newfound popularity with his congregation—until curiosity got the better of him and he opened the conjure bag to study its contents. In the end the preacher "tore up [the bag] and threw it away, and [was] never able to draw an audience since."[107]

In order to be successful, conjure doctors required extensive knowledge of roots, a matter of no small importance for a people displaced and enslaved in a new context, forced to resolve a new set of practical and pharmacological issues.[108] Art historian Michael Harris notes, "Here is the transplanted African learning to conjure with new roots, new herbs, and old meanings. . . . Here is that scorned dark woman gone into the woods, tearing off the burlap sack dress to clothe herself in the protective culture of her ancestral legacy."[109] The New World presented enslaved Africans with new herbs, oils, implements, plants, and roots with which ritual experts had to familiarize themselves.[110] Slaves often called upon conjure doctors to treat general ailments in the slave community, requiring conjure doctors to rely on their knowledge of various roots and other natural medicines. William Edwards made medicine from "King Physic [which] grows on duh salts an is bery plentiful, but yuh hab tuh know how tuh fine it."[111] Edwards also included insects in his medicinal arsenal: "Duh spiduh web is good fuh stoppin duh blood wen anybody git cut."[112] He used both the web and the spider itself, transforming them into medicine by "stooin eel skin in lawd wit it. Wen dis is done, I hab a saave dat will stop any kine uh pain."[113] George Little, a root worker and resident of Brownville, Georgia, reports that he studied the science of herbs from the time he was a little boy and listed his favorites: golden seal, yellow dust, golden thread, hippo root, pink root, lady slipper, yellow root, blood root, rattlesnake master, black snake root, and John the Conqueror.[114]

John the Conqueror was not only a medicinal root of some importance among the slave community but also a prominent figure in the folkloric experience of antebellum blacks. Cunning and clever, High John "could hit a straight lick with a crooked stick; he could beat the unbeatable."[115] Zora Neale Hurston, well-respected folklorist and novelist, maintains that "he was top superior to the whole mess of sorrow, and what made it so cool, finish it off with a laugh." Antebellum blacks "pulled the covers up over their souls which kept them from all hurt, harm and danger," and told High John stories, in secret.[116]

Hurston tells us that High John had come from Africa, walking on the waves of sound. He walked the very winds that filled the sails of the ships and followed those black and bound bodies huddled down there in the Middle Passage. Once he arrived "he left his power here, and placed his American dwelling in the root of a certain plant." One need only secure the root of the plant in which he has taken up his secret dwelling, dress it with perfume, and keep it on your person or in a secret place in your home to ensure good luck and health.[117] Minnie Dawson, of Pin Point, Georgia, reports that "jis day befo yestuhday a uhmun wuz right yuh tuh dis house sellin High John duh Conqueruh fuh fifty cent an she sho say it would bring yuf powuhful good luck." Unfortunately, Dawson "ain hab fifty cent" and was unable to purchase the root.[118] Perhaps some time later she collected the change needed to secure asylum against a powerful and potent oppressor, a small portion of hope in the body of a protective plant.

Conjurers certainly had the power to heal, but they also could inflict harm.[119] Due to the great influence of conjure in the antebellum South, the root doctor often enjoyed "even more importance than a preacher" because many regarded him with the respect that awe and fear excites. Charles Hunter of St. Simon's island in Georgia admitted, in reference to a local root doctor, "We's sked ub im wen we's boys an use tuh run wen we see im come."[120] Root doctors often assumed a mystical character, as illustrated in the following description:

> The consulting room is smoky, airless, and reeking with a queer pungent odor. The shades are drawn down tightly and the door is shut securely against intrusion. The furniture is scant, consisting of a lamp on a plain table, a couch for the visitor, and placed directly across the room a wooden armchair in which sits the dealer in magic. The most remarkable object in the room is a spirit picture, showing the head of one of the creatures of the shadow world. The eyes are closed, the face bears a rapt, exalted expression, and the picture fades off into a dim mist of clouds.[121]

Root doctors often drew their power by virtue of a peculiar birth. Lowcountry blacks regarded children born with a caul, a thin membrane adhered to the forehead, as specially gifted with psychic power. Removed at birth, the caul must thereafter be cared for and preserved, for if the caul tore, the owner would die. Many slaves believed the caul to be so powerful that even deaf people born with one can hear spirits talk.[122] James Washington reported that he "wuz bawn wid a double cawl wut wuz sabe fuh me till I wuz grown [and] duh spirit show me ebryting."[123]

In addition, the seventh son or the seventh daughter in a family was also deemed specially invested with the power to commune with the other world. A. T. Edwards certainly perceived of the power of seven as wonderfully portentous, as he explains in this 1860 advertisement: "A. T. Edwards is naturally a Doctor—having a gift from the Lord. My mother was her mother's seventh daughter, and I am her seventh son. . . . I am a seven months' child, and walked seven months after I was born, and have shed my teeth seven times."[124] Other root doctors enjoyed special ritual powers in line with their African birth. For slaves, the idea of Africa took on potent meanings, assuming a mystical character as the magical site of supernatural healing, the final destination for the souls of the deceased, and the ultimate cure for the pains and oppressions of plantation life.[125]

In addition to distributing sacred poisons and their remedies, the root doctor's role extended well beyond the strictly spiritual. As in any society, the slave community had to manage any number of grievances, tensions, jealousies, and competitions, both major and minor. Without access to the formal legal and political institutions of the master class, the root doctor served as a mediator, an enactor of social and community justice. Planters often lamented the root doctor's role as community mediator because they saw it as a hindrance to the operations of plantation production. For many slaveholders, the root doctor was as a "secret agent . . . gratifying all the animosities that find lodgment in [the slaves'] breasts, thus allowing them to reek their ill-feelings with absolute immunity."[126] As James Sweet argues in the case of enslaved Africans in Brazil, "an attack on another slave using African religious powers was always more than a personal attack; it was also a strike against the master's economic and social well being."[127] In this way, every act of conjure from one slave against another represented a critical form of resistance, and the depletion of the plantation workforce due to conjure amounted to a blow against the system.

Lowcountry slaves often articulated community grievances through the idiom of conjure so that "it [was] doubtful whether a violent contention ever [arose] between members of the race, that the parties . . . are not convinced . . . that an evil charm has been laid on him."[128] A former slave in South Carolina recounts the experience of his father, who after drinking from a spring in which a conjure bag had been hidden "wuz laid up on a bed o rheumatiz fer six weeks."[129] The victim quickly sought the aid of a conjure doctor, who, upon investigation, discovered the identity of the man who had inflicted the conjure. The root doctor's instructions were clear. He ordered the victim to return to the spring and secure a piece of a particular vine. The root doctor informed his client further that the guilty party must be beaten about the head with the vine and that, if done properly, the blows atop the head would free the victim of the conjure. And so it did. The victim "got up de next day and dey lows dat he nebber did have no mo' rheumatiz."[130]

So powerful, indeed, were the effects of conjure that once someone felt that he had been conjured he would "sink at once into despondency; his figure droops, his face becomes clouded and sad, while his general health declines; from the condition of a vigorous man . . . into an unwholesome melancholy which soon reduces him to a state of prostration."[131] According to C. C. Jones, the victim of conjure "became possessed of superstitious fears, and often complained of bodily 'miseries.'" Doctors were incapable of healing a patient convinced that he had been conjured.[132] For other victims, the effects were as one attacked by madness, "acting as wildly as if he had not only been deprived of his wits but was possessed of the devil" as he fell into paroxysms of anger alternating with fits of fear.[133]

These symptoms dissipated once payment was made to a conjure doctor to have the spell removed. Philip Bruce acknowledged that some cases of sickness were more readily treated by a conjure doctor than by a licensed physician because the cures that the conjure effected seemed almost miraculous, "the process of recuperation being so rapid as to be inexplicable."[134] One need only secure the services of a conjure doctor powerful enough to reverse the effects of the harmful spell and "[the victim's] form becomes erect once more; his old manner is resumed."[135] One victim of conjure consulted a root doctor who informed him that the "charm . . . was under the topmost loose brick of a certain old tomb, the fourth one from the gate, on the left hand side of the middle walk, going in." The victim found the offending charm and received specific instructions from the root doctor regarding the correct manner of discarding the bag. After completing the prescription, the victim was returned to good health.[136] Chloe West of Currytown, Georgia, recounts the time when a neighbor tried to conjure her. West enlisted the aid of root doctor Johnson, who "dig unduh [the] steps an take out a bunl. It hab some dut an some haih an sulphuh in it. Doctuh Johnson say it wuz grabe yahd dut."[137]

Root doctors practiced their art with such skill that they challenged the medical care administered by plantation doctors. One Georgia resident took his daughter to a medical doctor to treat an illness, and when, one year after the visit, the little girl fell sick again, he lamented, "I don't t'ink de Doctuh exceed so well wid de gal, 'cause, een de fus' week een dis same Jinnywerry—befo' de yeah well out—de gal tek wid mis'ry een 'e lef' han' foot, en' w'en I sen'um back tuh de doctuh 'e want'uh chaa'ge anodduh dolluh en' sebenty-fi' cent' fuh t'row mo' physic een de gal. . . . Eb'rybody know dat Doctuh Ba'nwell couldn' be exceed so well . . . elseso 'e wouldn' haffuh cyo' en' de same gal two time en' de same yeah!"[138]

In addition to attacks lodged by other slaves, many Lowcountry blacks maintained a deep trepidation regarding the presence of witches and hags in the community, for which they often sought the aid of conjurers. Witches were known to travel great distances during nighttime hours when they wreaked havoc by "riding" unsuspecting victims. A special type of assault, "riding" consisted of attacking an individual during sleep. Victims commonly reported being deprived of air while their bodies, especially their tongues, lay paralyzed, rendering them unable to escape or call for help. Often these assaults resulted in bruises, contusions, and scratches. In fact, the witch could be "so persistent in her persecutions of her victims that they sometimes pine away and die after a year or two of her nightly visitations."[139] The notion of riding was both metaphorical, connoting a special type of spirit possession, and literal, as witches fashioned special bits that they inserted into unsuspecting mouths, using the hair of their victims as reins and stirrups.[140] To wake in the morning with one's hair tangled or with scratches upon one's body might be a sign that a witch had visited during the night.[141] One could also detect the presence of a witch when, in the early hours of the morning or in the dead of night, one awakes to find oneself suffering from a bout of temporary paralysis.[142]

Before seeking out would-be victims, witches had first to remove their skin. Free of the constraints of their bodies, witches traveled magically over great distances in the nighttime hours, causing terror under the cover of darkness. But nocturnal flights succumbed to daytime restraints as the witch was required to return to the skin before daybreak. Would-be victims of a witch's attack took advantage of this vulnerability. If a would-be victim could find and properly treat the abandoned skin, the witch would not be able to return safely to her body. Thus one notes the following recipe common among slaves in the coastal region as a method of defending themselves against witches: "Rub pepper and salt into the skin left behind by a 'hag,' so that when she returns from her mischief and resumes her skin, as she must before daybreak, the burning pain will drive her out again to her death."[143] As noted earlier, salt warded off witches and evil doers—a belief commonly held among Kongolese converts to Christianity, as noted in chapter 2. So one discerns the development of a certain trope in Low-country folktales, often told and retold, of a witch unable to return to her skin because it had been treated with pepper and salt. When, in the early morning, she tries to jump back into her body, she suffers serious burns, screaming, "Skinny, skinny, you don't know me?"[144] More graphic is the tale of another witch who was unable to reenter her salt-laden skin and took refuge under bed sheets. When the sheets were snatched off, "dere she was raw like a beef."[145]

The attacks made by witches, hastened by the removal of their skin, reflect the idea of the body as a mere shell for resident spirits. The witch was much like any other person in appearance and could be a friend or family member. But once they removed their skin—when they discarded their shell—their true nature was revealed. Tales of witches in flight recall the perceptions of both Africans in Kongo and slaves in the Lowcountry who perceived of *minkisi,* medicine bottles, and conjure bags—and in some cases human beings themselves—as mere vessels housing abiding animating spirits. As discussed in chapter 2, many Kongolese regarded Christ as a most powerful *nkisi.* Even more, the Kongolese had a long tradition of regarding their king as a great *nkisi.* So reports Olfert Dapper in the late seventeenth century in reference to the power of the Kongolese monarch: "The subjects ordinarily give him the name Moquisie [Minkisi], as a title which expresses admirably well the limitless power by which he can, with a single word, impoverish or make rich, humble or elevate, put the provinces in trouble and men in the grave. . . . He makes it rain when he wants, transforms himself into a ferocious beast, makes a knot from an elephant's tooth."[146] Like *minkisi* or the other ritual objects discussed throughout this chapter, the shell is but a container, not unlike other like containers. The true nature of the object is revealed in the spirit. In many respects, the witch is but a person uncontained, left to move freely about the earth, inflicting pain and havoc in her wake.

Enslaved Africans further elaborated notions of containment in their prescriptions for capturing witches. In most cases, the witch who rides victims at night may be captured in the morning through the use of a well-greased bottle or jar placed close to the bed, causing the witch to slip and fall inside during her nighttime escapades.[147] Other prescriptions dictate that an empty bottle be placed near the bed at night along with a cork studded with nine needles. Witches were notorious for their obsessive counting, and after having attacked a victim a witch would be compelled to count the needles before leaving the room. Thus preoccupied, the intended victim must cork the bottle quickly before the witch completes her counting. If performed successfully, the witch would be trapped inside. If the properly corked bottle was then placed in a fire, then the assailant would burn in agony.[148] Or one might simply leave the corked bottle unharmed and wait patiently until "some old woman, faint and weak and nearly dead, will crawl into your house and entreat you to let her spirit out of the bottle or she must die. . . . If you keep the bottle corked, the poor old thing will gradually waste away and die."[149]

Women were more likely than men to be witches, and the old were more likely than the young. Older women, especially those in feeble health, might be especially vulnerable to accusations of witchcraft. Laura Towne, an abolitionist and homeopathic doctor who traveled to the Lowcountry to aid newly freed slaves, recounted the brutal beating of "Mom Charlotte" at the hands of a young man who feared that the old woman had "hagged" him. Towne noted that the man approached her as soon as she arrived on the scene "to beg my pardon and say he would [beat Mom Charlotte] no more." Towne failed to convince the man that Mom Charlotte "did not go every night to his house and 'hag' him, or that he ought to defend himself by beating her to make her stay away." Towne pointed out to the assailant that Mom Charlotte could not have walked half the distance he presumed her to have traveled to execute the attacks.[150]

If some Lowcountry blacks consulted conjurers to help them get rid of "riding" hags, others hired conjurers to hag an enemy. Notably, root doctors did not wantonly administer this more harmful form of conjure and internal systems served to check and balance these maleficent forms. In fact, hagging an enemy could be a painful and precarious undertaking, not only for the victim of such root work but also for the root worker. Often these doctors incurred the wrath of the community. After having administered harmful remedies with impunity throughout his community, one root doctor, a resident of Sandfly, Georgia, found himself "down on is knees" begging for forgiveness and promising not to practice the harmful art "no mo."[151]

Conjure as a Ritual of Resistance

Conjure played a crucial part in slave resistance and rebellion as fictionalized in Arna Bontemps's *Black Thunder,* a novel about the Gabriel Prosser 1800 slave conspiracy in Virginia. In the novel Bontemps introduces the reader to Pharaoh, who worried that he had been conjured. Pharaoh feared the wrath of his fellow slaves, who wanted to harm him as retribution for his having revealed the slaves' plot to the whites: "I been finding frogs' toes and like of that in my pipe. They keeps my bed sprinkled with conjure dust." His fears were confirmed when, after sipping a cup of coffee, he "suddenly began trembling violently. A moment later he was crying: 'see there. They fixed me. I done puked up a varmint. What is it—a snake or a lizzard? Lordy! They done fixed me.'"[152] Bontemps's fiction corresponds to historical sources in which slaves and former slaves recount their experiences with conjure. One Sea Island witness to this type of root work reports that "yuh could see lil animals runnin up an down uh ahm . . . duh tings all done come intuh duh finguhs."[153] Eventually he enlisted the aid of a root worker, who quickly went to work: "He ketch hol uh duh han an duh tings run out. . . . Dey wuz puppy dogs."[154] Indeed, some conjure doctors specialized exclusively in the manipulation of "ground puppies" and could afflict victims with tremendous muscular twitching.[155]

Notably, both men and women practiced as root doctors in a profession that seems to have exhibited remarkable gender equality. Women certainly played their part in slave resistance, as evidenced by the case of Sinda, a slave on the Georgia plantation of Pierce Butler. Described by Frances Kemble as a "hideous old negress," Sinda enjoyed such respect as a prophetess that, "having given out . . . that the world was to come to an end at a certain time, and that not a very remote one, the belief in her assertion took such possession of the people on the estate, that they refused to work; and the rice and cotton fields were threatened with an indefinite fallow, in consequence of this strike on the part of the cultivators."[156]

So strident were the slaves in their belief in the impending apocalypse that the white overseer readily "perceived the impossibility of arguing, remonstrating, or even flogging this solemn panic out of the minds of the slaves. The great final emancipation which they believed at hand had stripped even the lash of its prevailing authority, and the terrors of an overseer for once were as nothing, in the terrible expectation of the advent of the universal Judge of men." [157] Unable to force the slaves to work, the overseer eventually acquiesced on condition that should the prophecy prove false, he would punish Sinda severely. As the sun set without incident on the forewarned Judgment Day, the dawn of Sinda's own apocalypse fast approached. The overseer had Sinda brutally flogged as, on pain of death, Sinda's "spirit of false prophecy was mercilessly scourged out of her, and the faith of her people . . . reverted from her to the omnipotent lash again." Still, Kemble writes, "think what a dream that must have been while it lasted, for those infinitely oppressed people, —freedom without entering it by the grim gate of death, brought down to them at once by the second coming of Christ, whose first advent has left them yet so far from it." [158] Though Sinda's spirit expired, that of her fellow slaves persisted.

Not only her fellow slaves but also many whites acknowledged the efficacy of slave conjure. When Edmund Kirke, a traveler through the South, visited a conjure doctor in the late antebellum period he was initially skeptical, but after a brief interview with the woman, his attitude changed. As the conjure doctor fell deeper into a meditative state, her pipe fell suddenly from her mouth, "her bent figure became erect, and a quick, convulsive shiver passed over her." [159] She took a small conjure bag from her bosom and placed it in Kirke's pocket. When the conjurer accurately relayed some of the significant events of Kirke's past, he felt obliged to confirm her account, though he suggested that she might have learned some of the details of his past from others. As for the conjurer's predictions for his future, Kirke acknowledged, some twenty years after the meeting, that "the woman had a wonderful talent at guessing." [160] Though reluctant to acknowledge the power of the conjure doctor, Kirke grudgingly accepted the slave woman's powers.

Nor was Kirke alone among whites who acknowledged, even if grudgingly, the efficacy of black conjurers. In fact, "many planters who have observed their tenants closely come to have a certain faith in the procedures themselves. . . . They have seen the healing herb close wounds and the bitter tea allay fevers." [161] Edward Pollard, a white southerner, maintained a deep faith in what he termed the "superstitious" slaves, asserting "it is from the Negro that I have learned my superstitions. It is the slave that has given me these precious consolations. It is he that has taught me and persuaded me that the spirits of those mourned as dead are with me still." [162] Pollard had experienced the power of conjure for himself after one of his slaves, Aunt Matilda, relayed a message that had been sent from the otherworld:

"The old woman delivered it with an ominous look. . . . It was that [my angel-sister] was coming for me."[163] Pollard later reported the truth of that prophecy when the spirit of his deceased sister came to visit him from the land of the dead to share a loving moment.

One South Carolina slaveholder, Martin Posey, hired Jeff, a slave, knowing full well his reputation as a conjurer in hopes that he might "do something that would secretly cause his wife's death."[164] This incident and others like it identify slave conjure as an alternate juridical system for the enslaved, and any acknowledgment of or participation in the system by whites served to diminish the power of the more formal legal system of the antebellum United States.[165]

Despite the fact that many whites acknowledged the efficacy of the conjure doctor and even participated in it themselves, they still saw root work as a potential threat to plantation authority. Many southern whites regarded the control of slaves' medical treatment as an essential element in fostering plantation discipline and understood full well the ideological battle posed by slave ritual experts. Planters' adherence to new scientific methods was bolstered by the emergence of professionalized health care and the rise of botanical medicines, which came to replace earlier herbal remedies. As the burgeoning medical establishment developed in the South throughout the nineteenth century, white doctors became increasingly interested in the rational administration of medicine, of which slaves often served as the first subjects. For example, white doctors performed dangerous experimental procedures on slaves, including postmortems and Caesarean sections as southern medical schools "procured an illicit supply of corpses drawn disproportionately from populations of free and enslaved African Americans."[166] News of the novel techniques and mechanisms available to medical professionals circulated widely through the advent of mass print culture in the country, highlighting the role that scientific rationalism and secular medicine played in supporting slavery and white supremacy.[167]

Highlighting this conflict, Sharla Fett, in *Working Cures,* suggests that educated whites "put science to the service of proslavery ideology and white supremacy."[168] Indeed, the work of the root doctor stood in direct opposition to the burgeoning scientific medical establishment that developed during the nineteenth century, "the result [being] a dual system of health care, the two parts of which constantly conflicted with each other."[169] In order to avoid the failures and harshness of white remedies and to exert a degree of control over their own bodies, slaves developed their own systems of medicine and health care centered on the practice of conjure, despite planters' accusations of slave negligence and incompetence in the care of other slaves. When enslaved Africans sought out the medical aid of conjurors and root doctors, they inevitably flouted not only the presumptions of Western rational medicine but also the manifest authority of planters.

The rationalization and secularization of medicine during the nineteenth century proceeded in fits and starts with various medicinal "experts" from different healing traditions all claiming the efficacy and usefulness of their particular methods.[170] Throughout the antebellum period many Americans, black and white, held fast to remedies derived from homeopathy, allopathy, herbalism, and—in the case of slaves—conjure. Jon Butler, writing in *Awash in a Sea of Faith,* reconstructs the religious pluralism that characterized the American landscape during the colonial and early national period. Butler argues that while a burgeoning medical establishment along with Protestant missionaries decried the persistence of magic, witchcraft, and the occult among lower-class whites, the religious fervor that resulted in the Salem witch trials of the late seventeenth century did not continue through the eighteenth and nineteenth centuries.[171] Authorities failed to completely stamp out the practice of magic and the occult, but they eventually resigned themselves to the notion that "occultism did minimal harm to people of minimal importance."[172] As institutional congregations grew in the postrevolutionary period—often building huge religious edifices in the process—the folk medicine, magic, and rituals of lower-class Americans continued, though outside the halls of power, influence, and wealth.

But if authorities came generally to regard the practice of the occult as the harmless rituals of harmless (powerless) people, the same may not be said with regard to slaves. Indeed, the medical establishment, churches, and the courts continued to insinuate themselves into the religious lives of bondsmen. Well after the revolutionary period, and indeed throughout the antebellum era, American authorities engaged in a pitch battle against slave ritual medicine. The religious landscape of the United States in the nineteenth century was dotted with a variety of ritual beliefs, practices, and practitioners, both black and white, many of whom remained outside the purview of the established church. But amid this varied field of belief and ritual, the practice of conjure among enslaved Africans was held up in particular ignominy. In this sense, though conjure was itself a widely diverse practice (including herbal remedies, divination, poisoning, and

curses), one of its principal cohesive elements was its political relationship to the master class. That is, conjure functioned as a form of spiritual
resistance that not only challenged the authority of the master class but
also established an independent realm of criminality, justice, and authority
outside the immediate authority of whites. Conjure granted its practitioners and adherents an avenue to influence, power, health, and retribution
over which the master class had little influence. It constructed a singular,
though not monolithic, universe replete with spirits, graveyard dirt, shorn
hair, animal claws, skin, teeth, and bones difficult to access by whites. Even
as the bodies of slaves were bound under the constraints of slavery, their
spirits and minds acknowledged other authorities.

For its part, the burgeoning medical establishment was sharply divided
between several camps making varied and often oppositional conclusions
about the role of science in the administration of health. In this sense, the
tension that existed on the plantation between owners and black ritual
experts reflected a larger national tension between the rise of scientific
rationalism and the persistence of what might be regarded as a medical counterculture. Despite the rise of scientific rationalism in American
medicine, most whites, not to mention southern legislatures, yet regarded
slave ritual expertise as effective and worthy of trepidation.

This fear is illustrated in the antebellum South in the case of Macon, a
Tennessee slaveholder who permitted his slave Jack to go about the country
practicing medicine. Although Jack "performed many cures of a most extraordinary character," the state prosecuted Macon and found him guilty
of breaking a state law that prohibited slaves from practicing medicine. The
legislature had passed this law in order to guard against insurrectionary
movements on the part of slaves, fearing that "a slave, under the pretence of
practicing medicine, might convey intelligence from one plantation to another, of a complicated movement; and thus enable the slaves to act in concert
to a considerable extent, and perpetrate the most shocking massacres."[173]

The legal attacks on slave conjure seem to be attempts on the part of
whites to determine and define that which constituted valid medical practice.
White medical practitioners, many of whom perceived of slave conjurers
and root doctors as backward and primitive, used the law as an instrument to create, from a vast, varied, and complicated medical landscape,
an orthodox medical practice to which all practitioners were compelled
to adhere. Notwithstanding these varied attacks, both Western medical

practitioners and lay men alike (as illustrated in the Martin Posey case) acknowledged the effectiveness of slave medical practices. In its effectiveness, slave conjure posed a serious threat to the rational and secular administration of medicine and, by extension, the ideologies of power in the antebellum South that justified slavery in the first place.

Nor was slave conjure the site of a merely ideological battle. The root doctor played a critically important role in the slave community as revolutionary leader. Denmark Vesey of Charleston, South Carolina, for example, who carefully plotted his slave uprising, mindfully selecting his associates and gradually collecting arms, employed Gullah Jack, a conjurer, as one of his most important co-conspirators. Jack was a conjurer "who kept African religious traditions alive" by providing the rebels with African religious symbols that promised victory and invincibility. He was "regarded as a sorcerer, and as such feared by the natives of Africa, who believed in witchcraft."[174] Indeed, on his initial passage from Africa to South Carolina, Jack "had his conjuring implements with him in a bag which he brought on board the ship and always retained them."[175] Robert Starobin reports that "vast numbers of Africans firmly believed that Gullah Jack could neither be killed nor taken; and that whilst they retained the charms which he had distributed they would themselves be invulnerable."[176] Harry Haig, another co-conspirator, reports, "Gullah Jack calls himself a Doctor Negro—he charmed [me] and [I] then consented to join."[177] So frightened, in fact, was George, another slave conspirator, that he pleaded with the court to offer him protection: "If I am accepted as a witness and my life spared, I must beg the court to send me away from this place, as I consider my life in great danger from having given testimony. I have heard it said that whoever is the white man's friend, God help them, from which I understood they would be killed. . . . I was afraid of Gullah Jack as a conjurer."[178] Neither were blacks alone in their trepidation; many whites greatly feared Jack's influence among the slave population.[179]

Root doctors not only incited large-scale slave conspiracies but also encouraged resistance on a much smaller level. Frederick Douglass, in *Life and Times of Frederick Douglass,* describes Sandy, a root doctor who was "a genuine African" who "had inherited some of the so-called magical powers said to be possessed by the eastern nations."[180] Sandy offered to prepare a root for Douglass, which, if kept always in his possession, would prevent any white man from striking him. Although Douglass was initially skeptical about the professed power of the root doctor, he finally acquiesced. "I at first rejected the idea that the simple carrying of a root on my right side could possess any such magic power," Douglass wrote. "I had a positive aversion to all pretenders to *"divination."* But Douglass relented, noting that "if it did me no good it could do me no harm, and it would cost me nothing anyway."[181] In carrying the protective charm, Douglass joined many of his enslaved brethren who did the same. And so, C. C. Jones noted, "they have been made to believe that while they carried about their persons some charm with which they had been furnished, they were invulnerable."[182] The power of the root doctor to protect the slaves from the pains and oppression of plantation life created in some an obstinate defiance to slaveholders.[183] In one case the very lash of the overseer upon the back of the slave produced neither welt nor scar but elicited laughter on the slave being thus punished.[184]

Conjure and Slave Folklore

Enslaved Africans told and retold stories of the powers root doctors enjoyed on the plantation. One such story recounts the trials of John, a long-suffering plantation slave who looked to the root doctor for some relief:

> In slavery times John had done got to a place where the Master whipped him all the time. John was told to get a mojo to get out of his next whipping. So he went down to the corner of the Boss-man's farm, where the mojo-man stayed, and asked him what he had. Well, the mojo-man replied, "I have a pretty good mojo, a very good mojo and a damn good mojo." "What will the pretty good mojo do?" asked John. Mojo-man answered, "the pretty good one could turn you into a rabbit, a quail and a snake." John took it.[185]

That the mojo-man could be found at the corner of Boss-man's farm suggests that slave resistance in general, and the conjure arts specifically, resided at the periphery of power and authority symbolized by the big house. Though at the periphery of white cruelty, the mojo-man was close to slaves interested in securing his services. In this way, authority and its resistance existed in relative proximity. Just at the edge of the big house lived those who, like the mojo-man, concocted conjures to resist the demands of plantation life. The mojo-man was part of a much larger network of practitioners and participants who stood poised to oppose the authority of the master class.

Although John consulted the mojo-man in hopes of securing some protection against the lash, he was only able to obtain the pretty good mojo. Though John had access to systems of power outside the authority of the master class, his was still a compromised power, presumably lesser than that of Boss-man. As John leaves the mojo-man, the reader still wonders what clandestine hidden powers lay untapped in the very good mojo and what potential threats remain hidden in the damn good one. The second portion of the story implies that the slave master always had access to ultimate forms of authority, that he possessed the "damn good" conjure:

> Next morning, John slept late and refused to work: "I'm not working for you anymore." Boss-man decided to whip John and when old Boss-man returned to make good on his promise, John turned himself into a rabbit. Unbeknownst to John, Boss-man had a mojo of his own and used it to turn into a greyhound. The rabbit was in a heap a trouble when that greyhound took to the chase. John responded by turning into a quail and flew away from the fast approaching dog. But Boss-man wasn't quite finished and he turned into a chicken hawk and was just about to capture that bird. . . . Well, John changed into a snake in the nick of time and was slithering away to safety when Boss-man turned into a stick and vowed to beat John.

This tale figures slave resistance as malleable as slaves adapted to the systems of power mobilized against them. As the slave is a rabbit, so the master is a greyhound; as the slave is a quail, so the master is a chicken hawk; and as the slave is a snake, so the master is a stick, ready to inflict pain. Though the story ends here, we may rest assured that John will change shape once again and that Boss-man will follow suit soon after. The undying desire and ability of slaves to respond to the forms of violence and oppression on the plantation reflected a constant dialectic with the authority and power of the master class. The forms of oppression—the greyhound, chicken hawk, and stick—responded continually to the diversity of slave resistance. And in like manner, the forms of resistance—the rabbit, quail, and snake—must be sufficiently malleable to adapt to the ever changing forms of violence wielded upon the slave by the master class.

Occasionally root doctors used their ritual powers to enjoy special favor on the plantation. Such was the case for Dinkie, a root worker described in William Wells Brown's slave narrative. Dinkie was so favored that no one "remembered the last time that he was called upon to perform manual labor. In fact, no one dared interfere with him. Dinkie hunted, slept, roamed the woods, ate at mealtime, and went to the city as he pleased. Even more than this, some whites tipped their hats to him and the white patrollers allowed him free passage. With the power to see the unseen, Dinkie had become "his own massa."[186] When challenged by whites to fall in line, Dinkie simply threatened to have the devil take them away. So powerful were the conjure arts of slaves, and so roundly acknowledged as effective, that a skilled practitioner could live as his own master, though he was owned by slaveholders. Dinkie stood as an ultimate threat to the systems of power in the antebellum South, an oxymoronic figure who lived as a free slave. He inspired awe in other slaves on the plantation, who regarded him with fear, amazement, and astonishment.

In this, art imitates life, as Br'er Rabbit, perhaps envious of the lives of men like Dinkie, consulted a nearby conjure man. Br'er Rabbit did not much care for work and had already tried a "heap er scheme fuh git eh libbin outer edder people."[187] Rabbit's desire here speaks volumes about the nature of the slave system and the knowledge that slaves had that their own labors served to support other men. This notion is expressed beautifully, if but briefly, in a couplet oft repeated by slaves: "The big bee flies high, the little bee makes the honey; the black folks make the cotton, and the white folks get the money.[188] The very life of a slave, and certainly her survival, was determined by the degree to which others made a living out of her work. In this parasitic relationship, the few enjoyed the labors of the many. Br'er Rabbit wanted only to be his own boss, to be his own master, a dangerous desire indeed in the plantation South. So Rabbit visited the conjure man to learn the trade and thereby astonish others and make them believe that he was wise. Though the conjure man taught him many curious things, Br'er Rabbit was "greedy fuh knowledge" and demanded that the conjure man give him the full breadth of his wisdom. The conjure man agreed and set Rabbit upon a quest: "Ef you kin ketch one big rattle-snake an fetch um ter me live, me gwine do wuh you ax me fuh." Relying on cleverness and skill, Br'er Rabbit succeeded. He impressed the conjure man, who sent Rabbit out once more to perform the improbable, telling him, "You go fetch me er swarm er Yaller Jacket, an wen you bring um ter me, me prommus you tuh gie you all de sense you want." Br'er Rabbit had flare in his back pocket, and what he lacked in strength he made up for in sheer wit and determination. He returned to the conjure man with the deed done. The conjure man remarked, "Buh rabbit, you is suttenly the smartest ob all de animel, an you sense shill git mo an mo ebry day."[189] Br'er Rabbit received nothing from the conjure doctor save for a set of tasks. He completed the deeds with his own agility, cleverness, and guile. He already possessed all of the tools necessary to be a wise man, to be a conjure doctor, and, by extension, to be a free man.

In 1823 the Medical College of the State of South Carolina was established at Charleston as the first institution of its type in the South. Other southern states followed suit throughout the 1830s, and two decades later medical journals made their first appearance in several southern states. During the nineteenth century the Western medical establishment moved increasingly toward a notion of health and healing that emphasized the clinical treatment of disease. Committed to the scientific method, these physicians were certain that disease was both knowable and treatable. Their notions of health and healing were accompanied by a secularization of medicine whereby physicians regarded the diseases that act on the body as the result of pathogens that, if eliminated from the body, ensured overall health. They perceived of medicine as a purely scientific endeavor.

Slaves in the antebellum South developed wholly different notions of health and healing. First, they avowed the reality and immediacy of the spiritual realm as a factor in their overall health. In this formulation, disease was caused, in large part, by spiritual forces that could be manipulated by men in the material world. Moreover, slave conjure was more than medical in nature. It also was political and social, providing one of the vehicles through which slaves articulated group grievances, jealousies, and conflicts. Like slave conjure, the *minkisi* complex in Kongo was not only clinical but also political (the king was considered an *nkisi*), economic (in that it was supported by established networks of exchange), and legal (used to determine the relative guilt or innocence of accused).

Notably, both blacks and whites acknowledged the effectiveness of slave conjure in the Lowcountry. The same was true in Kongo with regard to the *minkisi* complex, a lesson that the Portuguese traders who nailed Kikokoo learned the hard way after their ship sank. On both sides of the Atlantic, these ritual practices posed a tremendous threat to notions of rationalism and threatened the theoretical underpinnings of slavery and modernity. In justifying American slavery, elite whites established, on the one hand, certain categories of people who were esteemed for their reliance on reason and science and, on the other, developed categories of beings, considered subhuman, whom they derided for their presumed lack of reason and rationality. They were considered backward, superstitious. Theirs was the religion of the past, the idolater, the pagan. Enter the religious practices of slaves with their pins and needles, feathers and bones. According to the theories of rationalism, the use of so-called fetishes by slaves proved their primitive nature and further disqualified them from the fruits of civilization (i.e., freedom). Ironically, the responses of white elites and black clergymen to the practice of conjure among slaves maintained both the absurdity and the effectiveness of slave ritual practice. Most reporters reconciled this contradiction by suggesting that slave conjure operated on a psychosomatic level, noting that once someone felt that he had been conjured, he would "sink at once into despondency . . . while his general health declines."[190] Some observers regarded the psychosomatic effects of conjure as some remnant of so called primitive peoples: "ignorant people, when they get the slightest ailment, are often demoralized by fear, so that reassurance, whether it comes in the form of an herb tea or the mild pills of a physician, does more to restore vigor that pharmacopoeia."[191] This explanation fails to explain the effectiveness of a presumably absurd ritual practice. For in fact, the psychosomatic effects of medicine would not have been greater with regard to slave conjure than they were in the scientific medical establishment, where the psychological effects of medicine and treatment are key. The usefulness and potency of these rituals was proven day after day by the ritual experts who performed the cures and curses and by their clients, who repeatedly and persistently sought out their services. Indeed, in its efficacy, slave ritual practice challenged the ideology of slavery. That slaves were regularly healed by conjure, and that some planters even invoked conjure for their own healing demonstrates that conjure could not be easily dismissed as superstition and that rationalism was not a complete system, invulnerable to attack.

4

Burial Markers and Other Remembrances of the Dead

That night slaves from all about came to the cabin and sat around while they sang and prayed. People kept coming and going all night long . . . now that Sister Dicey was freed from all the trials and tribulations of slavery and was safe in Heaven. . . . And so the sitting up went on all night. . . .

The womenfolk put flowers and ribbon grass on top and put colored bottles, broken glass, and sea shells all around the grave of Sister Dicey. In that way they showed their love for her. . . . No man could own their souls or keep them from loving one another. These gifts came only from God.

William J. Faulkner, *The Days When the Animals Talked*

During the era of the slave trade, Kongolese notions of the soul maintained that the body existed as a container for a composite set of inhabiting souls that, though independent, existed simultaneously in each person, animating the body and investing it with breath and life. The *moyo* pertained to the perishable aspect of the soul. When one died, the *moyo* slowly dissipated and eventually quit the corpse. Along with the heart and the liver, the Kongolese perceived of blood (which is transported and cleansed by these organs) as the source of life, the spark that motored the body. The relationship between blood and *moyo* was crucial to the extent that any loss of blood weakened and damaged the *moyo*.[1] As a result, mourners did not formally consider the deceased dead until all of the humors of the body dried up, a process that could last for months.

A second manifestation of the soul, the *nsala,* was commonly thought of as the seat of reason and was responsible for thoughts and ideas. After one died, the *nsala* moved to the otherworld, where it remained vital until such time as the living relatives and friends of the deceased no longer remembered his or her name. Once the name of the deceased was forgotten, the *nsala* was transformed into a more distant spirit, leaving only the deceased's *mwela,* which represented the breath of life and was the power element of the soul. When one died, the *mwela* did not die but moved to either the realm of good ancestors *(mpemba)* or the realm of evil ancestors *(bankuyu).*[2]

Rituals concerning death and burial acknowledged the composite nature of the body and ensured the easy transition of the soul from this world to the next. Caretakers of the deceased prepared and cleansed the body for the journey into the otherworld. They carried the corpse to the marketplace or another public site and subsequently elevated it on a large block. Mourners gathered to view the body, honor the deceased with song and dance, and inquire as to the possible cause of death. This mourning period lasted for several days and nights. After this initial mourning period, the body was shaved and painted red with a dye made of *takula* wood, a substance used often in Kongolese ritual. The color red signified the nether space between this world and the otherworld, and its application to the body of the deceased suggested the impending movement of the soul from this world to the next. In addition, mourners anointed the body with a balm of varied herbs and ritual medicines.[3] In the case of kings and some noblemen, the body was smoked for several days. Abbé Proyart, a missionary in Kongo in the eighteenth century, noted the dessication of a recently deceased person: "They set a fire which makes a thick smoke. Once the cadaver has been sufficiently smoked, they expose it for several days in open air, leaving someone next [to the corpse] who has no other duty but to chase away any flies that might approach."[4]

The process of smoking the body hastened the movement of the soul out of this world and into the otherworld by drying up all of the humors of the body, leaving the *moyo* to make its transition more quickly. In addition, the smoking of the corpse reflected a sense of perdurance, illustrating the analogy in Kongolese thought that wet is to transient as dry is to durable.[5] In this sense, the drying of the corpse stabilized the legacy of power and authority that the deceased enjoyed when alive. After the interment, mourners continued to gather at the grave site to greet the deceased with song.[6] Father Bernardo da Gallo decried the *Chittampi* ritual he witnessed in Kongo, which consisted of a large feast at which the living shared food and drink with the dead by placing a meal atop the burial mound.[7] This practice is documented widely, and some reports maintain that these feasts were held regularly and that family members "cried over the tomb at each new moon," after which they ate as much as they could and shared their meal with the departed.[8]

Though these rituals ensured the movement of the soul from this world to the next, notions concerning the actual location of that otherworld were nonspecific. The dead were thought to exist in wooded areas, under the ground, or under water. The specific location of the city of the dead was contextual, so that any body of water (the Congo River, the Atlantic Ocean, a local stream), any wooded area, or any underground space could be interpreted as the realm of the dead.[9] Rather than marking the land of the dead spatially, the Kongolese described it differentially. It always existed elsewhere. The land of the dead is where we are not. As the living live in cities and towns, so the dead inhabit the woods; as the living occupy the land, so the dead dwell in the water. The Kongolese also marked this distinction temporally, for the time of the dead reflected an inversion of the time of the living. When the noontime sun prevails in the land of the living, midnight reigns in the realm of the dead. While living men sleep through the night, the dead are active.[10] In this way the dead are not only *where* we are not but also *when* we are not. Yet they are always imminently present in the lives of men and available for guidance and advice, both spiritual and mundane. This duality—that the realm of the dead is always elsewhere yet ever present—evokes a particular geography of power and its operation in the world. For in fact the natural world was full of portals (streams, rivers, forests) through which communication and travel between this world and the next were possible, thus obscuring any clear demarcation between the living and the dead.

House of the *Nkisi* (the Grave)

As discussed in chapter 2, Kongolese ritual experts often buried, that is, awakened *minkisi* through burial in strategic places, thus highlighting a symbolic connection between the powers of *minkisi* and the graves of the dead. While ministering in rural Kongo, Father Caltanisetta came upon a burial mound built by an *nganga*. Small palm-nut-filled packets peppered the mound along with other spiritual elements including ritual ash and wooden *minkisi*. The burial mound served as a portal of sorts, allowing the *nganga* to commune with the devil.[11]

Just as the *nkisi* object was a focal point allowing for communication between this world and the next, the gravesite acted as a portal through which members of a given lineage group communicated with their ancestors. In Kongo thought, burial sites comprised a special category of *nkisi*. Like other *minkisi,* the grave was a contained space within which resided an inhabiting spirit that could be invoked to effect changes in the material world. This sense of containment was reflected in the practice of wrapping the deceased in expensive white fabrics. Proyart noted that

Kongolese mourners often wrapped the body of the deceased in a large quantity of foreign and domestic fabrics and that one judged the relative wealth of the deceased and those that survived him by the quality and quantity of the fabric used.[12] The wrapping of the deceased in expensive fabrics evoked a sense of the containment of the embodying spirit, and white predominated as the color of burial shrouds because it connoted the realm of the dead.[13] For chiefs, burial in this world reflected investiture in the otherworld. The fabrics, grave decorations, and other materials connected with funerary ritual earned honor for the deceased not only in this world but also in the next.[14] The notion of containment was reflected even further in the very earth itself, which was trod upon by relatives during the burial in order to seal the body and soul within its confines, ensuring that the dead would not wreak havoc upon the living.[15] If funerary rites were not performed with care, the deceased could return to trouble the living. In these cases, the *nganga* exhumed and resurrected the body in a public ceremony, making it appear to move and speak. Only after the proper observance of all aspects of the burial ritual could the deceased be again laid to rest.[16]

Mourners regularly placed the last used implements of the dead atop the grave in order to excite the burial mound, to invest the soil with something of the spark of life and the power of the deceased. These objects identified the occupation or special status of the dead. Chairs, bows, arrows, elephant tusks, dishes, utensils, animal skulls, and bones could be placed atop graves. Caltanisetta recounted one such burial site at Mbanza Nsundi in 1697: "I saw a grave at the head of which someone had placed a porcelain cup [from the Netherlands] from which the deceased had drunk; at the foot of the grave there was, fixed in the ground, a musical instrument called an *mpungu* ... because this was the instrument played by the deceased."[17] The porcelain cup and the *mpungu* linked the deceased metonymically with the objects he had used when alive. The objects placed on the grave served as visual reminders of the powers, status, and influence that the deceased enjoyed when alive. The gravesite of a fallen warrior might be decorated with weapons and other implements of war, around which soldiers might gather in order to ask for guidance from their fallen compatriot as they prepared for battle.[18]

When Caltanisetta encountered gravesites decorated with animal bones, musical instruments, and the like, he resolved to rid the country of what he deemed superstitious practices. On one occasion he found such objects, along with a pot resting on two sticks, planted in the shape of an X and immediately destroyed them. On another occasion, he saw two pots full of superstitious objects on a tomb in *Mbanza Mpangu* that he knocked over without hesitation.[19] Later, he approached a gravesite with the intention of removing the objects from the grave until an interpreter dissuaded him, warning that such an act might provoke the villagers. Caltanisetta decided to speak directly to the village leader in order to reprimand him for allowing such practices but was disappointed when the village leader defended the practice by saying that the deceased was, in fact, an honorable and respectable man and that no one, save for a priest (read: *nganga*), could remove the items. Upon hearing this, Caltanisetta, assuming the role of *nganga,* immediately scooped up the items.[20] The practice of dressing gravesites with sacred implements was ubiquitous, and Caltanisetta remained diligent, even if woefully unsuccessful, in his attempts to rid the country of this ritual.

These brazen actions on the part of Christian missionaries could invoke the ire of both the community and the ritual objects themselves. So discovered Jesuit missionary Pero Tavares, whose experience of having been struck by lightning was related in an earlier chapter. While traveling the countryside, Tavares came across a large wooden *nkisi* standing guard at the entrance of a cemetery. The *nkisi* oversaw a large pyramid-shaped mound flanked by a large hollowed-out beam that had been filled with "fetishistic ingredients."[21] Beside the beam stood a small hut with holes in the walls through which people passed food and drink to the deceased. Tavares had seen other cemeteries constructed in a similar manner and was determined that this one would be destroyed in dramatic fashion. The following morning he gathered all of the villagers at the entrance of the cemetery and berated them for their spiritual "blindness and idolatry."[22] Then, to the amazement of the onlookers, he set fire to the *nkisi* that guarded the cemetery. When the legs of the *nkisi* failed to burn, Tavares attempted to push the figure to the ground; the missionary not only failed to knock the figure over but also suffered serious burns for his efforts. The onlookers laughed loudly at this turn of events and maintained that the *nkisi* had burned Tavares in retaliation for the assault. To this, Tavares redoubled his efforts but still could not fell the figure and was forced, once again, to retreat due to the flames while "the bursts of laughter increased." Finally, Tavares threw himself headlong into the fire and, despite suffering terrible burns, threw the *nkisi* to the ground.[23]

Not yet satisfied with his show of force, Tavares continued his assault by tying the *nkisi* to the tale of a horse and dragging it as he beat it with sticks. Soon after, he climbed a tree and cut two branches with which he fashioned a cross as well as some brooms. He erected the cross and used the brooms to sweep up all of the ashes that he, in turn, cast into the bush. In so doing, he unwittingly reinforced Kongolese notions concerning *minkisi* and funerary rites. By dragging and beating the *nkisi,* he acknowledged that it was more than a lifeless and powerless object, that it was a willful agent, subject not only to punishment and death but also to humiliation. In like manner, the burning of the *nkisi* object and the casting of its ashes is consistent with the practice of smoking the corpse, of releasing its resident animating spirit. And the placement of the cross where the *nkisi* once stood did not deny the efficacy of the latter but established the former as a corollary object of ritual potency.

House of the *Nkisi* (the Church)

Catholic missionaries in Kongo made a significant error when they translated church into kiKongo as *nzo a nkisi,* or "house of the holy." For, in fact, *nzo a nkisi* was the common word used by the Kongolese to mean "grave."[24] The Roman Catholic Church was translated as *nzo a nkisi a Roma,* or the "Roman grave."[25] Couple this with the common Catholic practice of burying popes and other men of high status either on the grounds of the church or inside the church itself and the full meaning of *nzo a nkisi* becomes clear. Members of the Kongolese elite adopted the practice of burying notables inside the church, and by the seventeenth century all of the mission churches in Mbanza Kongo contained tombs. King Alvaro III (1615-22) was buried in a church, and his funeral procession included provincial governors, a full complement of musicians, and Catholic priests. With a golden cross placed across his chest, Alvaro III was carried by six noblemen to St. Jacques Church and buried beside his father, who also was laid to rest there.[26]

For the Kongolese nobility, the church—along with its attendant rituals (mass, funerals, festivals)—represented a site for ancestor reverence, a central place where the living could mourn the deceased and communicate with those who had made the transition to the otherworld.[27] Because only kings and nobles were buried there, the church became a significant seat of political authority and legitimacy. But even more than this, the church was yet another *nkisi,* a contained space invested with all of the power and authority of the kings and nobles buried therein. This power was sedimented into the very walls of the church, in the bodies of those buried inside the church and in the burial plots that surrounded the church. Members of the Kongolese nobility clearly saw the church as a final resting place reserved expressly and solely for the nobility. When a Portuguese sailor died in a Kongolese coastal town, Portuguese missionaries sought to bury the deceased inside the church. They carried the sailor's body to the church and buried it without incident, but soon after the prince's guard arrived at the church and demanded that the body be removed on the grounds that the prince had not consented to the burial. Although the priests initially refused to allow the deceased to be exhumed, they eventually relented in the face of four hundred Kongolese soldiers, who disinterred the body and transported it to another cemetery.[28]

The Kongolese sometimes referred to a Christian missionary as *nganga nzo a nkisi,* that is, a "priest of the grave."[29] Christian priests further cemented this appellation when they participated in the funerary rites of deceased Kongolese nobility. Father Pero Tavares reports the death of a provincial priest: "The [chief] died recently, that is to say, he went to hell because he was a pagan and, if not a pagan, he was a Christian only by name."[30] Still, Tavares gave religious instruction to the chief's successor and was present at what he called a "diabolical funeral" attended by nearly six thousand Kongolese from both the local town and the surrounding areas.[31]

Kongo kings of the era took part in many of the rituals of Christianity in an effort to foster communication between the living and the dead. Churches at Mbanza Kongo operated under the authority of the king, and some churches—Saint-Jacques and Saint-Joseph, for example—were actually adjacent to the royal palace, thus visibly marking their connection to the political center of power. While Alvaro IV (1631–36) attended mass regularly at Saint-Jacques and Saint-Joseph, other churches at Mbanza Kongo fell into disrepair.[32] Kongolese nobility demonstrated the connections between political authority and ritual power when they adopted weekly mass as an opportunity to highlight their own dominance. They arrived at church services accompanied by an impressive entourage outfitted with "bows, arrows, drums and other varied instruments."[33] Garcia I (1624–26) "was dressed in black with a clerical hat" while leading rituals of ancestor reverence and conducting funeral ceremonies where he "celebrated the soul of Alvaro II (his uncle) (1587–1614) and other members of the nobility."[34] During the same period a daily mass was held in remembrance of King Afonso I's soul. Moreover, evidence suggests that the pattern of church construction at Mbanza Kongo coincided with filial and lineage connections and that each of the major royal clans undertook the construction of a church.

The connections between political authority, funerary rites, and Christian missionaries were striking. The official announcements of the death of the king as well as the name of the kings' successors were made at the church.[35] As early as 1526 King Afonso wrote to his counterpart in Portugal to request that several stonemasons and carpenters be sent to Kongo to help with the construction of a certain church, Notre-Dame de la Victoire: "We need five or six stonemasons and ten carpenters to complete [construction of the church] . . . we began in a dense forest where, in the past, Kongo kings were buried, according to idolatrous customs."[36] The "idolatrous customs" to which Afonso referred consisted of the common practice of burying the deceased in wooded areas, called *infinda,* generally perceived to be the cities of the dead.[37] Trees played an important role in Kongo funerary ritual because they were thought to connect the land of the living with the dead, the subterranean roots inhabiting the otherworld and the branches occupying the realm of the living.[38] Thus the construction site for the church in a wooded area reflects Kongolese notions of the church as a grave, the placement of cemeteries in *infinda,* and of Christianity as a religion designed to honor and respect the dead.

In the late eighteenth century Father Dicomano offered a detailed description of the funeral rite, noting that Kongolese nobleman went to some lengths to be buried in either one of the churches of Mbanza Kongo or where a church used to stand. Even during this period, riddled with political destabilization and warfare, Mbanza Kongo held significance for those in the central kingdom as well as those in the outlying regions. Many Kongolese regarded the capital city as a crucial symbol of national unity, an ancestral site linking the many different peoples that comprised the kingdom. The earliest tales of the founding of the kingdom refer to Mbanza Kongo as a central site from which power and political legitimacy radiated. Indeed, the nobility validated and justified their claims to power through references to ancestral and lineal links to the capital city. In many cases these links were fictive, even if commonly accepted and acknowledged. In this way, the central kingdom along with all of its outlying tributary states were connected through a system of ancestral links that contributed to the unification of the kingdom. In this capacity the capital served as a place of ancestral mourning and reverence. The connections between Mbanza Kongo as an ancestral site (a city of mourning) and the Christian practices of building churches (read: graves) as places to worship the dead would not have been lost on the Kongolese elite.[39]

So powerful was this connection that even members of the provincial nobility stationed among the many far-away outposts of the Kongo kingdom desired greatly to be buried at the capital city, despite the dangers and difficulties that travel to the capital city entailed. Porters quite literally risked their lives when they carried the bodies of nobles through villages and other potentially hostile areas to ensure that the nobility might be laid to rest at the capital. Given the frequent civil wars, succession battles, and minor skirmishes that plagued Kongo during the late eighteenth century, securing these mourning parties often required small armies. So difficult was the passage to Mbanza Kongo that some families waited more than ten years before they conducted a proper burial at the capital city.[40]

This analysis of Kongolese funerary rite enhances our understanding of Christian conversion in the region, especially for the elite at Mbanza Kongo. That the Kongolese viewed the church as a grave that was itself a special category of *nkisi,* that Kongo kings were buried inside, and that Christian priests were regarded as ministers to the dead all point to the development of a novel set of meanings associated with the Christian faith. Attendance at mass, rituals of royal investiture, Christian festivals, and confraternities in Kongo must all be seen through the lens of Kongo Christianity, a set of ritual practices that revolved, at least in part, around communications with and reverence for the dead. Moreover, this reading of the gravesite and even the body itself as a *minkisi* encourages us to expand our notions of the *minkisi* complex in Kongo. That is, the complex consisted of more than a set of manufactured ritual objects and the beliefs that attend them. For, in fact, almost any item could be transformed into an *nkisi,* including carved objects, pots, burial mounds, churches, and the human body itself. Rather than defining *minkisi* by the objects themselves, we might focus on the larger theories of power that support them. Particular notions of invocation, containment, symbolism, and metonym link all of the different *minkisi* treated thus far.

The Specter of Death and Articulations of Pain during the Middle Passage

Before continuing on to a discussion of burial, death, and funerary ritual among Lowcountry slaves, this chapter treats the specter of death and burial as it relates to the Middle Passage. Scholars have had some difficulty in offering broad outlines of mortality during the Middle Passage because the rates of death varied according to port of (dis)embarkation, the time period in question (mortality rates seems to have dropped steadily throughout the seventeenth and eighteenth centuries), and the particular vessel in question.[41] Estimates regarding the mortality for slaves during the Middle Passage suggest that between 15 and 20 percent died on board, along with a significant percentage of the crew. These numbers, however, are somewhat misleading. Slave ship captains tended to underreport the number of slaves taken aboard and overreport the number of deaths en route in hopes of selling Africans on their own—independent of the company charter—and pocketing the profits.[42] In addition, the Middle Passage accounts for a limited number of total deaths in the overall slave trade. Many African captives perished on the long trek from the interior to the African coast or in holding pens in port towns. The following discussion of death and the slave trade does not treat the raw numbers of mortality during the Middle Passage—the number of ships that set sail, their average capacity, or the captain's log. Instead, this treatment addresses the manner in which the specter of death was treated in the cultures and societies affected by the slave trade.

The specter of death constitutive of the trade caused a crisis for the peoples involved that was articulated in varied ways throughout the Atlantic rim. In the realm of art, politics, folklore, and society, Africa, Europe, and the Americas each produced its own aesthetic understandings of the Middle Passage. In one sense, notions regarding the slave trade were an important aspect in the development of the Atlantic World, representing a transatlantic crisis in the bodies politic of the three regions involved. The nature of this crisis in Europe—debates that pitted proslavery factions against abolitionists—was neither the same as that which characterized Kongo (heightened cycles of violence, civil strife, and the loss of uncounted lives) nor that which prevailed in the U.S. South (chattel slavery, racism, and sectional strife). It is important to note that the cultural memory and recollection of the slave trade continue to be highly charged matters, informing artistic production and political debate to the present day. An investigation into some of these articulations of pain—visual images, political tracts, folklore, and written verse—affords us an understanding of the manner in which Africans in Kongo, European traders, and Lowcountry slaves understood the specter of death as it related to the Middle Passage.

The Kongolese perceived of the Atlantic Ocean as the land of *mpemba*, a vast body of water in which the spirits of the dead resided.[43] The Atlantic marked the barrier between the land of the living and that of the dead, and the Middle Passage itself was perceived as a journey into that watery underworld. The Kongolese understood European slave traders and the trade itself in terms of cannibalism, and many thought that the red wine the traders drank so heavily was made from the blood of captives, that olive oil was produced by pressing the bodies of slaves to extract the necessary humors, that cheese was culled from the brains of captives, and that bullets were manufactured from human bones.[44] In each instance the bodies of slaves were thought to be transformed into commodities—objects of trade and profit—that were consumed by Europeans.

John Atkins, an eighteenth-century slave trader, wrote a cautionary note against complacency to his fellow slave traders: "When we are slaved and out at Sea, it is commonly imagined, the Negroes ignorance of navigation, will always be a safeguard; yet, as many of them think themselves bought to eat . . . there has not been wanting examples of rising and killing a ship's company."[45] Enslaved Africans throughout the continent made similar connections between the slave trade and cannibalism.[46] Olaudah Equiano, whose world famous description of enslavement continues to define the slave trade for many, expressed his own fears: "When I looked round the ship too, and saw a large furnace of copper boiling, and a multitude of black people, of every description, chained together, every one of their countenances expressing dejection and sorrow, I no longer doubted of my fate. . . . I asked them if we were not to be eaten by those white men with horrible looks, red faces and long hair."[47] And Quobona Ottobah Cugoano writes, "The next day we traveled on, and in the evening came to a town, where I saw several white people, that made me afraid they would eat me, according to our notion as children in the inland parts of the country."[48]

In Kongo, cannibalism served as a metaphor for unbridled greed and selfishness. To be a cannibal was to exercise power and authority in excess. Those who held high political office, owned wealth in goods or people, or had the power to attack others violently were thought to be witches, to have accessed the powers of evil known as *kindoki*. In Kongolese thought, power itself was neutral, though the Kongolese drew distinctions between power used for the good of the community and that used for the good of the individual. When individuals amassed wealth or held high office, they were thought to have subverted the public good in favor of the private. In effect, Kongolese notions of the Middle Passage as cannibalism speak to the very real operation of systems of capital, wealth, and profit that motored the trade. In a metaphorical sense, the bodies of slaves were transformed into consumable commodities: sugar, tobacco, cotton, and indigo. The image of European slave traders consuming the bodies of captive Africans highlights a certain system of power relations in which whites became the beneficiaries of profit and wealth garnered by the slave trade.

In Europe a set of political tracts and visual images emphasized the cruelty of the slave trade. British abolitionists in particular mobilized images of slave cargoes in their efforts to see an end to the trade. Of these, the most famous and widely reproduced and adapted image representing slave conditions during the slave trade ever made is the 1789 engraving *Description of a Slave Ship,* which is a graphic overview of the slave ship *Brookes.*[49] The *Description* emphasized the staid, organized and static image of enslaved Africans in the hold of the ship. In purely aesthetic terms, the captives have no human presence at all; "in terms of compositional balance the white spaces where the slaves are not are as important as the black spaces of ink which represent their bodies."[50] In fact, the captives are little more than spaces of ink, the one not markedly different from the other. The *Description* was part of an abolitionist political agenda intended to depict Africans as passive and helpless victims, thus heightening the culpability of proslavery advocates and engendering a sense of remorse and sympathy for the viewing public. But at the same time, the image erases any sense of personal and individual torment. The holds of the ship are void of all pain. The sterility of the image, the standardization of the bodies renders the slaves into muted and sanitized objects.

In lieu of descriptions of pain and torment, many European observers resorted to a certain mathematical articulation of the slave trade: "The slaves lie in two rows, one above the other, on each side of the ship, close to each other, *like books upon a shelf.* I have known them so close, that the shelf would not, easily, contain one more.[51] Captain Parrey of the Royal Navy was commissioned in 1788 to make a set of measurements of the

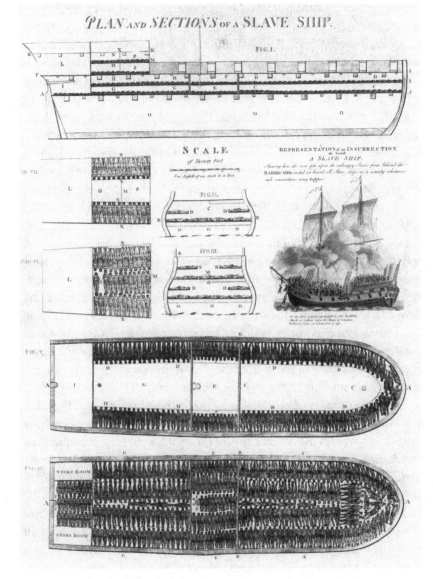

Description of a Slave Ship (1789)

Reprinted from C. B. Wadstrom, *An Essay on Colonization*, 1794. Courtesy of the Library Company of Philadelphia.

Brookes and report his findings to the House of Commons. His measurements were meticulous, mapping the dimensions of the ship from bow to stern. Based in large part on these measurements, many abolitionists conducted numerous calculations regarding the number of captives that could be humanely carried on board. One such commentary notes:

> Let it be supposed that . . . every man slave is to be allowed six feet by one foot four inches for room, every woman five feet ten by one foot four, every boy five feet by one foot two, and every girl four feet six by one foot, it will follow that the annexed plan of a slave vessel will be precisely the representation of the ship Brookes, and of the exact number of persons neither more nor less, that could be stowed in the different rooms of it upon these data . . . if counted will be found to amount to *four hundred and fifty one.* Now if it be considered that the ship Brookes is of three hundred and twenty tons, and that she is allowed to carry by act of Parliament four hundred and fifty four persons, it is evident that if three more could be wedged among the number represented in the plan, this plan would contain precisely the number which the act directs. . . . If when four hundred and fifty one slaves are put into different rooms of the Brookes, the floors are not covered with bodies, but these bodies actually touch each other, what must have been their situation when six hundred were stowed in them at the time alluded to by Dr. Trotter, who belonged to this ship, and six hundred and nine by the confession of the slave merchants in a subsequent voyage.[52]

These descriptions belie the violence inherent in the slave trade, replacing it with a certain commodified efficiency. The image of stacked books connotes an orderly and motionless set of bodies that neglects the brutality inflicted upon African captives. Moreover, the comparison drawn between slaves and books further cements the notion of the slave as commodity. Through a mathematical objectivity, these descriptions of the slave trade contribute to an erasure of violence, a cultural and social amnesia related to death and the Middle Passage.

These descriptions call to mind the difficulty of rendering accurate and adequate treatments of violence and pain. James Stanfield, in *Observations on a Guinea Voyage,* suggests that "no pen, no abilities, can give more than a very faint resemblance of the horrid situation. One *real* view—*one minute,* absolutely spent in the slave rooms on the Middle Passage, would do more for the cause of humanity than . . . the whole collective eloquence of the British senate." [53]

The specter of death made up a significant part of the content of slave folklore. Folktales, such as the following, concerning the initial capture of Africans and their experiences on board ship circulated widely throughout the slave community:

> Dey been pack in dere wuss dan hog in a car when dey shippin' 'em. An' every day dem white folks would come in dere an' ef a nigger jest twist he self or move, dey'd cut de hide off him wid a rawhide whip. An' niggers died in de bottom er dat ship wuss dan hogs wid cholera. Dem white folks ain' hab no mercy. . . . Dey drag dem dead niggers out an' throw 'em overboard. An' dat ain' all. Dey th'owed a heap er live ones wha' dey thought ain' guh live into de sea.[54]

This account highlights the experience of Gullah Joe, born in Africa and brought as a slave to the Congaree River Valley, a region in South Carolina close to Columbia. His understanding of the specter of death on board the slave ship is important not only for those who survived to tell the tale but also for those who survived to hear it. Unlike the *Description,* this treatment is wrought out of the very real and personal experience of pain that attended the slave trade. The specters of death and disease are central in this tale, as are bodies being thrown overboard. Gullah Joe found nothing orderly in the packaging of bodies; the captives, real living persons suffering the conditions on board in very personal and immediate ways, writhed, twisted, and moaned.

Death during the Middle Passage continues to inform more contemporary notions of slavery, which are seared not only into the consciousness of the descendants of slaves in the Americas but also into the very psyche of those societies that participated in the transatlantic trade. In recent years calls for reparations for slavery have looked, in part, to the violence of the Middle Passage to justify the necessity of redress and recompense for the descendants of slaves in the United States. In July 1999 the Middle Passage Monument, a fifty-foot stainless-steel arch of cubist inspiration was dropped into the Atlantic Ocean some 260 miles off the coast of New York Harbor. The monument was sponsored by the Homeward Bound Foundation, whose founder, St. Croix-born Wayne James, intended to create a gravestone to memorialize the bodies of those Africans whose remains lie along the ocean floor. The Homeward Bound Foundation created six replicas of the monument to be placed on lands affected by the Middle Passage: Africa, the Caribbean, Central America, Europe, North America, and South America. The project garnered the support of Kofi Annan, secretary general of the United Nations, as well as the Congressional Black Caucus. That the project enjoyed support from such an international body of individuals and organizations testifies to the continued potency of the memories of the Middle Passage in contemporary times.

Indeed, the specter of the bodies strewn along the sea floor played a significant role in the ceremony that marked the installation of the monument. After having placed the monument in the ocean, the crew along with the participants headed back to New York Harbor. Soon after, many of the mechanical devices on board failed, and by nightfall the ship had drifted back to the point at which the monument had been lowered into the ocean. There the engine failed, the rudder broke, and more than half of the ship's fresh water supply was lost. In addition, the ship's radio and telephone services were damaged. For three days this cycle was repeated: The ship headed toward New York Harbor by day only to be returned each night to the location where the monument had been dropped. Several people on board reported seeing visions of men and women, and others heard mysterious voices. Capt. Scott Chew reported on record that he heard voices on several occasions but saw no one. For Wayne James and others aboard ship, those voices bear witness to the presence of the souls of those lost during the Middle Passage. "That experience . . . was our ancestors' way of saying 'thank you' for the monument, 'we are happy you came out, we want you to stay a little longer,'" says James.[55]

Contemporary visual artists have also been compelled by the Middle Passage and its significance for the present. Visual artist Tom Feelings produced a series of strikingly painful representations of the transatlantic trek in *The Middle Passage,* a collection of sketches that narrate the movement of captured Africans from the interior of West Africa to the coast, over the Atlantic and into the plantation societies of the New World. Technically, the sketches represent experiments in contrast: of light opposed to dark, of haziness and shadow versus stark lines etched in black and white; of motion against stillness. Feelings began the project after a Ghanaian friend asked him, "What happened to all of you when you were taken away from here?" Feelings initially responded in silence as "muted images flashed across [his] mind."[56] Some things are unspoken and—more to the point—unspeakable. Unlike the *Description,* Feelings work engages the humanity of enslaved Africans directly, marking the person and individual experience of pain and the specter of death constitutive of the slave trade. The Middle Passage was but a passage through death, the Atlantic Ocean but a watery grave—the litter of bones on the sea floor pointing the way to the New World. Many slave traders themselves acknowledged this connection when they adopted the term "floating tombs" for slave ships and the mortality rates on board ship for both the enslaved as well as their enslavers confirms the specter of death on board.

Grave Decoration and the African Atlantic Religious Complex

For more than a century, scholars have noted that the funerary rituals of the slave South closely resembled those of Kongo. In particular, commenters addressed the striking similarities that characterize the decoration of gravesites in the two locales. In the late nineteenth century H. Carrington Bolton described the graves of South Carolina blacks, noting that "numerous graves are decorated with a variety of objects, sometimes arranged with careful symmetry, but more often placed around the margins without regard to order. These objects include oyster-shells, white pebbles, fragments of crockery of every descriptions, glass bottles, and non-descript bric-a-brac of a cheap sort,—all more or less broken and useless." [57]

During the same period, observers of African burial customs were making very similar remarks regarding funerary rites on the other side of the Atlantic. In 1891 *Century* magazine published E. J. Glave's "Fetishism in Congo Land," accompanied by an engraving of a Kongolese gravesite. "The natives," the article noted, "mark the final resting-places of their friends by ornamenting their graves with crockery, empty bottles, old cooking-pots, etc., all of which are rendered useless by being cracked, or perforated with holes." [58] That mourners broke the items signified on both sides of the Atlantic a certain and necessary rupture that need be made between the living and the dead. For the deceased, the perforations connoted a liberation of movement, a freedom to travel between worlds. For the survived, those broken dishes ensured that the chain of death would be broken: "Yuh see, duh one pusson is dead an ef yuh dohn break duh tings, den duh udduhs in duh fambly will die too. Dey will folluh right along." [59]

Contrary to the opinions of many observers, the bereaved did not carelessly place items around the graves of their lost loved ones. Take, for example, the chips of blue China situated atop the grave of Old John along the coastal region of Georgia during the early twentieth century. That blue china had once belonged to the plantation "Missis" who had given it to one of her slaves to be filled with water at a nearby spring. After filling the pitcher the slave girl was heading back to the Big House when she tripped and dropped the pitcher, causing the mouth of the vessel to break, thus spilling its contents on the path. Undaunted, she returned to the spring, filled the pitcher again, placed it atop her head and set off for home. As she returned, the pitcher leaked from its broken mouth and tiny rivulets of water dribbled down the slave girl's face. By the time she returned home, the pitcher was empty, but the girl's face was streaming with what looked to the Missis to be sorrowful tears. Feeling that the girl was crying of despair and regret at having broken the vessel, the "Missis" took pity on the girl and not only abstained from beating her but also gave her the broken vessel. So the vessel stayed in the young girl's possession until she grew up, married Old John and watched him die. To prepare for the burial, the girl took a hatchet and finished the job she had started decades earlier, breaking the pottery to pieces, laying its remains carefully atop her deceased husband's grave. This blue china, then, held decades of memories highlighted by a moment when a slave owner refrained from an expected brutality, a moment when a river of tears saved a slave from a beating.[60]

In addition to these items, medicine bottles (of the sort described in chapter 3) also adorned the graves. Typically, these bottles stood "upside down with the corks loosened so that the medicine may soak into the grave."[61] This connection emphasizes the very close relationship between ritual objects and death. In Kongo, the status of the deceased body was ambiguous. On the one hand, the corpse was but an empty vessel, an object not easily differentiated from other mundane objects, yet when invested with certain ritual prescriptions, that vessel might be animated and empowered to effect change in the here and now. In the same manner, the placement of medicine bottles and other implements atop burial mounds in the slave South marked the deceased as an object of reverence, requiring special care and ritual observance as well as an agent capable of supernatural power and influence. That the deceased, once animated, became a force to be reckoned with is illustrated in the use of "goofer dust"—dirt taken from a burial mound—as a central item in the construction of conjure bags.[62] The term "goofer" derives from the kiKongo *kufwa,* meaning dead person.[63]

The use of graveyard dirt throughout both the slave South as well as in Kongo connoted a relationship between the arts of conjure and the spirits of the dead that continued to operate in the realm of the living.[64]

As was the case for Kongo, the varied shells, pots and other items placed atop gravesites in the Lowcountry evoked complex symbolisms, metaphors and metonyms reflecting the power of the spirit of the deceased. The color white was ubiquitous on and around the burial mounds, establishing the connection between the land of the dead (*mpemba*) and the graves of the recently departed. Seashells were also common as a decorative implement, their spiraling curves signifying not only the cyclical arcs of life and death but also the very close relationship between the burial mound and a watery otherworld. In the Lowcountry, seashells were so closely identified with death that many residents considered it bad luck to possess or use the shells in any other context.[65]

Slaves further elaborated this water motif in the commonly held view that after death, the soul of the slave would travel across the Atlantic in a glorious return to Africa. The last used implements that decorated the grave helped to identify the deceased, to invest the soil with the spirit of the recently departed. This sort of identification could be metonymic: a watch standing in for its owner or a necklace in place of the woman who adorned it. Moreover, these items helped the dead make the transition to the otherworld, ensuring that they would not be found wanting any item formerly used in life and be forced, therefore, to wander about in search of treasured articles.[66] Indeed, the practice of placing seashells, decorative items, and the last used implements of the deceased atop the grave is found in other regions of the African Atlantic with significant populations of enslaved Kongolese. In Jamaica, for example, a late-seventeenth-century commenter noted the presence of varied smoking paraphernalia including pipes and a fire kit atop a grave mound intended to ease the transition into the otherworld.[67]

Scholarly treatment of the similarities between grave decoration in Kongo and the slave South began as early as the 1920s and 1930s and gained significant attention in 1926, when, writing in *Folk Beliefs of the Southern Negro*, Newbell Niles Puckett acknowledged the African antecedents of grave decoration in the Deep South.[68] During the 1940s Melville Herskovits and Roger Bastide took up the matter, and in more recent years art historians, anthropologists, and others have studied these rituals. Most notable of the more recent work in this vein are the studies of African

American gravesites conducted by art historian Robert Farris Thompson, who noted the persistence of seashells, the last used objects of the dead, and other decorative implements atop the graves of African Americans as late as the 1960s and 1970s.[69] On the basis of the formal and visual affinities between these African American gravesites and the descriptions of Kongo gravesites from the late nineteenth and early twentieth centuries, Thompson maintains that "nowhere is Kongo-Angola influence on the New World more pronounced, more profound, than in black traditional cemeteries throughout the South of the United States."[70]

While the treatments offered by Thompson and others deal with the aesthetic similarities that attend grave decoration in the two locales, they are less interested in the manner in which the historical dynamics of slavery and the transatlantic slave trade conspired to produce a set of funerary rituals that spread throughout the African Atlantic and tend not to treat questions regarding the manner in which funerary ritual and grave decoration changed over time in either Kongo or in the New World. In order to articulate the relationship between funerary ritual in Kongo and the New World, we must begin to draw not only aesthetic links but also temporal connections between the practices in the two locales. This calls for a treatment of funerary ritual in light of the transatlantic slave trade, relying on sources from that period. In this way the late-nineteenth-century engravings of E. J. Glave are less an end point from which we might draw comparisons and conclusions than a starting point from which we might gaze backward in order to better understand Kongo funerary ritual in an earlier period. These investigations allow one to continue to chart the development and maintenance of an African Atlantic religious complex both in Kongo and in the Deep South.

It is perhaps in our treatment of the dead that we learn the most about the living, in our caring for the deceased that the living are most closely bound together, one to the other. Michael Blakey suggests as much when he contends that African American "identities are entombed, marked, fought for, preserved, celebrated, symbolized, mourned, and incorporated in the cemeteries they describe."[71] Such seems to be the case for antebellum slaves, for whom burial rituals and grave decoration constituted a principle realm of resistance.

Slaves utilized the spirits of the deceased to affect circumstances in the land of the living and constructed, in the process, networks of power and authority outside the purview of the master class. The dead had an influence over the living that simply could not be checked by members of the master class. The dead could be satiated with food and drink or angered by neglect. The burial mound itself could be manipulated to highlight group grievances among slaves, especially in the use of "goofer" dust. Or that same dirt could be directed against members of the master class as part of poisonous recipes. The dead were a source of power and authority that challenged the authority of the master class. As a result, the rituals of burial and death among slaves addressed alternate sources of power and influence. In the song and dance that often accompanied funerals, or in the spirit possession that attended the rituals of death, slaves exploded the myth that their bodies were valuable only in its labor and profit potential. Even in death the bodies of deceased slaves maintained a value of the highest order by influencing the realm of the living.

The Movement of the Body from Life to Death

Some extreme care was required in order to ensure the easy transition of the recently deceased from this world to the afterlife. As soon as someone died, mourners immediately covered all of the mirrors and pictures in the home of the deceased.[72] Explanations for this practice vary, and although some informants report that the reflection of the corpse, once captured in the mirror, would be forever set, others maintain that the mirror would tarnish if not properly covered or turned to the wall. At least one resident of St. Helena Island, upon pointing out some irregular spots on her mirror, suggested that they were the "eyes of spirits which came back because the mirror" had not been covered after a recent death.[73] The moment when death claimed a life was a very dangerous and vulnerable time for the living; the passageways and portals connecting this world and the next were open during these times, allowing death to move about freely. Care had to be taken to close those portals, to regulate the movement between the world of the living and that of the dead. For if the dead were allowed to roam freely, their grasp might claim more lives.

Before the nineteenth century the Kongolese used the reflecting surfaces of water as an avenue to communicate with the dead, indicating the dual significance of water in Kongolese thought. First, gazing into pools and ponds was tantamount to looking into the realm of the dead, the watery underworld where the deceased resided. Second, the water's surface also reflects the image of the viewer and places it under the water's surface, situating him or her in the otherworld so that the image, as reflected by water, appears to originate from under the water's surface. Wyatt MacGaffey notes that "to see something in a mirror is to see something which is not there, which is elsewhere."[74] The viewer, then, is placed mystically at the crossroads of opposing worlds, simultaneously occupying the world of the living, of flesh and bone, and the realm of the dead, glimmering in rippled water. During the nineteenth century, European traders introduced glass mirrors into Kongo and the Kongolese transposed their notions of watery reflection onto the mirrors, applying them to the bodies of *minkisi* and using them to acquire knowledge of the otherworld.

This helps to explain the ubiquity of glass, mirrors, shiny metallics and the like placed atop burial mounds in the Lowcountry. These items facilitated the reflection so necessary for communication between the living and the dead. Thus equipped with the powers of reflection, gravesites acted as passageways through which one might "see" the otherworld symbolically. But for the body yet unburied, for the recently departed, the powers of reflection need be muted. The sick bed and the home need not be transformed, through the powers of reflection, into open passageways between the living and the dead. For the sake of the living the home must not become an open avenue for the dead, and so reflective surfaces—glass, mirrors, and the like—were covered.[75]

As part of the preparation for burial, mourners washed and placed the body atop a cooling board, a table covered with white cloth. Until rigor mortis set in, a cloth was commonly tied around the chin of the deceased to keep the mouth closed. Once the body became stiff, a longer cloth was wrapped around the body, thus explaining the plaintive prayers recorded by the black faithful, "Lord, I thank thee for permitting me to rise this morning and that my bed was not my cooling board [and] that my cover was not my winding sheet."[76] Caretakers placed coins on the eyelids to keep the eyes firmly shut and placed salt underneath the corpse of the recently deceased in order to prevent the newly released spirit from wreaking havoc on the living.[77] One former slave from Georgia recalled that "they put a pan of salt on de corpse to keep . . . de witches away."[78] The salt consumed whatever disease afflicted the deceased and so protected the survivors from succumbing to a similar fate. Just as the Kongolese perceived of "salt baptism" as a security against the reprisals of witches, so Lowcountry blacks continued to use salt as a substance suitable for protection from dysphoric spirits.

Once the body was sufficiently prepared, the "drums of death" sounded, summoning the community to gather. Indeed, drums could be used to communicate various messages in the slave community and as a result, a certain rhythmic lexicon developed so that listeners could distinguish the varied messages that they received: "Dey hab a diffunt beat wen dey call um tuh a settin-up aw fewnul frum duh one dey use tuh call um tuh a dance."[79]

As nighttime approached, slaves arrived at the home of the deceased to pay "deir 'spects to de fambly of de dead." In fact, "folkses sot up all night wid de corpse and sung and prayed."[80] Mourners commonly laid hands on the deceased, a ritual that represented both a final and kind farewell and a plea that their own lives be spared. Many thought it bad luck not to touch the corpse. This laying of hands upon the corpse ensured that the body would "lie-easy," that is, not return to haunt the living. The soul of the deceased was thought to hover about the body for approximately three days and after being interred it lingered about the burial site for three days more. During this time the dead could hear the conversation of the living, could see their comings and goings. The "settin' up" was an opportunity to communicate final thoughts, to put the dead to rest before those portals that connected the living and the dead closed. So continued the settin' up, a ritual of remembrance and song until well into the night.[81]

Maureen Warner-Lewis documents similar rites performed by blacks in Columbia called *lumbalú,* which consisted of a "musical death rite the purpose of which is to demonstrate condolence and love for the deceased.... Around the corpse are assembled professional mourners, drummers and singers to intone ... the religious chants of the *lumbalú.*"[82] The *lumbalú* typically took place at the home of the deceased and was punctuated by singing and dancing as well as general merriment, laughter, and chatter. Many of the lyrics and exclamations commonly sung during the ritual derived from Kongo lexical traditions including *mame* "alas," *tantwe* "great sorrow" and *muhià* "calamity."[83]

In the Lowcountry, the "drums of death" followed the settin' up, signaling the procession to the burial site. It moved slowly, solemnly; moaning marked the way. Regarding her own experience as the daughter of a planter in Georgia, Telfair Hodgson noted that even decades after the end of slavery the "sound of dreary wailing from the cabins when someone died" still filled her ears. She observed, "I can still see these mournful processions, led by dim lanterns through the moss-covered trees, at midnight, when they went to the Negro cemetery on the hill beyond the pines."[84] Upon arrival, the assembled circled the burial site and formed a ring. This manner of movement also characterized the settin' up in which mourners often circled around the cooling board itself, passing any infants of the house offer the coffin so as to break the cycle of death.[85] Because many slaveholders forbade the use of drums by slaves, the drumming often was conducted in secret:

> Now, ole man Dembo he use tuh beat duh drum tuh duh fewnul, but Mr. Cooper he stop dat. He say he dohn wahn drums beatin roun duh dead. But I watch em hab a fewnul. I gits behine duh bush an hide an watch an see wut dey does. Dey go in a long pruhcession tuh du buryin groun an dey beat duh drums long duh way an dey submit duh body tuh duh groun. Den dey dance roun in a ring an dey motion wid duh hans. Dey sing duh body tuh duh grabe an den dey let it down an den dey succle roun in duh dance.[86]

Mourners placed the body in the ground with the head facing West, so that on that "great getting up morning" the deceased will face Gabriel as he blows his trumpet in the East. Thomas Wentworth Higginson, a colonel in the Union army, described the funeral of several black soldiers under his command: "Just before the coffins were lowered, an old man whispered to me that I must have their position altered,—the heads must be toward the west; so it was done,—though they are in a place so veiled in woods that either rising or setting sun will find it hard to spy them."[87]

On the plantation owned by Pierce Butler, the husband of Frances Kemble, a slave funeral began when the preacher offered a word over the body before the congregation proceeded to the slaves' burial ground. Once they arrived at the gravesite, the congregation gathered around the body and "uplifted their voices in a hymn, the first wailing notes of which—sung all in unison, in the midst of these unwonted surroundings—sent a thrill through" Frances Kemble's nerves.[88] The initial wails of the mourners often gave way to more demonstrative expressions. Some regarded emotional ecstasy as the sine qua non of black funerals: "A negro funeral without an uproar, without shouts and groans, without fainting women and shouting men, without pictures of triumphant deathbeds and judgment day, and without the gates of heaven wide open and the subjects of the funeral dressed white and rejoicing around the throne of the lamb, was no funeral at all."[89] Through the intensity of the songs and the passion of dance, slaves achieved an altered state of consciousness, which the mourners used as a mode of communication with the dead, a means through which they articulated their grief. For a people whose bodies were so constrained,' this enactment of grief offered a brief freedom of movement. The emotion exhibited during the ritual marked the conscious refusal of slaves to have their bodies defined and restrained as merely objects of labor, capital accumulation, sexual assault and profit.

After the burial was complete, the bereaved continued to care for the departed. The practice of leaving food for the deceased was quite common for slaves in the Sea Island region. Florence Postell, of Brownville, noted that food placed on the grave keeps the spirit of the deceased from returning to the house. Some mourners went so far as to carry dishes to the burial mound and set a proper table for their dearly departed. Emma Stevens of Sunbury asserted that the spirits of the dead get hungry just as the bodies of the living, noting that "yuh hab tuh put food in duh ruhm fuh duh spirit tuh com eat . . . ef duh spirit is hungry, it will sho come back an hant yuh." [90]

If performed properly, the funeral ceremony ensured that the soul of the deceased would finally and forever be free from the pain and persecution of this world: The "spirit and the skin been together like the smoke and the ashes in the wood; when you dies, they separates. The smoke goes free [and] can't nobody hurt smoke." [91] This notion is illustrated in at least one slave spiritual, which suggests that the soul of the deceased becomes embodied in dust and ashes that fly upward from the gravesite as the soul flies upward to heaven. [92] According to Mary Stevens, a resident of the Georgia Sea Islands, the spirit "nebuh go in duh groun wid duh body, it jus wanduh roun." [93]

After the initial burial, many Lowcountry slaves celebrated a second funeral held for the deceased that occurred perhaps weeks or even months after the initial interment. This was, to many, the "real funeral," the initial gathering being only the burial. [94] Jane Lewis, a former Sea Island slave, recalled that there were always two funerals for the deceased, one immediately after death in the manner described above and a second that took place annually and acknowledged all of those who had passed in the previous year. [95] James Bolton, a former slave in Oglethorpe County, Georgia, recalled, "Sometimes it were two or three months after the burying before the funeral sermon was preached." [96] The practice of "second burials" was common throughout West and West-Central Africa during the era of American slavery and the transatlantic slave trade. One thinks immediately, for example, of the much-delayed burials of Kongo provincial nobility who might not be interred for months and, sometimes, years due to their desires to be buried at Mbanza Kongo. Among the Ibo the typical practice was to bury the deceased quickly, with preliminary ceremonies: "Then after a year or less, sometimes more, the second burial would take place with a lot more elaborate ceremonies than the first. It was believed that this second burial was the one that helped the spirit of such departed elderly persons to rest comfortable with the ancestors in the land of ancestral bliss, from where they plead effectively with the gods for the well-being of their children on earth."[97]

So crucial were these memorial services that the slave folk tradition even includes examples of the dead gathering at convenient places to hold remembrance services for the dead who had been forgotten: "Though the living have forgotten, the dead do not forget."[98] Slaves did not intend for the rituals of burial to mark a final separation between the living. Some observers remarked of slaves that they "dwell as much in a visionary world as in the material world; he is constantly passing in thought the debatable ground that divides the natural from the supernatural, and he is unconscious of the stage of transition, for his spirit moves with as much freedom in the domain of the one as in that of the other."[99]

Those gifted with second sight or otherwise invested with the powers of the otherworld could readily access the dead. In fact, some slaves maintained that they not only saw the dead but also walked with them along the road and talked to them in the bush.[100] July, a Sea Island resident and former slave, recalled a time when he came across Miley, a departed friend. Miley said he had been wanting to ask a question then suddenly darted toward the graveyard. July followed closely behind, and when Miley arrived at his own plot, he put his head down, twirled around two or three times and down he went, disappearing into the grave. July approached the grave, and though he thoroughly inspected it for traces of his old friend, he could not figure out how Miley had entered it. The grass remained undisturbed and there was no hole in the ground. "An yet me see um, wid me own yeye," July said, "gone down, head foremose, een eh grabe."[101] So confident was July in his ability to see the dead that he asserted, "Ef I bin know dem befo dey dead, I kin know dem now. Me kin see dem dist es plain es me kin see you know."[102]

If July could see the dead unaided, other Lowcountry blacks used special implements to do the same. Some Lowcountry residents report that tree branches could be used to locate hidden treasures or see the unseen. Using the branch as a divining rod, some Lowcountry blacks stated that they could see the "shell" of dead persons hovering about, thus illustrating further the body as a mere covering—a shell—for resident animate spirits.[103]

The notion, commonly held in Kongo, that the realm of the dead operated as the mirror opposite of the land of the living was elaborated by Lowcountry slaves in the idea that the dead walked backward, that their faces were turned backward atop their bodies, and that their feet were turned around such that the toes pointed backward. The very hours of the day and night intimated the close relationship between the living and the dead. When asked to reckon the time of day, Lowcountry blacks referred to the following schema: "Fus' fowl crow" was followed by "day clean," "sun up," "attanoon," "sun da lean fuh down," "fus dus' da'k," "bull bat time," "deep dus," "night time," "plait eye prowl," and "hag hollerin' time."[104] Thus the nighttime hours are regarded as the provenance of the dead and are so respected. Kongolese understandings of the otherworld were not simply replicated in the Americas but embellished by Lowcountry slaves, pointing once again to the idea of tradition first mentioned in chapter 1.

The collections of famed folklorist John Bennett highlight the powers of the dead to blur and even to disregard the barriers that separate their world from ours:

> Suddenly the earth cracked under his feet, and from the crack came the sound of voices singing underground. . . . The dead were singing in their graves! He could hear all round him the sound of rotten planks crumbling and coffin lids crackin under the upheaved sand. A cold wind blew on him out of the graves, and the earth cracked wide the length of the graveyard. And, as the crack widened he could see within it the dead stretching themselves and sitting up in their coffins, singing. The newly dead had garments. The old dead had nothing but the rubbish of the grave. Some wore ragged shrouds; some tattered gravecloths; some had only the sand and clay between their brown bones. . . . Next day came the earthquake. The dog and the dead knew.[105]

According to the slave spiritual tradition, that "great getting' up morning" is also marked by an erasure of the lines separating the living from the dead.[106] We will know that moment when trumpets sound to wake the nations underground; the very graves of the earth will come undone, as coffins burst open and the dead rise up to take their place with the living to be judged and abide in the bosom of the Lord:[107] *"I'll be somewhere sleepin' in mah grave; when He calls me I will answer, I'll be somewhere sleepin' in mah grave."*[108]

Some slaves perceived of death as a final resting place, away from the brutalities of life, an opportunity to reconstitute community, even to see their loved ones but one more time. So closely linked were this world and the otherworld that some slaves passed messages to loved ones through the recently deceased: "When a woman dies some friend or relative will kneel down and sing to the soul as it takes flight."[109] This desire to maintain contact with those who had died before is illustrated in the following spiritual:

> I Got some friends on de ober shore
> Do love de Lord!
> I want to see 'em more an' more when I die
> Do love de Lord.[110]

If death connoted rest and reconnection for the slaves, it meant something entirely different for the enslavers who paid for the sins of this world once they reached the afterworld. Drawing on folk tales collected by E. C. L. Adams, Sterling Stuckey argues that slaves used folklore to redress the pains of plantation life. In its construction of a nether world of horrid retribution for those who profited from slavery and the slave trade in this world, many Sea Island blacks established a juridical system of crime and punishment that meted out justice in the spirit realm for people whose crimes were never prosecuted in earthly courts. In "Ole Man Rogan" and "King Buzzard," Lowcountry blacks detailed the life, death, and final punishment for a slaveholder and an African seller of slaves whose spirits roamed the nether world without rest or comfort.[111]

In his masterful *Congaree Sketches*, Adams reveals a Lowcountry region full of signs of the nefarious dangers of the natural world.[112] For example, Adams introduces Thaddeus Goodson—Tad—who through the power of his storytelling, brings black lore to life. "I been down in de big swamps on de Congaree," Tad tells us, "wey God's mornin' leads to de devil's night . . . where owls on a dead limb talks of de dead, talks wid de dead and laughs like de dead . . . way down in de big swamps of de Congaree, de home of de fever wey death is de king."[113]

In his mention of owls, Tad echoes the trepidation of F. J. Johnson, a resident of Grimball's Point along the Georgia coastal islands who reported to WPA interviewers that "duh owl is a true messanjuh uh det."[114] Relaying similar sentiments, George Smith of Sapelo Island warns, "If an owl hoots on top of the house or near the house, it is supposed to be a sign of death."[115] In this sense the Congaree swamps, like the graveyard, were a space that required careful steps and sure footing, for there were spirits down in that murky wetness.

Recounting yet another excursion into the swamps, Tad recalled, "I lay down back there in de swamp wid my head on a log and drapped asleep." Before long, "I open my eye [and] one of dese here owls been settin' on a limb of a dead snag right by me, an' he look right down in my eye an' laugh." Soon enough Tad realized that "he ain' no owl, but he been people. Dat ole bird tell me when he been in dis world, he been ole man Smart Daniel' daddy, en he say he don't res' none. An' he say some un um takes on other shapes an' lives in de form of different birds and animals."[116]

Another of Adams's informants, Leck, had a similar experience in the Congaree swamp: "De ole river sho' is ragin' I look down on de yaller water and I see wey buzzard cast his shadow. Everywhere I look I see buzzard." So violent, in fact, were the raging waters that Leck concluded, "When de Congaree gets riled, it mighty nigh look like Jesus hisself forgits de poor critters, it look like he stan' back and give de devil a chance to do he do." The swamps, "dey 'stroy your body and if dey ain't 'stroy it, look like dey' 'stroy your soul."[117]

The buzzard, like the owl, signaled death. Dye Williams of Old Fort, Georgia, suggested as much when she claimed that "deah's udduh signs uh det too, sech as ef yuh sees a buzzud sailin' roun, das a sho sign."[118] Moreover, buzzards are intimately connected to the practice of black magic. Lawrence Baker, another Sea Island resident, reported that witches "can take all kine uh shape."[119] He recalled the day when a local resident shot a buzzard that subsequently careened into the chimney of a house. When onlookers went to observe the fallen bird they "fine a ole uhmun wid uh ahm broke."

So horrid, in fact, were these swamps that there was, deep in its recesses, a place from which a man can never return. The swamp attracted people "like a trap draws files, an' people dies in de big swamps like flies dies in traps. An' you meets unknown men an' dey ain' right an' dey takes on ways of things dat ain' nat'ral"[120] There was a "lake o' water wey all humans an' beasts perish on its shores which are strewed wid de dead." Buzzards hovered around the lake "for no purpose but to make the place look more dreadful. Dey looks like some'n dat's dead wid de power to walk slow an' dey walks like dey counts dey footsteps, an' dey footsteps is de footsteps of de dead."[121] Lowcountry blacks used depictions of the lake of the dead to warn listeners to lead righteous and good lives, careful never to succumb to the evil: "Stay 'way my brother, stay 'way from de path of de buzzard; for ef you walks in dey path an' wanders too far, you'll land on de shores of de Lake of de Dead. An' men has walked on de shores of dis lake."[122]

The swamps may be likened unto a way station between this world and the next—a curious middle ground where the living interact with the displaced deceased.[123] Indeed, only those spirits that are neither burning in hell nor basking in Heaven's glory reside in the swamp. They are the lost souls who, no longer occupying human forms, take shape in the bodies of swamp creatures: the owl that hoots, or the sinister snake that slivers in the murky marsh. The inhabitants of the swamp "ain't 'lowed in heben and can't get in hell. Dey punishment is to wander in de bad place an' dey ain't get no res.'"[124]

These tales suggest that slaves developed alternate systems of authority and punishment. For those who traded in slaves in life, a dismal and eternal punishment awaited them in death. Ole man Rogan, King Buzzard, and others paid dearly in death for the pains they caused in life. Without access to legal or constitutional retribution, slaves extended the latitude of redress such that crimes committed in life would be paid for in death. More generally, the very close relationship between the living and the dead extended the specter of death onto the very plantation itself and into the deepness of the swamps. As in Kongo, the physical world was full of passageways and portals through which the dead could be contacted and called up to affect circumstances in the lives of men. Ras Michael Brown argues that, given the central role of the natural world in West-Central Africa, memories of the feenda encouraged the development of similar spaces in the slave South, such that "the wooded areas of the Lowcountry became a kind of African domain distinct from plantation society and inhabited largely by enslaved hunters, woodsmen, herders, guides, travelers, and maroons."[125]

As discussed above in reference to slave baptism, Lowcountry blacks regarded death as more than a mere idea, a state of being, or a freedom from slavery. Rather, death was regarded as a real, living entity. When asked to define death, one former slave retorted, "I ha' done seen it in times er sorer, in times er sickness. Hit's er shader en er darkness; hit's like er spider's web, 'cept 'ez hit's black, black ez de long hours er night—dee legs uv it, dar whar hit hangs o'er de wool' by, dee air—long—long—long . . . en dat shader en darkness hit comes drappin' down onyer, creepin' up on yer. . . . Dat reap hook hit gi's er wrench ter de breaf er yo' mouf, en dar! Yer gone—caze yer breaf hit's yer soul."[126] Death also resembled a man in the following slave spiritual:

> Of deat' he is a little man,
> Death he ain't nothin' but a robber, don't you see?
> Death came to my house and he didn't stay long,
> I looked in de bed an' my mother was gone
> Death he ain't nothin' but a robber, don't you see?[127]

One of the most striking instances of death as an immediate presence in the lives of the living is evident in the recollections of Gullah Joe, who detailed the importance and potency of the natural world through the symbolic meanings attached to the *infinda*. Gullah Joe, discussed earlier in this chapter, recalled, "I is a ole man now, but I has a longin' to walk in de feenda. I wants to see it one more time. I has a wife an' chillun here but when I thinks er my tribe an' my friend an' my daddy an' my mammy an' de great feenda, a feelin' rises up in my th'oat an' my eye well up wid tear."[128]

Sterling Stuckey argues that Joe's use of the feenda in this instance reflects the tensions that some enslaved Africans felt "between longing for one's tribe and attachment to new relations in the American environment."[129] But Gullah Joe's reference may be even more subtle, more cryptic. While his statement reads as a plea to be surrounded by the familiarities of home, it may also point to Joe's feelings about his own mortality. Certainly, the feenda is no ordinary place but a site specially reserved as the habitation for the spirits of the deceased. King Afonso of Kongo established the connection between the infinda and death when he constructed a church in a wooded area that formerly had been used as a ritual burial ground. In invoking the feenda, Joe calls to mind a particularly Kongolese conception of the geography of power, death, and rebirth in the natural world. Joe implies that his tribe, friends, mammy, and daddy are in the feenda and their spirits roam in its expanse. That Joe, who by his own admission is "an ole man now," desires "to walk in de feenda" suggests that he seeks a freedom from the pains and oppressions of life and that he too awaits an impending death.[130]

Also in this connection, one notes among some Lowcountry blacks a prohibition against planting cedar trees for fear that it might cause death. One Lowcountry resident warns, "Plant a cedar an dis 'e sta't fuh pint up somebody gwine to dead."[131] Notably, the same stricture did not apply to trees planted in graveyards, where it is figured that little more can befall the occupants. Much like Joe's memory of the feenda, the proscriptions related to cedar trees illustrate the clear connections that enslaved Africans made between trees and death. So in Kongo trees played an important role in funerary ritual. The Kongolese maintained a reverence for trees in line with the notion that they connected the land of the living with the dead, the roots extending into the otherworld, the branches growing in this one.[132] Notably, the term *infinda* has been documented in other African Atlantic locales. In Cuba, one of its meanings is "cemetery," indicating the close connections that pertain between death and forested areas through-out the Americas and in Kongolese theology.[133] Edward Pierce described the geography of burial grounds, noting that they were generally located "in an open field, under a clump of some dozen or twenty trees, perhaps live-oaks, and not fenced. There may be fifty or hundred graves, marked only by sticks eighteen inches or two feet high."[134] Unlike cemeteries for whites, slave burial grounds were rarely organized along linear patterns. Graves might be scattered, and in some cases slaves devoted little atten-tion to manicuring the grounds, which often left white observers with the impression that black burial sites were haphazardly arranged.[135] But as Pierce observed, "these lowly burial-places, for which art has done noth-ing, are not without a fascination, and . . . they take a faster hold on the sentiments than more imposing cemeteries, adorned with shafts of marble and granite, rich in illustrious dead."[136]

Slave Funerary Ritual Reactions of the Master Class

Nowhere and at no time during the history of American slavery was "the slave funeral legally protected as a human right and only rarely was it pro-tected in limited ways."[137] In fact, the record of the master class as it related to slave funerals is mixed. Some slaveholders tolerated or even encouraged slave funerals, though this seems to have been the case for only a select group of slaves. Favored slaves, lauded in life for their patience, obedience, and value, occasionally enjoyed in death elaborate services attended by both blacks and whites. While in Savannah, Georgia, Frederick Law Olmsted noted a grave marker set in marble and erected by "whites to the memory of favourite servants":[138] "To record the worth fidelity and virtue of Reynolda Watts . . . reared from infancy by an affectionate mistress and trained by her in the paths of virtue, she was strictly moral in her deportment, faithful and devoted in her duty and heart and soul."[139]

Masters occasionally attended or officiated over slave funerals in an effort to exert some control over the affair. When Frances Kemble attended a slave funeral with her husband, their presence was duly noted by the slaves as "every pair of large white-rimmed eyes turned upon [Mr. Butler] and myself."[140] At one point during the ceremony, "all the people knelt down in the sand, as I did also, Mr. [Butler] alone remained standing in the presence of the dead man and of the living God to whom his slaves were now appealing."[141] That Butler remained standing concerned Kemble deeply: "There was something painful to me in [Butler]'s standing while we all knelt on the earth. . . . Here I wished he would have knelt, to have given his slaves some token of his belief that—*at least in the sight of that Master* to whom we were addressing our worship—all men are equal."[142] But Butler would not be moved. Even in the sight of the heavenly Master, he relented nothing of his own powers on earth.

Some missionaries took full advantage of slave funerals to preach the Gospel and render an impression of the uncertainty of life: "What' says the not-to-be-disturbed-at-night pastor of a Chapel of ease, 'put yourself to the trouble of burying a *dead* Negro?' Why Not? We have unsuperable objections to burying a *living* one, but see no reason why the last sad office of the Church should not be performed over the remains of the black man. Has he no affections, are there no weeping friends to be consoled[,] . . . but apart from this, may not the living be effectually warned."[143] By highlighting the patience and obedience of some recently departed slaves, on the one hand, and emphasizing the uncertainty of life on the other, slaveholders hoped to mitigate against slave resistance by warning slaves of the importance of leading humble and obsequious lives on Earth.

Occasionally, slaveholders provided some of the materials for the funeral, including nails, a coffin, or paint. Slaves on the Butler plantation applied to Frances Kemble for cotton to cover the body of a recently deceased slave.[144] Some slaveholders inscribed an affectionate note on the tombstone of a departed slave. More often they went to no such trouble. One former slave recalls that "dey didn't have no funerals for de slaves, but jes' bury dem like a cow or a hoss, jes' dig a hole and roll 'em in it and cover 'em up."[145] Even worse, some slaveholders left the bodies of slaves unburied, as did Charles Manigault when a slave drowned while attempting to escape: "The body was left floating in slack water until tides took it away so that others might be deterred from resistance."[146] In 1856 one Georgia planter did pay for the funeral expenses of George, a hired slave, but not without promptly suing George's owner to recuperate the lost monies.[147] Indeed, so mixed is the record of the master class in providing for slave funerals that paternalism fails as an adequate explanation for the persistence of slave burials in the slave South.[148]

Funeral Sermons

Perhaps nowhere else is the close connection between art and death in black life more poignantly drawn than in the African American funeral ritual, the sermons of which highlight the frailties of this life and the imminence of the next:

> De body of Silas
> Stiff on de coolin' board lies . . .
> His soul has passed
> To his far off home . . .
> His soul's gone forward,
> But his body is left
> For de weepers and mourners,
> For de singers of songs
> And de prayer of prayers
> He passed in de night,
> In a heavenly flight,
> By a holy light.
> He's gone to his home
> His far off home.[149]

In a few lines, the image of dear Silas crystallizes the distinct separation that attends the death of a loved one. His body, a mere shell, lies on the cooling board for the benefit of the mourners. It remains in the world so mourners might pray and sing and pay their respects. But Silas is already elsewhere, his soul gone off to some far away place, upward to the celestial realm, eastward to Africa. A former slave now hovers in death,

> above the lowly things of the earth.
> She's at rest where the angels
> sweetly sing . . . and her spirit rests
> far above the mists.[150]

Though reserved and pensive, the tone of this memorial is not somber. Implied in most slave funeral sermons is the notion that the loss of life invites the reward of freedom. So the life of another Sea Island resident is remembered: "She's at rest, asleep and free; her soul from sorrow is lifted far above the trials of this world with its joys and its tears."[151] The same was true for so many others, and it was certainly true during the memorial services for Elizabeth Coleman, a Lowcountry resident who sleeps out in de graveyard, "free from de world and its sins."[152]

It is interesting also to read these funeral sermons in light of subsequent artistic creations that were heavily based on the slave folklore experience. So writes James Weldon Johnson:

> And God said: Go down, Death, go down
> Go down to Savannah, Georgia,
> Down in Yamacraw,
> And find Sister Caroline.
> She's labored in my vineyard,
> And she's tired
> She's weary
> Go down, Death, and bring her to me . . .
> While we were watching around her bed . . .
> She saw what we couldn't see;
> She saw old Death . . . coming like a falling star
> And she whispered to us: I'm going home.[153]

The slave funeral sermon drew the attention of the mourners to what, for the slaves and their progeny, were the most crucial aspects of the death experience: flight, freedom, and home. These themes eased the pain of transition and emphasized particular and specific notions about the afterworld, the body, and the body's movement in that realm.

Taken together, this reading of slave funerals highlights not only the similarities between ritual practice in two Atlantic locales but also the centrality of death in the formation of the African Atlantic religious complex. In graphic detail, the two locales were linked by the blanched bones laid strewn along the ocean's floor, by the unknown numbers of captive Africans who died on the way to the coast. Death persisted in the antebellum South in both the mortality rates of slaves and the very fact that the system of slavery was based, in large part, on the powers of life and death that the master class held over bondsmen. The specter of death remained a central element in the lives of Lowcountry slaves even though the mortality rates for American slaves were lower than those for Caribbean or South American slaves. The life of a slave continued to be a disposable commodity, valued mainly in its profit potential. In the end, the powers of life and death constituted the predominant factor in the relations between slaves and slaveholders.[154]

In each of this book's preceding chapters, the metaphor of death persists. As discussed in chapter 2, slaves considered baptism a symbolic death, a journey under the water's surface and into the afterworld, with a subsequent return into the land of the living. As discussed in chapter 3, a set of ritual objects, *minkisi* in Kongo and conjure bags in the Deep South, acted as tools to access the otherworld so that the dead could affect circumstances in the realm of the living. This discussion continues in relation to death in this chapter with the notion that the very practice of burial and its attendant rituals were linked between Kongo and the slave South. Not only in the decoration of graves but also in the very theories that attended funerary ritual one notes a very close relationship between Kongolese belief and practice and that of the Lowcountry. In both locales similar preparations for the postmortem body and corollary notions regarding the continued potency of the spirits of the deceased persist. Moreover, the realm of the dead was inscribed into the natural landscape itself such that wooded areas, waterways, and swamps revealed portals and passageways through which communication with the other realm was made possible. The blurring of the demarcation between the world of the living and that of the dead characterized ritual in both locales. Yet funerary ritual in the Lowcountry was not a mere replica of Kongolese ritual practice. Instead, innovation and elaboration characterized New World ritual to the degree that slaves formed practices that were novel yet still conversant with Kongolese ritual.

Conclusion

The preceding chapters propose the development of an African Atlantic religious complex that developed during the era of slavery and the slave trade. Linked through a constellation of interrelated sites, varied African Atlantic peoples managed and, in many cases, manipulated the oppressive slavery regimes under which they suffered by drawing on a wellspring of cultural resources rooted both in their own memories of Africa and innovative New World community creations. While not eliding the very real distinctions that existed throughout the plantation Americas, the notion of an African Atlantic serves useful purposes. By inviting continued comparative study in the region, this formulation encourages discussions of not only the manner in which the cultures of Africa affected the Americas but also the varied ways in which different American locales affected one another. As noted by Julius Scott, transatlantic connections between both free and enslaved blacks during the era of slavery created extensive avenues of information exchange.[1] In this book I have investigated but one strand in this network, charting the rise of a certain historical trajectory that linked ritual practice in the Kongo region of West-Central Africa to that of the slave societies of the U.S. South, especially the Lowcountry region of Georgia and South Carolina.

The early development of this African Atlantic space is illustrated in light of Christian conversion. On both sides of the Atlantic, Lowcountry blacks converted to Christianity, creating a particular religious and ritual practice in the process. In this sense, would-be converts manufactured a faith of importance and relevance based on their own religions and cosmological assumptions and used it to address the very specific conditions of their lives. The prior exposure that some Kongolese captives had with Catholicism colored the subsequent encounter that New World slaves had with the mandate of Christian conversion in the Americas, thus complicating the ultimate meaning of Christian conversion. In Kongo, many converts believed that baptism offered a spiritual protection against not only death but also the very real threat of being taken as a slave and sent to the New World; others reinterpreted Christian theology to argue that Jesus was Kongolese and that Jerusalem was located in the capital of Kongo. In the Lowcountry, many enslaved Africans thought of baptism and the spiritual possession that often attended Christian practice as an opportunity to escape slavery by taking refuge in the otherworld. In both cases, blacks drew on a shared set of ritual practices, beliefs, and presumptions to mobilize Christianity as a crucial space for cultural resistance, community construction, and identity formation.

The nature of the African Atlantic religious complex is also revealed in the construction and use of ritual objects. As they circulated around the Atlantic rim, African-inspired ritual objects maintained not only formal and aesthetic relationships but also, and perhaps more importantly, theoretical, symbolic, and cosmological connections. In this sense, African ritual objects were not simply remade in the New World but were elaborated in creative and innovative ways by slaves. Further, these objects played a crucial role as a form of resistance both in Kongo, against the demands of the slave trade, and in the slave South, against the brutalities of plantation slavery. By relying on their own theories of otherworldly power and its effect in the natural world, enslaved Africans reinvested their lives with meaning and countered the dehumanization that they suffered at the hands of plantation mangers, owners, overseers, and physicians. Much like ritual objects, burial rites in West-Central Africa and the Lowcountry reveal not only formal and aesthetic relationships between Kongo and the American South but also shared theoretical and symbolic meanings regarding notions of the body, the spirit, and the movement of the postmortem soul from this world to the next.

The preceding chapters brought several themes into sharp focus. First, each of the spiritual practices discussed is persistently resistant. Many Kongolese mobilized and interpreted Christianity, ritual objects, and burial practices in a pointed critique against slavery and the slave trade. In the slave South, the rituals of resistance were put to use as weapons aimed at the alleviation of the pains and oppressions of plantation life.

I argue that slaves resisted more than the conditions of slavery and the slave trade. Instead, the ritual resistance of slaves existed alongside, and often times in opposition to, the ideologies of labor expropriation, global capital, and a burgeoning age of enlightenment, reason, and rationality that justified slavery in the first place. In its insistence on a world of retribution, power, and justice outside the purview of the master class, enslaved Africans lodged a critical blow to the spiritual and theoretical presumptions that undergirded slavery. Their ecstasy along the banks of baptismal rivers, their use of conjure and divination, and their broken glass over burial sites affirmed their own notions of the world, their bodies, and their bodies' movements.

The remarkable flexibility and adaptability of black Atlantic cultures also stands out in graphic relief in the preceding chapters. So crucial was this cultural dynamism that *Rituals of Resistance* adopts a broad conception of cultural transmission and connection. When they found themselves in the plantation societies of the Americas, enslaved Africans reconstituted certain cultural forms. In myriad ways slaves *remembered* Africa, as in the reconstruction and reconfiguration of language, gestures, dance, and material culture. But even more than this, enslaved Africans maintained certain symbolic and theoretical principles in the construction of slave cultural practices. In this sense, while the actual practice of certain rituals might look quite different in various New World plantation societies, they were each rooted in similar cosmological conceptions common throughout the African Atlantic. Innovation, then, followed the requirements dictated by the machinations of daily life and the particular imperatives of various plantation regimes.

In recent years, scholars have argued for increased specificity in the study of African cultural continuities in the slave societies of the plantation Americas. Moving away from notions of culturally monolithic Africans or of masses of unspecified amorphous African crowds, these scholars, many of whom were first trained as Africanists, have shed considerable light on the social, economic, political, and cultural landscapes from which captive Africans originated. In like manner, scholars of American slavery have been mining sources in the New World to paint more clearly the picture of African cultural resonances in the plantation Americas. These efforts have not gone without significant criticism. Michael Gomez argues that studies into "the cultural and social transformations of transported Africans tend to invite a quality of critique unique in its level of elevated scrutiny, emphasizing distance and lacunae in the substance and circumstances separating Africa and the Americas."[2] These oppositions are often articulated "in doubts about the ability of Africans to transfer collective perspectives to the Americas, and in ruminations that arguably overdetermine the conditions of slavery and the slave trades."[3] In the end, this opposition, often accompanied by notions of creolization, suggests that the study of African cultural continuities in the New World is a misguided if not futile attempt. When argued further, some of these oppositions have questioned the validity of any "category of collective identity in Africa" prior to the transatlantic slave trade.[4] Ironically, this hesitation to ascribe to Africans any collective identity before slavery runs the risk of, on the one hand, combining all Africans (or at least those from Senegambia to West-Central Africa most directly affected by the slave trade) into large, unwieldy "crowds"[5] or, on the other hand, of reducing them into so many innumerable tribal parts. Neither of these depictions is accurate; both echo older notions of Africans as both generic and provincial, ubiquitous though invisible.

That these debates ultimately reflect political orientations is evident in the statements of Richard and Sally Price, who in *Maroon Arts* offer a cautionary missive to those interested in the relationships between African and African American cultures. They warn that any "determined researcher, intent on proving a point, can almost always locate similar formal design styles or patterns in two different locales, even if the people in those locales have had little or no historical connection with each other."[6] In this view, much of the interest and scholarship related to the long arm of Africa in the lives of American slaves is ideologically driven.[7] More recently, Gwendolyn Midlo Hall writes in a spirited defense of the crucial importance of Africa in the study of American slavery that her work is "inevitably . . . highly political."[8]

While I disagree with those who would read *Rituals of Resistance* as merely ideologically driven, I cannot pretend to ignore the political implications of my conclusions, namely, that the cultures of West-Central Africa played an early, significant, and persistent role in the religious and spiritual practices and beliefs of enslaved men and women in the Lowcountry. I have suggested a method for acknowledging and even embracing the diversity and variation that marked slave cultural formation in the Americas while yet attempting to identify discernible contributions from particular groups of Africans. I maintain a view of slave culture as composite, the product of various distinct elements that are neither hermetically sealed nor hopelessly dissolved into a hazy cultural mist. Crucial in this study has been the use of African historical sources from the time period under investigation. Perhaps the most significant legacy of the recent interest in mapping specific and particular connections between the cultures of Africa and the slave cultures in the Americas is the manner in which the sources, methods, and interests of Africanists and African Americanists are converging. Increasingly, students of American slavery will need to look to contemporary African sources to fully understand developments in the plantation Americas. Notably, this sort of historical investigation promises to shed light on not only American slavery but also the nature of African society between the fifteenth to the nineteenth centuries. Novel and intriguing avenues of African historical investigation are bound to open up as Americanists approach African materials with questions, approaches, and orientations different from those previously adopted by Africanists.

This manner of investigation is particularly crucial for the study of slavery in the United States, where scholars have long regarded the cultural relationships between Africans on the continent and those transplanted over seas as especially tenuous and fleeting as compared to those in the Caribbean or South America. I suggest that blacks in the United States maintained their own deep and longstanding connections to Africa, which they used to their own benefit and in line with their own needs. These connections reflected both the formal affinities between certain ritual implements, practices, and rites, as well as a large set of metaphorical and symbolic resonances that were no less important.

Beyond this, the African Atlantic continues to resonate to the present day. This is certainly true with regard to contemporary African American visual arts, music, and dance, which continue to draw on not only slave art but also the artistic traditions of Africa. Visual artist Renee Stout recalled the reach of the long arm of Africa in her own sculpture: "I say it's Central Africa specifically. I don't know why. I have an interest in the rest of the continent, but there's something about the things that come from that region that I just react to the most, and I don't know why. I would like to know that myself, what it is, what is that connection that is almost like I can look at this and immediately understand something?"[9] The Middle Passage Monument, discussed in chapter 4, and the recent discovery and debate over the Negro Burial Ground in New York highlight the persistence of Africa in the construction of contemporary African American identities.

If the cultures of the African Atlantic are bound together by the similarities of their religious and cultural expression, they are also bound, sadly, by the specter of death. Indeed, death pervades this project. Enslaved Africans were beset on all sides by the specter of death, which was both literal, in the high mortality rates during the Middle Passage, and figurative, in the struggle to maintain viable cultural, religious, and social practices. Not surprisingly, bondsmen invested tremendous meaning in death and dying and shared with their Kongolese counterparts an understanding of the intimate connections between the realm of the dead and the realm of the living. Now, after having tormented the victims of slavery and the slave trade, Death now visits the children of Africa on the continent and in the diaspora. This is evident in the high level of violence and instability that have affected blacks in postcolonial African states as well as in the inner cities of the United States or the outer cities of Europe. The persistence of the specter of death in the lives of black Atlantic peoples is perhaps no more evident than in the scourge of AIDS, which has ravaged the African continent and affected blacks disproportionately around the Atlantic rim.

In a sense, art and death are bringing blacks from all around the Atlantic rim into closer contact. The rise and spread of hip-hop culture in recent years has certainly accelerated the linkage of black communities around the Atlantic in important ways. In the wake of the violent murders of hip-hop artists Tupac Shakur and Notorious B.I.G., a friend of mine traveled to Ghana, where a group of interested youths asked him, "What are you . . . East Coast or West Coast?" When he told the young men that he was born and raised in New York City, half of the group responded defiantly by waving their hands high in the air as they imitated Los Angeles gang signs and yelled, "Westside!" in tribute to Tupac, their fallen leader. This sense of connection has also been heightened in recent years by the high rates of black emigration around the Atlantic, which has brought the cultures of the African Atlantic into close and, in some cases, conflicted contact. Candomblé, Vodou, and Santería are now found not only in Brazil, Haiti, and Cuba but also in New York, London, and Paris. The African Atlantic, then, comprises a constellation of cultural interaction that continues to operate as a living, breathing space whose relevance is in no way limited to the era of slavery.

This topic is replete with possibilities for further study. As noted in chapter 1, scholars from various disciplines have traditionally treated the Lowcountry as a particular, and in many cases peculiar, unit of analysis. But the peculiarity of the region is coming increasingly into question, and scholars may need to reconceptualize the boundaries that separate this region from other areas of study. This is certainly true with regard to colonial Florida, to which many Sea Islanders fled in efforts to escape plantation slavery. The work of Jane Landers and others implies that the cultural zone of the Lowcountry may need to be extended outward.

In much the same way, the richness of black cultural expression far to the north in New York (and related areas) bears the mark of slave-inspired artistic production. Some study, then, into the connections between Low-country culture and the black cultures of the North may bear substantial fruit. Such study may begin to revise long-held notions that though re-markable, Sea Island culture was largely atypical when compared to the rest of the slave South and the free North.

In the longer view these connections suggest that national boundaries may be ill fit to consider fully the construction and development of slave cultures. When followed to its logical extent, the African Atlantic implies not only the connections between Africa and the Americas but also the vast interaction and circulation of ideas, materials, and symbols on all of the continents directly affected by slavery and the slave trade. The focus this book places on ritual practice suggests that other areas of research, including language, labor, and material culture, would likely be interest-ing avenues of inquiry that might flesh out further the ultimate meanings, functions, and development of the Atlantic as an organizing unit of analysis in the study of slavery and the slave trade.

Epilogue

Looking over here from beyond the bridge, you might believe some of the more far-fetched stories about Willow Springs: the island that got spit out from the mouth of God, and when it fell to earth it brought along an army of stars. He tried to reach down and scoop them back up, and found Himself shaking hands with the greatest conjure woman on earth. "Leave them here, Lord," she said. "I ain't got nothing but these poor black hands to guide my people, but I can lead on with light."

Gloria Naylor, *Mama Day*

The people of Willow Springs have been celebrating Candle Walk on the twenty-second night of December for some time now, though nobody really knows why or exactly when the ritual began. But they do know that it has been this way since before they were born—and even before the ones before them were born. They have been observing the holiday since way before that outside preacher, Reverend Hooper, tried to stop it altogether, and they kept right on going strong after he left.

In some ways the holiday has never changed. But even if it feels like Candle Walk has always been the same, the truth is that it has always been changing. The young folks now carry kerosene lamps or sparklers in lieu of the old-fashioned candles preferred by the elders. The residents of Willow Springs used to use Candle Walk Night as a way of sharing the fruits of their hard labor: fresh vegetables, a cured side of meat, a homemade cake, or a freshly brewed tea. But now, with more and more people crossing the bridge to earn a living, there are fewer fresh vegetables to be had. Instead, some of the young ones have taken to buying each other gadgets and other such things from the catalogues. Some have refused to bake their own sweets, opting instead for store-bought ginger snaps. Worse still, some have even stopped walking during Candle Walk altogether, choosing to drive instead, with headlights blazing.

Some older residents argue that, taken together, all of these changes spell the end of Candle Walk. But the wisest ones remember that when they were youngsters, Candle Walk was different still, that they used to gather on the main road and "hum some lost and ancient song." Back then you heard talk of "a slave woman who came to Willow Springs, and when she left, she left in a ball of fire to journey back home east over the ocean." Indeed, the elders remember that their parents' celebrations of Candle Walk were different still. In the end, it will take generations before Willow Springs stops celebrating Candle Walk, and more generations will pass after that before people stop talking about it. By then, "it won't be the world as we know it no way—and so no need for the memory."[1]

In her brief portrait of Candle Walk, Gloria Naylor illustrates some of the most important themes explored in *Rituals of Resistance*. To a certain extent, the ritual beliefs and spiritual practices explored throughout this project have been the same for some time. In both Kongo and the Low-country blacks responded to Christian missionaries and their attendant theologies through the lens of their own immediate concerns. On both sides of the Atlantic they decorated graves in a similar fashion and constructed medicine bags and bottles from the rough cloths and wood carvings available to them. On both coasts they resisted slavery and the transatlantic slave trade. They did it for centuries—and they continue to do it. But the slave cultures of the Americas were no mere replica of a presumed African precedent. American slaves valued innovation and creativity. Still, this innovation of blacks around the Atlantic, like the improvisation in be-bop, carried its own rules and discipline. One had to play the music, as in the Candle Walk, according to tradition. As Toni Morrison explains, "Black Americans were sustained and healed and nurtured by the translation of their experience into art, above all in the music. That was functional. . . . My parallel is always the music because all of the strategies of the art are there. All of the intricacy, all of the discipline. All the work that must go into improvisation so that it appears that you've never touched it."[2] Tradition is not bound by inheritance. Rather, people create tradition out of a certain legacy of principles, practices, and theories, none of which determine the ultimate outcome or form of artistic expression. When faced with changing circumstances and the particular conditions of life, people rely on their traditions when creating cultural forms that are both old and new, ancestral and innovative.

Indeed, the preceding chapters suggest a vision of culture that is fluid and multidimensional, allowing for such novelty and transformation as to avoid ongoing debates about cultural provenance and authenticity in the plantation Americas. Cultural practice in the Lowcountry was neither monolithic nor hermetic, and though West-Central Africans played a major role in the construction and maintenance of slave culture in the Lowcountry, people from other areas of Africa, along with Native Americas and European Americans, contributed in the process. While some have analyzed this cultural matrix as evidence of creolization, the preceding chapters suggest a possible avenue of research whereby the particular contributions of different peoples and cultures can be acknowledged without references to culture as the product of a nebulous postmodernity. Related to this is an idea of cultural transmission that, rather than demanding an adherence to a presumed authentic prototype, allows for greater degrees of innovation, dynamism, and creativity.

Moreover, this study emphasizes multidirectionality as a central theme and driving force of the African Atlantic. Rather than a linear progression from African homelands to New World plantations, this book highlights the African Atlantic as a constellation of sites, each ever conversant with the others. So one notes a certain reverberation of themes, practices, and beliefs among North America, the Caribbean, South America, and Africa, all in relationship with one another. This multidirectionality is highlighted also in the manner in which enslaved blacks throughout the Americas put Africa to use as they meditated on the role and importance of the continent in their own lives. This conceptual movement "back to Africa," as it were, served as the ideological foundation upon which later pan-Africanist ideologies were laid.[3]

Artist Carrie Mae Weems's *Sea Island Series* is a multimedia installation of images and texts that highlight life and history in the Sea Islands. Principle among her concerns is the relationship between Africans and their progeny in the Americas. To illustrate this relationship, Weems offers the following progression:

> Gola
> Angola
> Gulla
> Gullah
> Geechee[4]

Part of the series consists of Weems's photographs of the islands, which capture a landscape, in stark back and white, living and breathing with the beliefs and rituals of its inhabitants. Perhaps most important, the natural landscape, the tress, grass, and sky, are dotted and decorated with the ritual practices of Sea Island residents—medicine bottles and bags, seashells, and hubcaps—which all inscribe particular spheres of sanctity in an otherwise mundane landscape. The people of the Sea Islands are insinuated in the natural landscape such that the rituals that they perform on the land—ceremonial burial, praise-house worship, yard decoration—define the landscape itself. In this sense, little separates the landscape and that which is performed on it. Or put another way, the landscape is an active member and a willing participant in the congregations and communities that comprise the Sea Islands. Indeed, the *Sea Island Series* is as much about the living people of the Sea Islands as it is about the living land of those islands, breathing and moving of its own accord.

In her series, Weems addresses one of the central themes in this book. In each chapter I have noted the uses to which blacks in different Atlantic locales put the natural landscape. In Kongo, wooded areas, rivers, and deep ocean waters were all negotiated as sites of interstitial power and communication between the world of the living and that of the dead. In the Lowcountry, slave burial grounds and swamps held portentous meanings for the enslaved, and any murky river or stream could be called upon to reflect the river Jordan during slave baptismals. Blacks around the Atlantic further mobilized the natural world in the construction of *minkisi* and conjure bags, which were filled with dirt, blood, bone, and the found objects that lay strewn about the ground.

In addition, Weems's *Sea Island Series* is peppered with text drawn from the black folk tradition: "A baby born near midnight or with a veil over the eyes will be able to see ghosts." Challenging the notion that these beliefs represent merely the long since abandoned and vestigial superstitions of a presumably modern people, Weems asserts, "RIGHT NOW, I KNOW LOTS OF YA HAVE DIMES TIED ROUND YO ANKLES. DON'T YA!" To a certain extent Weems explodes the distinctions between the past and the present. A traditional plantation praise house is figured in a photo juxtaposed against a community store and restaurant offering, among other things, fresh greens, smoke meats, neck bones, and a "Wash & Dry" service.[5] So *Rituals of Resistance* moves away from notions of Africa as ever situated in the past and the Americas as always the more contemporary recipient of its cultural and religious practices, themes, and tropes. This book has focused on the relationships and connections between people and places separated by the Atlantic. I am interested in not only the way Africa informs our study of blacks in the Americas but also the manner in which our study of the Americas enhances our perceptions of Africa.

Indeed, Weems explores the importance of Africa in a series of ceramic plates, the faces of which are the subject of a particular antiphony (call and response). In bold letters one sees a phrase underscored, *"Went Looking For Africa,"* underneath which Weems offers a multitude of possibilities:

> and found Africa here
> in the proverbs
> of McIntosh
> in the voices
> of Sapelo
> in the songs
> of St. Simons.
> Along the highways
> of Jekyll
> in the gardens
> of John's
> in the grave-yards
> of Hilton Head.

In another plate, Africa is found in "uncombed heads / acrylic nails & / Afrocentric attitudes / Africans / find laughable." Africa is in "gumbo, fried fish, the blues, King Cotton, butterbeans, newspapered walls and neck-bone eatin' cornbread smacking negroes."[6]

Indeed, the search for Africa is central to Weems's project. Yet this search for Africa does not render images of a static, timeless homeland. Instead, it is in our search for Africa, in our search for ancestors, that we find ourselves, in cornbread and cornrows, in cemeteries and a song.

NOTES

ABBREVIATIONS

BIHBR   *Bulletin de l'Institut Historique Belge de Rome*
GHS   Georgia Historical Society, Savannah
JAF   *Journal of American Folklore*
SCHS   South Carolina Historical Society, Charleston
SCL   South Caroliniana Library, University of South Carolina, Columbia

INTRODUCTION

1. Drawn from Gloria Naylor's discussion of Reema in her *Mama Day* (1988; reprint, New York: Vintage Books, 1993), 7.

2. Ibid., 8.

3. Ibid.

4. Ibid., 7, 8.

5. Frantz Fanon, *Black Skin, White Mask* (New York: Grove Weidenfeld, 1967), 112.

6. Brent Hayes Edwards, *The Practice of Diaspora: Literature, Translation, and the Rise of Black Internationalism* (Cambridge: Harvard University Press, 2003), 10.

7. Although I focus especially on the kingdom of Kongo (the political and economic structure of which is defined in more detail in chapter 1), I make regular references to smaller polities, tributary states, and neighboring kingdoms that maintained various relationships with Kongo proper between the sixteenth and nineteenth centuries. At times, these states existed under the direct purview of the Kongo kingdom; at other points they enjoyed political autonomy. When referring not to Kongo proper but to a larger zone of related, though by no means homogenous, cultures, languages, and belief systems, I use the term "West-Central Africa."

8. For the former, see, for example, E. Franklin Frazier, *The Negro Family in the United States* (Chicago: University of Chicago Press, 1939), 21; Kenneth Stampp, *The Peculiar Institution: Slavery in the Ante-bellum South* (1956; reprint, New York: Vintage, 1989), 375; and Sidney Mintz and Richard Price, *The Birth of African-American Culture: An Anthropological Perspective* (Boston: Beacon Press, 1992). For the latter, see Joseph Roach, *Cities of the Dead: Circum-Atlantic Performance* (New York: Columbia University Press, 1996).

9. David Scott, *Refashioning Futures: Criticism after Postcoloniality* (Princeton, N.J.: Princeton University Press, 1999), 108.

10. Melville Herskovits, *The Myth of the Negro Past* (1941; reprint, Boston: Beacon Hill Press, 1958), 1–2. Notwithstanding Scott's critique, one must acknowledge, at the outset, the tremendous importance of the work of Herskovits and a mere handful of others who so vociferously opposed the leading historical interpretations as regards African American history. Herskovits's investigations were truly foundational in the field of African American history, generally, and certainly with respect to African American culture. In this sense, the present discussion should be read more as a criticism of the constraints under which Herskovits and others worked and less as a criticism of their groundbreaking investigations.

11. Scott, *Refashioning Futures,* 108, 111.

12. Ibid., 108.

13. Ibid., 111.

14. Herskovits, *Myth of the Negro Past,* xiii, 6.

15. Ibid., 6, 12. Some notable exceptions include W. E. B. Du Bois, *Black Folk Then and Now* (1939; reprint, Millwood, N.Y.: Kraus-Thompson, 1975); and Carter G. Woodson, *The African Background Outlined* (Washington, D.C.: Association for the Study of Negro Life and History, 1936).

16. David Scott, "That Event, This Memory: Notes on the Anthropology of African Diasporas in the New World," *Diaspora* 1, no. 3 (Winter 1991): 268.

17. Scott, *Refashioning Futures,* 117.

18. Ibid., 115, 124, 126; see Kobena Mercer's "Black Hair/Style Politics," in *Welcome to the Jungle: New Positions in Black Cultural Studies,* by Kobena Mercer (New York: Routledge, 1994), 97–130.

19. Stuart Hall, "Cultural Identity and Diaspora," in *Identity: Community, Culture, Difference,* ed. Jonathan Rutherford (London: Lawrence and Wishart, 1990), 226.

20. Scott, *Refashioning Futures,* 109; see also Kamau Brathwaite, "The African Presence in Caribbean Literature," in *Roots,* by Kamau Brathwaite (Ann Arbor: University of Michigan Press, 1993), 190–258.

21. Sterling Stuckey, *Slave Culture: Nationalist Theory and the Foundations of Black America* (New York: Oxford University Press, 1987); William Bascom, *African Folktales in the New World* (Bloomington: Indiana University Press, 1992); Roger Bastide, *African Civilizations in the New World* (London: C. Hurst, 1972); Herskovits, *Myth of the Negro Past.*

22. Linda Heywood, ed., *Central Africans and Cultural Transformations in the American Diaspora* (New York: Cambridge University Press, 2002), 8.

23. Jan Vansina, "The Kongo Kingdom and Its Neighbors," in *General History of Africa,* ed. B. A. Ogot (Berkeley and Los Angeles: University of California Press, 1998), 5:546, 550–557.

24. For studies that consider the West-Central African presence in the Americas, see Stuckey, *Slave Culture,* esp. chap. 1; Margaret Washington Creel, *A Peculiar People: Slave Religion and Community-Culture Among the Gullahs* (New York: New York University Press, 1988); Robert Farris Thompson and Joseph Cornet, *The Four Moments of the Sun:*

Kongo Art in Two Worlds (Washington, D.C.: National Gallery of Art, 1981); Robert Farris Thompson, *Flash of the Spirit: African and Afro-American Art and Philosophy* (New York: Vintage Books, 1984), 103–145; Michael Gomez, *Exchanging Our Country Marks: The Transformation of African Identities in the Colonial and Antebellum South* (Chapel Hill: University of North Carolina Press, 1998), esp. chaps. 8–9; John Thornton, *Africa and Africans in the Making of the Atlantic World, 1400–1800,* 2nd ed. (1992; reprint, New York: Cambridge University Press, 1998); Heywood, *Central Africans,* esp. chaps. 11 and 13; Herskovits, *Myth of the Negro Past;* Peter H. Wood, *Black Majority: Negroes in Colonial South Carolina from 1670 through the Stono Rebellion* (New York: Alfred A. Knopf, 1974); Daniel Littlefield, *Rice and Slaves: Ethnicity and the Slave Trade in Colonial South Carolina* (Baton Rouge: Louisiana State University Press, 1981); Maureen Warner-Lewis, *Central Africa in the Caribbean: Transcending Time, Transforming Cultures* (Barbados: University of West Indies Press, 2003); Monica Schuler, *Alas, Alas, Kongo: A Social History of Indentured African Immigration into Jamaica, 1841–1865* (Baltimore: Johns Hopkins University Press, 1990); and James Sweet, *Recreating Africa: Culture, Kinship, and Religion in the African-Portuguese World, 1441–1770* (Chapel Hill: North Carolina Pres, 2003).

25. Albert Raboteau, *Slave Religion: The "Invisible Institution" in the Antebellum South* (New York: Oxford University Press, 1978), 87–88, 271–272; Melville Herskovits, "African Gods and Catholic Saints in New World Negro Belief," *American Anthropologist* 39:635–647; Herskovits, *Myth of the Negro Past,* 16, 220. For an interesting discussion of the connection between African spiritual pantheons and Catholic saints, see Zora Neale Hurston, *Tell My Horse: Voodoo and Life in Haiti and Jamaica* (1938; reprint, New York: Harper and Row: 1990), 113–114.

26. Herskovits, *Myth of the Negro Past,* 16.

27. See, for example, Richard Price and Sally Price, *Maroon Arts: Cultural Vitality in the African Diaspora* (Boston: Beacon Press, 2000).

28. Jon Butler, *Awash in a Sea of Faith: Christianizing the American People* (Cambridge: Harvard University Press, 1990), 159–160, 161–163.

29. Mintz and Price, *Birth of African-American Culture,* 15, 60.

30. Butler, *Awash in a Sea of Faith,* 158–159.

31. Roach, *Cities of the Dead,* 25.

32. Saidiyya Hartman, *Scenes of Subjection: Terror, Slavery, and Self-Making in Nineteenth-Century America* (New York: Oxford University Press, 1997), 74.

33. Sweet, *Recreating Africa,* 228.

34. Ibid., 116.

35. Ibid., 123, 126.

36. Ibid., 115.

37. See, for example, Lorenzo Dow Turner, *Africanisms in the Gullah Dialect* (1949; reprint, Columbia: University of South Carolina Press, 2002); Georgia Writers' Project, *Drums and Shadows: Survival Studies among the Georgia Coastal Negroes* (Athens: University of Georgia Press, 1940), esp. appendix.

38. Price and Price, *Maroon Arts,* 300.

39. The historiography on American slavery and resistance is long and varied. The following represents a mere sampling of relevant sources. For investigations into the role

that community, culture, and art played as forms of resistance, see Stuckey, *Slave Culture;* Gomez, *Exchanging Our Country Marks;* Creel, *Peculiar People;* Charles Joyner, *Down by the Riverside: A South Carolina Slave Community* (Urbana: University of Illinois Press, 1984); Raymond Dobard and Jacqueline Tobin, *Hidden in Plain View: The Secret Story of Quilts and the Underground Railroad* (New York: Bantam Books, 1999); Sylvia Frey, *Water from the Rock: Black Resistance in a Revolutionary Age* (Princeton, N.J.: Princeton University Press, 1991); Michael Mullin, *Africa in America: Slave Acculturation and Resistance in the American South and the British Caribbean, 1736–1831* (Urbana: University of Illinois Press, 1992); Michael Mullin, *Flight and Rebellion: Slave Resistance in Eighteenth-Century Virginia* (New York: Oxford University Press, 1992); Norrece T. Jones, *Born a Child of Freedom, Yet a Slave: Mechanisms of Control and Strategies of Resistance in Antebellum South Carolina* (Middletown, Conn.: Wesleyan University Press, 1989); Richard Price ed., *Maroon Societies: Rebel Slave Communities in the Americas,* 3rd ed. (Baltimore: Johns Hopkins University, 1996); and John Hope Franklin and Loren Schweninger, *Runaway Slavery: Rebels on the Plantation* (New York: Oxford University Press, 1999).

40. See, for example, Joyner, *Down by the Riverside;* Roger D. Abrahams, *African American Folktales: Stories from the Black Tradition in the New World* (1985; reprint, New York: Pantheon Books, 1999); James C. Scott, *Domination and the Arts of Resistance: Hidden Transcripts* (New Haven, Conn.: Yale University Press, 1992); and Lawrence Levine, *Black Culture and Black Consciousness: Afro-American Folk Thought from Slavery to Freedom* (Oxford: Oxford University Press, 1978).

41. Stuckey, *Slave Culture,* 12 and passim.

42. Gomez, *Exchanging Our Country Marks,* 3–4.

43. Washington, *Peculiar People,* 4.

44. Scott, *Hidden Transcripts,* xii.

45. Ibid., xiii.

46. Ibid., 15.

47. Slavery is, of course, not the only system of forced labor of which villeinage, indentured servitude, and others might also be included. For an in-depth discussion of the differences between various forms of forced labor, see Orlando Patterson, *Slavery and Social Death: A Comparative Study* (Cambridge: Harvard University Press, 1982); Peter Kolchin, *American Slavery, 1619–1877* (1993; reprint, New York: Hill and Wang, 2003); Oscar and Mary Handlin, "Origins of the Southern Labor System," *William and Mary Quarterly,* 3rd ser., 7 (April 1950); and Winthrop Jordan, *White Over Black: American Attitudes Toward the Negro, 1550–1812* (Chapel Hill: University of North Carolina Press, 1968).

48. Hartman, *Scenes of Subjection,* 23.

49. Ibid., 24.

50. E. P. Thompson, *The Making of the English Working Class* (New York: Pantheon, 1963), 199–201.

51. Interestingly, Max Weber foresaw, in the increased rationalization of the modern world, an impending order marked by the development of new mechanisms designed to coerce labor from the populace: "The Puritan wanted to work in a calling; we are forced to do so." This new order was bound to machine production, which determined "the lives of all the individuals who are born into this mechanism . . . with irresistible force." So

restrictive was this new order that Weber likened it to "an iron cage," a condition of life with which the enslaved were all too familiar not only because their labor was coerced but also because they operated under the constraints of a veritable "iron cage." Max Weber, *The Protestant Ethic and the Spirit of Capitalism*, trans. Talcott Parsons (New York: Scribner's, 1958), 181.

52. David Brion Davis, *The Problem of Slavery in the Age of Revolution, 1770–1823* (New York: Oxford University Pres, 1999), 560–564.

53. Fanon, *Black Skin, White Masks*, 163.

54. For a classic study of the centrality of slavery and the slave trade to the rise of industry in England and the United States, see Eric Williams, *Capitalism and Slavery* (1944; reprint, Chapel Hill: University of North Carolina Press, 1994), 85–107; see also Joseph Inikori, *Africans and the Industrial Revolution in England* (Cambridge: Cambridge University Press, 2002), 156–215; C. L. R. James, *Black Jacobins: Toussaint L'Ouverture and the San Domingo Revolution* (1938; reprint, New York: Vintage Books, 1963), ix; T. H. Breen, *Tobacco Culture: The Mentality of the Great Planters on the Eve of Revolution* (Princeton, N.J.: Princeton University Press, 1985), 69; and Peter Hamilton, "The Enlightenment and the Birth of Social Science," in *Modernity: An Introduction to Modern Societies,* ed. Stuart Hall, David Held, Don Hubert, and Kenneth Thompson (Cambridge: Blackwell, 1996), 23–24.

55. Max Weber, "Science as a Vocation," in *From Max Weber: Essays in Sociology,* ed. and trans. H. H. Gerth and C. Wright Mills (New York: Oxford University Press, 1946), 129–156; see also Robert Bocock, "The Cultural Formations of Modern Society," in Hall, *Modernity,* 175. Notably, this increased emphasis on reason enjoyed only mixed and uneven success in the United States and Europe. While some elite whites espoused the new rational age, members of the lower and working classes largely adhered to a world of wonders. For example, well into the nineteenth century spiritualism was on the rise among middle-class whites. See Butler, *Awash in a Sea of Faith,* esp. chapter 8.

56. Some scholars view the religious expressions of slaves as passive, if not entirely impotent. Writing in *Roll, Jordan, Roll,* Eugene Genovese suggests that slave religion inspired docility and submission. That is, many slaveholders came to believe that religion might be used as an effective means of control. Genovese asserts that Christianity enabled the slaves to do battle against the slaveholder's ideology, but defensively within the system it opposed; offensively it proved a poor instrument. In short, Christianity softened the slaves by drawing the hatred from their souls, and without hatred there could be no revolt. See Eugene Genovese, *Roll, Jordan, Roll: The World the Slaves Made* (New York: Pantheon Books, 1974). That Christianity could be used, in some cases, to dissipate resistance and revolt is certain. Still, I am arguing that Christianity was also mobilized by slaves not as a means of dissolving potential resistance but as a tool for harnessing and focusing that resistance.

57. For treatments of the body as a category of academic inquiry, see Michel Foucault, *History of Sexuality: An Introduction* (New York: Vintage, 1990); and Pippa Brush, "Metaphors of Inscription: Discipline, Plasticity and the Rhetoric of Choice," *Feminist Review* 58 (Spring 1998): 22–43. For specific treatment of the slave body, see Hartman, *Scenes of Subjection.*

58. Paul Gilroy, *The Black Atlantic: Modernity and Double Consciousness* (Cambridge: Harvard University Press, 1993), ix.

59. It must be noted that the relationship between slavery and modernity is complicated. We are well to remember Deborah Gray White's contention—"The Black Atlantic exists at once in antipathy to and as an integral part of western modern life"—a matter explored most fully in Paul Gilroy's *Black Atlantic*. See Deborah Gray White, "'Yes,' There Is a Black Atlantic," *Itinerario* 23, no. 2 (1999): 128.

60. For some works that treat the African diaspora, consult the following list, which is by no means exhaustive. For studies into the African contributions to American society, see Stuckey, *Slave Culture;* Gomez, *Exchanging Our Country Marks;* Creel, *Peculiar People;* Joseph Holloway, *Africanisms in American Culture* (Bloomington: Indiana University Press, 1990); Thornton, *Africa and Africans*. For theoretical treatments of the black diaspora, see Gilroy, *Black Atlantic;* Paul Gilroy, "It Ain't Where You're From, It's Where You're At," *Third Text* 13 (Winter 1991): 3–16; Mercer "Black Hair/Style Politics," 97–130; Darlene Clark Hine and Jacqueline McLeod, eds., *Crossing Boundaries: Comparative History of Black People in the Diaspora* (Bloomington: Indiana University Press, 1999); Hall, "Cultural Identity and Diaspora"; White, "Black Atlantic"; Eduoard Glissant, *Caribbean Discourse: Selected Essays* (Charlottesville: University Press of Virginia, 1989); Robin D. G. Kelley, "'But a Local Phase of a World Problem': Black History's Global Vision, 1883–1950," *Journal of American History* 86 (3): 1055–1058; Michael Hanchard, "Racial Consciousness and Afro-Diasporic Experiences," *Socialism and Democracy* 3 (1991): 83–106; and Brent Hayes Edward, *The Practice of Diaspora: Literature, Translation, and the Rise of Black Internationalism* (Cambridge: Harvard University Press, 2003).

61. See Edward Blyden, *African Life and Customs* (1908; reprint, Boston: Black Classics Press, 1994); W. E. B. Du Bois, *The World and Africa: An Inquiry into the Part Which Africa Has Played in World History* (New York: Viking Press, 1947).

62. Vincent Thompson, *The Making of the African Diaspora in the Americas, 1441–1900* (Harlow, Essex: Longman, 1987), 1.

63. Michael Gomez, *Reversing Sail: A History of the African Diaspora* (Cambridge: Cambridge University Press, 2005), 1–2.

64. Isidore Okpewho, ed., *The African Diaspora: African Origins and New World Identities* (Bloomington: Indiana University Press, 1999), xiv, xii. See also Thomas C. Holt, "Slavery and Freedom in the Atlantic World: Reflections on the Diasporan Framework," in Hine and McLeod, *Crossing Boundaries,* 35.

65. Kristin Mann and Edna Bay, eds., *Rethinking the African Diaspora: The Making of a Black Atlantic World in the Bight of Benin and Brazil* (Portland, Oreg.: Frank Cass, 2001), 10.

66. Gilroy, *Black Atlantic,* 4.

67. Julius Sherrard Scott III, "The Common Wind: Currents of Afro-American Communication in the Era of the Haitian Revolution" (Ph.D. diss., Duke University, 1986), 60.

68. Ibid., 67–68; see also Peter Linebaugh and Marcus Rediker, *The Many-Headed Hydra: Sailors, Slaves, Commoners, and the Hidden History of the Revolutionary Atlantic* (Boston: Beacon Press, 2000).

69. This contention is much in line with that of nineteenth- and early-twentieth-century black writers whose perspectives remained transnational. Indeed, well before current academic interest in the Atlantic world as a unit of historical analysis, black scholars were formulating theories regarding the transatlantic connections between blacks in different regions of the diaspora. Sterling Stuckey argues convincingly that throughout the nineteenth century and into the twentieth century, black intellectuals persistently referred to themselves and their organizations as African. See Stuckey, *Slave Culture,* esp. chap. 4, "Identity and Ideology: The Names Controversy"; Du Bois, *World and Africa;* James, *Black Jacobins;* Williams, *Capitalism and Slavery;* Alain Locke, *The New Negro* (New York: Atheneum, 1992 [1925]); Marcus Garvey, *The Philosophy and Opinions of Marcus Garvey, Or, Africa for the Africans* (Dover, Mass.: Majority Press, 1986); and Edward Blyden, *Christianity, Islam and the Negro Race* (Edinburgh: Edinburgh University, 1967).

70. Glissant, *Caribbean Discourse,* 67.

71. Robin D. G. Kelley, "How the West Was One: On the Uses and Limitations of Diaspora," *Black Scholar* 30, nos. 3–4 (2000): 32.

72. White, "Black Atlantic," 132.

73. Patterson, *Slavery and Social Death,* 5, 337; see also Claude Meillasoux, *The Anthropology of Slavery: The Womb of Iron and Gold,* trans. Alide Dasnois (Chicago: University of Chicago Press, 1991), esp. chap. 5.

74. W. E. B. Du Bois, *The Souls of Black Folk* (1903; reprint, New York: Penguin Books, 1989), 212.

75. Sterling Stuckey has made signal contributions in this field beginning with the publication of "Through the Prism of Folklore: the Black Ethos in Slavery," *Massachusetts Review* 9, no. 3 (Summer 1968): 417–437. In this article, Stuckey first articulated the uses to which folklore could be put in the study of American slavery. Stuckey expanded this thesis in *Slave Culture.* Other scholars, following Stuckey's lead have continued the tradition, including, for example, Levine, *Black Culture and Black Consciousness;* Joyner, *Down by the Riverside;* Genovese, *Roll, Jordan, Roll;* and, more recently, Gomez, *Exchanging Our Country Marks.*

76. E. C. L. Adams, *Tales of the Congaree* (Chapel Hill: University of North Carolina Press, 1987); Georgia Writers' Project, *Drums and Shadows;* Lydia Parrish, *Slave Songs of the Georgia Sea Islands* (Hatboro: Folklore Associates, 1965); Julia Peterkin, *Roll, Jordan, Roll* (New York: R. O. Ballou, 1933); and Elsie Clews Parsons, *Folklore of the Sea Islands, South Carolina* (Cambridge, Mass.: American Folklore Society, 1923) are among the most valuable of this type of folklore collections.

77. Scott, *Hidden Transcripts,* 163.

78. Ibid.

79. See Bascom, *African Folktales in the New World.*

80. With regard to the idyllic image of slavery, refer to U. B. Phillips, *American Negro Slavery* (New York: D. Appleton, 1918); Thomas Dixon, *The Clansman: An Historical Romance of the Ku Klux Klan* (New York: Grosset and Dunlap, 1905); and D. W. Griffith's classic film *Birth of Nation* (1915).

81. Scott, *Hidden Transcripts,* 160.

82. Wyatt MacGaffey, *Kongo Political Culture: The Conceptual Challenge of the Particular* (Bloomington: Indiana University Press, 2000), 17.

83. Hartman, *Scenes of Subjection*, 24; for an opposing viewpoint, see Patterson, *Slavery and Social Death*, 22–23.

NOTES TO CHAPTER 1

1. Edward Ball, *Slaves in the Family* (New York: Farrar, Straus and Giroux, 1998), 135.

2. See, for example John Thornton, "The African Experience of the '20 and Odd Negroes' Arriving in Virginia in 1619," *William and Mary Quarterly*, 3rd ser., 55, no. 3 (July 1998); and John Thornton, "African Dimensions of the Stono Rebellion," *American Historical Review* 96, no. 4 (October 1991).

3. See Heywood, *Central Africans*; Thornton, *Africa and Africans*; Sweet, *Recreating Africa*; Warner-Lewis, *Central Africa*; and Schuler, *Alas, Alas, Kongo*.

4. Warner-Lewis, *Central Africa*, 333–335.

5. See Stuckey, *Slave Culture*, 12; Gomez, *Exchanging Our Country Marks*, 1–4.

6. John Thornton, *The Kingdom of Kongo: Civil Wars and Transition, 1641–1718* (Madison: University of Wisconsin Press, 1983), 15–16.

7. Ibid., 20, 23, 31.

8. Anne Hilton, *The Kingdom of Kongo* (Oxford: Clarendon Press, 1985), 33–37.

9. Ibid., 9.

10. Hilton, *Kingdom of Kongo*, 40, 44–46; David Birmingham, *Central Africa to 1870* (Cambridge: Cambridge University Press, 1981), 53–54.

11. Pierre du Jarric, *De l'Histoire des Choses les Plus Mémorables . . . (seconde partie)*, vol. 2 (Bordeaux, 1610), 79; António Brásio, *Monumenta Missionaria Africana* (Lisbon: Agência-Geral do Ultramar, 1951), 3:228, quoted in W. G. L. Randles, *L'Ancien Royaume du Congo: Des Origines à la fin du XIX Siècle* (Paris: Mouton, 1968), 58.

12. "Rapport de la visite *ad limina* de François de Villanova, évêque de S. Tomé," in *L'Ancien Congo d'après les Archives Romaines*, by Jean Cuvélier and Louis Jadin (Brussels: Académie Royale des Sciences Coloniales, 1954), 223–224. See also Joseph Miller, *Way of Death: Merchant Capitalism and the Angolan Slave Trade* (Madison: University of Wisconsin Press, 1988), 265; Thornton, *Africa and Africans*, 74, 87–91. For a treatment of slavery in Africa, see Meillassoux, *Anthropology of Slavery*.

13. Hilton, *Kingdom of Kongo*, 55–60.

14. "Le Roi Afonso à Dom João III," in *Correspondance de Dom Afonso, Roi du Congo, 1506–1543*, by Louis Jadin et Mireille Dicorato (Brussels: Académie Royal des Sciences d'Outre-Mer, 1974), 156. Afonso's opposition to the trade is likely based both on a principled concern regarding the deleterious effects of transatlantic slavery along with his own pecuniary concerns at having lost a royal monopoly.

15. "Le Roi Dom Afonso à Dom João III," 168.

16. Only after Afonso reestablished a monopoly over the slave trade in the mid-sixteenth century—due to the establishment of markets on the eastern border of the country—did he reverse his position on the slave trade. See Hilton, *Kingdom of Kongo*, 59–60.

17. Joseph Miller, "Central Africa During the Era of the Slave Trade, c. 1490s–1850s," in Heywood, *Central Africans*, 28, 34.

18. Jan Vansina, *Paths in the Rainforests: Toward a Political Tradition in Equitorial Africa* (Madison: University of Wisconsin Press, 1990), 204–206.

19. Susan Broadhead, "Beyond Decline: The Kingdom of the Kongo in the Eighteenth and Nineteenth Centuries," *International Journal of African Historical Studies* 12, no. 4 (1979): 635.

20. Ibid.

21. Vansina, *Paths in the Rainforests,* 204.

22. Ras Michael Brown, "Walk in the Feenda: West-Central Africans and the Forest in the South Carolina–Georgia Lowcountry," in Heywood, *Central Africans,* 300.

23. See Wood, *Black Majority,* 302; John Thornton, *The Kongolese Saint Anthony: Dona Beatriz Kimpa Vita and the Antonian Movement, 1684–1706* (Cambridge: Cambridge University Press, 1998), 210.

24. Wood, *Black Majority,* 302.

25. Ibid., 301–304, 334–335.

26. David Richardson, "Slave Exports from West and West-Central Africa, 1700–1810: New Estimates of Volume and Distribution," *Journal of African History* 30, no. 1 (1989): 1–22; David Eltis, Stephen Brehendt, David Richardson, and Herbert Klein, eds., *The Trans-Atlantic Slave Trade: A Database on CD-ROM* (New York: Cambridge, 1999). For the role that these Africans played in the Stono Rebellion of 1739, see Thornton, *Kongolese Saint Anthony,* 212–214; Walter Rucker, *The River Flows On: Black Resistance, Culture, and Identity Formation in Early America* (Baton Rouge: Louisiana State University Press, 2006), 94–97.

27. Quoted in Peter Wood, *Strange New Land* (Oxford: Oxford University Press, 2002), 39.

28. Gomez, *Exchanging Our Country Marks,* 136; Wood, *Black Majority,* 302, 314.

29. Creel, *Peculiar People,* esp. chaps. 8 and 9.

30. Brown, "Walk in the Feenda," 304.

31. Joseph Holloway, "Origins of African-American Culture," in Holloway, *Africanisms,* 6–10; Gomez, *Exchanging Our Country Marks,* 137–140, 150–151.

32. Holloway, "Origins of African-American Culture," 7.

33. Joyner, *Down by the Riverside,* 14, 205.

34. Gomez, *Exchanging Our Country Marks,* 33.

35. James McPherson, *Battle Cry for Freedom* (Oxford: Oxford University Press, 1988), 98; Charles Montgomery, "Survivors from the Cargo of the Negro Slave Yacht Wanderer," *American Anthropologist,* new ser., 10, no. 4 (October–December 1908): 611–623. While nearly half of all Africans imported into Carolina stayed there to work as slaves, the remainder was reexported through the port at Charleston to subsidiary Lowcountry ports. Savannah, Georgia, for instance, received reexported enslaved Africans throughout the eighteenth century and supplemented that supply with other captives received through overland sources and Caribbean shipping. Georgia began to trade more directly with merchants in the last quarter of the eighteenth century and eventually outfitted a modest number of slaving voyages itself. In 1805, the slave ship *Montezuma* cleared from Savannah

carrying 328 captive Africans from Congo to Charleston. See Gomez, *Exchanging Our Country Marks,* 20; James Rawley, *The Trans-Atlantic Slave Trade: A History* (New York: W. W. Norton, 1981), 410; Brown, "Walk in the Feenda," 299.

36. Margaret Washington, for example, while noting very similar importation rates, argues for the critical importance of West Africans, especially those from Senegambia and Sierra Leone, based on the notion of "hearth areas." She argues that "the complex formation of African-American Gullah culture involved, in some ways, the concept of 'hearth areas,' that is, those who arrive earlier may have as strong an impact as latecomers of more numerical strength." In this sense, the numerical dominance of enslaved Africans from West-Central Africa did not smother the contributions of Africans from other regions, even though Kongo culture "served as incubator for many Gullah cultural patterns." See Washington, *Peculiar People,* 44.

37. Philip Morgan, *Slave Counterpoint: Black Culture in the Eighteenth-Century Chesapeake and Lowcountry* (Chapel Hill: University of North Carolina Press, 1998), 32.

38. Julia Floyd Smith, *Slavery and Rice Culture in Lowcountry Georgia, 1750–1860* (Knoxville: University of Tennessee Press, 1985), 7.

39. See Wood, *Black Majority.*

40. Lisa Gail Collins, *The Art of History: African American Women Artists Engage the Past* (New Brunswick, N.J.: Rutgers University Press, 2002), 67.

41. Willie Lee Rose, *Rehearsal for Reconstruction: The Port Royal Experiment* (Indianapolis: Bobs Merrill, 1964), 9.

42. Mason Crum, *Gullah: Negro Life in the Carolina Sea Islands* (1940; reprint, New York: Negro Universities Press, 1968), 4–5.

43. DuBose Heyward, "The Negro in the Low-Country," in *The Carolina Low-Country,* ed. Augustine Smythe, Herbert Ravenel Sass, Alfred Huger, Beatrice Ravenel, Thomas Waring, Archibald Rutledge, Josephine Pinckney, Caroline P. Rutledge, DuBose Heywood, Katharine C. Hutson, and Robert W. Gordon (New York: Macmillan, 1931), 186.

44. C. R. Tiedman, "Low Country Gullah," WPA D-4-27-A, SCL.

45. See Wood, *Black Majority,* 171–172; Creel, *Peculiar People,* 16–18.

46. Winifred Kellersberger Vass, *The Bantu Speaking Heritage of the United States* (Los Angeles: Center for Afro-American Studies at the University of California at Los Angeles, 1979); Turner, *Africanisms in the Gullah Dialect;* Joyner, *Down by the Riverside;* Gomez, *Exchanging Our Country Marks,* 102.

47. Collins, *Art of History,* 78.

48. Heyward, "Negro in the Low-Country," 186.

49. Rossa B. Cooley, *School Acres: An Adventure in Rural Education* (New Haven, Conn.: Yale University Press), x.

50. Brown, "Walk in the Feenda," 292.

51. Ibid., 293.

52. Adams, *Tales of the Congaree,* xiii.

53. E. C. L. Adams Papers, Folder 44 a/b, SCL; DuBose Heyward, *Mamba's Daughters: A Novel of Charleston* (Columbia: University of South Carolina Press, 1995), Peterkin, *Roll, Jordan, Roll;* Joel Chandler Harris, *The Complete Tales of Uncle Remus,* compiled by Richard Chase (New York: Houghton Mifflin, 2002).

54. Julia Mood Peterkin Papers, 28–614, no. 2, SCHS.

55. Sterling Brown, *Opportunity Magazine* 10:223.

56. Sterling Brown, *Opportunity Magazine* 12:60.

NOTES TO CHAPTER 2

1. Charles Raymond, "Religious Life of the Negro," *Harpers New Monthly Magazine* 27, no. 162 (November 1863): 816–817.

2. Ibid., 816.

3. Ibid.

4. Georgia Writers' Project, *Drums and Shadows*, 113.

5. The Spiritual Baptists in Trinidad, Haitian Vaudun, Santéria in Cuba, and the Candomblé traditions of Brazil would be other examples.

6. Newbell Niles Puckett, *Folk Beliefs of the Southern Negro* (New York: Dover Publications, 1926), 545–546.

7. See Holloway, "Origins of African-American Culture," 6–10.

8. Thomas Turpin, "Missionary Sketch," *Christian Advocate and Journal*, January 31, 1834. For a different reading of the same, see Creel, *Peculiar People*, 180–182.

9. Soi-Daniel W. Brown, "From the Tongues of Africa: A Partial Translation of Oldendorp's Interviews," *Plantation Society* 2, no. 1 (April 1983): 51.

10. Jane Landers, *Black Society in Spanish Florida* (Urbana: University of Illinois Press, 1999), 113.

11. Cuvélier and Jadin, *Ancien Congo*, 16.

12. The stability afforded by this system of royal succession ultimately failed in the mid-seventeenth century when foreign invasion and European colonial efforts combined with a succession dispute to destabilize the once-centralized Kongo, which subsequently fell into a long period of civil war that lasted until the beginning of the eighteenth century.

13. *Dom Afonso aux Seigneurs de Son Royaume (1)*, in Jadin et Dicorato, *Correspondance*, 61.

14. Ibid., 61.

15. Ibid., 62.

16. Ibid.

17. *Dom Afonso à ses Peuples (1)*, in Jadin and Dicorato, *Correspondance*, 58.

18. That is, thirty-seven Christian lords along with their servants.

19. *Dom Afonso à ses Peuples (1)*, 58.

20. *Dom Afonso aux Seigneurs de son Royaume (1)*, 55.

21. Ibid.

22. Ibid., 62.

23. For more on the reign of Afonso, see Hilton, *Kingdom of Kongo*, 53–65; Cuvélier and Jadin, *Ancien Congo*, 283–292; Randles, *Ancien Royaume du Congo*, 97–105; and Georges Balandier, *Daily Life in the Kingdom of Kongo, from the Sixteenth to the Eighteenth Century*, trans. Helen Weaver (New York: Pantheon Books, 1968), 42–64.

24. Cuvélier and Jadin, *Ancien Congo*, 17; *Dom Afonso au Roi Dom Manuel (1)*, in Jadin and Dicorato, *Correspondance*, 82.

25. Randles, *Ancien Royaume du Congo,* 99–100; *Dom Afonso au Roi Dom Manuel (1),* 78, 91.

26. Cuvélier and Jadin, *Ancien Congo,* 202.

27. Louis Jadin, "Rivalités Luso-Néerlandaises du Sohio, Congo, 1600–1675," *BIHBR* 37 (1966): 306.

28. Randles, *Ancien Royaume du Congo,* 154.

29. Thornton, *Kingdom of Kongo,* 65, 67.

30. Randles, *Ancien Royaume du Congo,* 162–164.

31. Luca da Caltanisetta, *Diaire Congolais (1690–1701),* trans. François Bontinck (Kinshasa: Publications de l'Université Lovanium de Kinshasa, 1970), 69.

32. The reference to Christian priests as *nganga* points to the manner in which Kongolese converts adapted Christianity to conform to their own spiritual traditions. When Christian priests first arrived in Kongo in 1483, the Kongolese regarded them as emissaries of the otherworld in line with the general practice in Kongo of venerating albinos as incarnations of the water and earth spirits. As a white-skinned peoples who emerged from vast waters, the characterization of albinos may well have been applied to Christian priests. Wyatt MacGaffey, *Religion and Society in Central Africa: The Bakongo of Lower Zaire* (Chicago: University of Chicago Press, 1986), 198; A. Fu-Kiau Kia Bunseki-Lumanisa, *N'Kongo Ye Nza Yakun'zungidila: Nza Kongo, Le Mukongo et le Monde Qui l'Entourait,* Cosmogonie- Kongo no. 1 (Kinshasa: Office National de la Recherche et de Developpement, 1969), 118; Hilton, *Kingdom of Kongo,* 50.

33. Thornton, *Kingdom of Kongo,* 65.

34. Broadhead, "Beyond Decline," 633.

35. Cuvélier and Jadin, *Ancien Congo,* 202; Sweet, *Recreating Africa,* 195–196; Thornton, *Kongolese Saint Anthony,* 17; Hilton, *Kingdom of Kongo,* 98.

36. Sweet, *Recreating Africa,* 195–197; see also Hilton, *Kingdom of Kongo,* 98.

37. Caltanisetta, *Diaire Congolais,* 112.

38. Hilton, *Kingdom of Kongo,* 13.

39. Ibid., 14.

40. Ibid., 14–15.

41. Ibid.

42. Thornton, *Kongolese Saint Anthony,* 17; Hilton, *Kingdom of Kongo,* 98.

43. Hilton, *Kingdom of Kongo,* 98.

44. Francesco da Pavia, "Temoinage du P. Francesco da Pavia," in "Le Congo et la Secte des Antoniens: Restauration du Royaume sous Pedro IV et la 'Saint Antoine' Congolaise (1694–1718)," by Louis Jadin, *BIHBR* 33 (1961): 437.

45. Bernardo da Gallo, "Relations de Bernardo da Gallo," in Jadin, "Congo et la Secte," 481, 555.

46. Ibid., 481.

47. Richard Gray, *Black Christians and White Missionaries* (New Haven, Conn.: Yale University Press, 1990), 4, 6.

48. John Thornton, "On the Trail of Voodoo: African Christianity in Africa and the Americas," *Americas* 44, no. 3 (1988): 267.

49. John Thornton, "Perspectives on African Christianity," in *Race, Discourse, and the Origin of the Americas: A New World View*, ed. Vera Lawrence Hyatt and Rex Nettleford (Washington, D.C.: Smithsonian Institution Press, 1995), 177–179.

50. Thornton, "On the Trail of Voodoo," 267.

51. J. Van Wing and C. Penders, *Le Plus Ancien Dictionnaire Bantu* (Louvain: J. Kuyl-Otto, 1928), 279; see also Vansina, *Paths in the Rainforests*, 96, 298. Vansina suggests that term originated well before A.D. 1500 and referred to a particularly powerful or supreme spirit, perhaps the first of all ancestors, perhaps a first Creator spirit or prime cause.

52. Van Wing and Penders, *Dictionnaire Bantu*, 279.

53. MacGaffey, *Religion and Society*, 205.

54. "Bonaventura d'Alessano à Mgr Ingoli," in Louis Jadin, "L'Ancien Congo et l'Angola, 1639–1655, d'après les Archives Romaines, Portugaises, Néerlandaises et Espangnoles," *BIHBR* 22 (1975): 661.

55. MacGaffey, *Religion and Society*, 205; Thornton, "The Development of an African Catholic Church in the Kingdom of Kongo, 1491–1750," *Journal of African History* 25 (1984):157.

56. Vansina, "Kongo Kingdom and Its Neighbors," 564. Between 1660 and 1793 the volume of slave exports continually increased along with slave prices. During this period one million slaves were exported from Kongo's Loango port. See Vansina, *Paths in the Rainforests*, 204.

57. Caltanisetta, *Diaire Congolais*, 79. Caltanisetta continues: "Nevertheless, they want to be baptized without too much trouble, that the priest comes to administer it to them in their *libata*." Many in this number clearly saw themselves as Christian. See Olfert Dapper, *Description de L'Afrique* (Amsterdam: Wolfgang, Waesberge, Boom & Van Someren, 1686), 357.

58. Giovanni Francesco da Roma, *Brève Relation de la Fondation de la Mission des Frères Mineurs Capucins du Séraphique Père Saint François au Royaume du Congo, et des Particularités, Coutumes et Façons de Vivre des Habitants de ce Royaume*, trans. François Bontinck (Louvain: Éditions Nauwelaerts, 1964), 119.

59. Ibid., 119–120.

60. Van Wing and Penders, *Dictionnaire Bantu*, 279; MacGaffey, *Religion and Society*, 205; Thornton, "Development of an African Catholic Church," 157.

61. Da Gallo, "Relations," 556.

62. Heywood, *Central Africans*, 84.

63. Thornton, "Development of an African Catholic Church," 161.

64. On the relationship between the colonizer and the missionary, see V. Y. Mudimbe, *The Invention of Africa: Gnosis, Philosophy, and the Order of Knowledge* (Bloomington: Indiana University Press, 1988), 44–64.

65. Thornton, "Development of an African Catholic Church," 154.

66. See ibid., 148, 150, 152; Thornton, "Perspectives," 178; Heywood, *Central Africans*, 83. The role of the fetish in European thought is treated in detail in a subsequent chapter.

67. Thornton offers perhaps one of the best examples of this critical reading of missionary motivations in Thornton, "Development of an African Catholic Church," 149.

68. Da Gallo, "Relations," 473.

69. Ibid.

70. Ibid., 482.

71. For a book-length treatment of the life of Dona Beatriz, see Thornton, *Kongolese Saint Anthony.*

72. Da Gallo, "Relations," 501.

73. Wyatt MacGaffey and Michael D. Harris, *Astonishment and Power: The Eyes of Understanding Kongo Minkisi* (Washington, D.C.: National Museum of African Art, 1993), 49.

74. Da Gallo, "Relations," 515.

75. Lorenzo de Luca, "Relation du P. Lorenzo de Luca, sur les Événements de 1706 au Congo," in Jadin, "Congo et la Secte," 541. These recurrent experiences with death were accompanied by an increased seclusion on the part of Dona Beatriz, whose close relationship with one of her primary supporters resulted in pregnancy.

76. Ibid. See also Wyatt MacGaffey, "Cultural Roots of Kongo Prophetism," *History of Religions* 17, no. 2 (1977): 164–165, 184. Spirit possession in Kongo was a normal and acceptable form of revelation. See Thornton, *Kongolese Saint Anthony,* 124. Many of the details of Beatriz' possession resemble the cult of the *bisimbi,* local spirits that reside in various bodies of water. If not adequately propitiated, *bisimbi* might enact violent retribution. The *bisimbi* belong to the larger class of the dead that consists of all the forces who inhabit the other or invisible world and mediate between God and living beings.

77. Thompson and Cornet, *Four Moments of the Sun,* 43–52.

78. Da Gallo, "Relations," 499.

79. Ibid.

80. Ibid., 516–517.

81. Ibid., 516. For a translation and treatment of the text, see Thornton, *Kongolese Saint Anthony,* 215–220.

82. De Gallo, *Relations,* 538, 530; see also Laurent de Lucques, *Relations sur le Congo du Père Laurent de Lucques,* trans. Jean Cuvélier (Brussels: Institut Royal Colonial Belge, 1953), 232–236.

83. Da Gallo, "Relations," 500. See also Warner-Lewis, *Central Africa,* 180.

84. Fu-Kiau, *N'Kongo,* 122; John M. Janzen and Wyatt MacGaffey, *An Anthology of Kongo Religion: Primary Texts from Lower Zaïre* (Lawrence: University of Kansas, 1974), 34.

85. In 1491, upon the baptism of Kongo's first Christian king, João I, a nobleman found a perfectly shaped stone cross described as "black and unlike any other in the country." Both the Christian missionaries and Kongolese officials present at the baptism revered the stone cross as a sign of otherworldly confirmation for the newly baptized king. Writing in *The Kongolese Saint Anthony,* John Thornton contends that the finding of the stone cross was an important revelation, confirming for King João the validity of Christianity. Others, however, have conceived of the stone-cross quite differently. Writing in *Kingdom of Kongo,* Anne Hilton argues that Kongolese leaders thought the stone cross related not to Christianity but to the *mbumba* dimension of Kongolese spiritual thought. According to this reading the propitious finding of the object authenticated the monarch's baptism in

terms of *mbumba* and the water and earth spirits. Both positions suggest the complexity of cross iconography in the region, encouraging sensitivity to the diversity of ritual practice in the region. Clearly, Christian signs, symbols, and terms carried multiple meanings such that both Christian and Kongolese cosmological conceptions were supported under its rubric. See Brásio, *Monumenta Missionaria Africana* 1:124–125; Thornton, *Kongolese Saint Anthony*, 56, 86; Hilton, *Kingdom of Kongo*, 51; Thornton, "On the Trail of Voodoo," 266; Adrian Hastings, "The Christianity of Pedro IV of the Kongo," *Journal of Religion in Africa* 28, no. 2 (May 1998): 157; John Thornton, "I Am the Subject of the King of Congo: African Political Ideology and the Haitian Revolution," *Journal of World History* 4 (1993): 189.

86. Ibid; Fu-Kiau *N'Kongo*, 122; Janzen and MacGaffey, *Anthology of Kongo Religion*, 34.

87. MacGaffey, "Cultural Roots of Kongo Prophetism," 184.

88. Broadhead, "Beyond Decline," 619.

89. Da Gallo, "Relations," 494–495.

90. Ibid., 495–496; see also MacGaffey, "Kongo Prophetism," 184–185; Thornton, *Kongolese Saint Anthony*, 108; Thornton, *Kingdom of Kongo*, 107, 111–112.

91. Balandier, *Daily Life in Kingdom of the Kongo*, 256–257.

92. Vansina, "Kongo Kingdom and Its Neighbors," 564; Vansina, *Paths in the Rainforests*, 204.

93. See Jadin, "Congo et la Secte," 499, 517, 578, 592, 596, and 599 for Dona Beatriz's perceptions of race and slavery.

94. Ibid., 417.

95. Cuvélier and Jadin, *Ancien Congo*, 88–89; see also Miller, *Way of Death*, 402. Miller's account does not address fully the preslave trade experience of some slaves, particularly those of the Kongo region. Hugh Thomas, *The Slave Trade: The History of the Atlantic Slave Trade, 1440–1870* (New York: Simon and Schuster, 1997), 398.

96. Miller, *Way of Death*, 403.

97. Ibid., 403.

98. Ibid., 269, 404.

99. Thornton, "On the Trail of Voodoo," 272.

100. Cuvélier, *Relations sur le Congo*, 283–284.

101. Francis Le Jau, "Slave Conversion on the Carolina Frontier," in *African American Religious History: A Documentary Witness*, ed. Milton Sernett (Durham, N.C.: Duke University Press, 1999), 27; emphasis added. See also Annette Laing, "'Heathens and Infidels' African Christianization and Anglicanism in the South Carolina Low Country, 1700–1750," *Religion and American Culture: A Journal of Interpretation* 12, no. 2 (Summer 2002): 197. Le Jau's comment comes from the early eighteenth century and is not included here as suggestive of an uninterrupted black Catholic community in South Carolina. It is noteworthy, however, as an example of the transatlantic commercial, and in this case, religious links that pertained to South Carolina and Kongo. Moreover, the document offers a glimpse into the longstanding tensions that marked the Catholic and Protestant missionary enterprises throughout the colonial and antebellum periods.

102. Laing, "Heathens and Infidels," 197.

103. Sernett, *Religious History*, 26.

104. Francis Le Jau, St. James Goose Creek, to the SPG, 1 February 1709, quoted in Frank J. Klinberg, *An Appraisal of the Negro in South Carolina* (Washington, D.C.: Associated Publishers, 1941), 16–17.

105. Robert Olwell, *Masters, Slaves and Subjects: The Culture of Power in the South Carolina Lowcountry, 1740–1790* (Ithaca, N.Y.: Cornell University Press, 1998), 111.

106. Ibid., 113.

107. Sernett, *Religious History*, 26, 29.

108. Raboteau, *Slave Religion*, 107.

109. John K. Thornton, "African Dimensions of the Stono Rebellion," *American Historical Review* 96, no. 4 (October 1991): 1105, 1109, 1111–1112.

110. Mark M. Smith, "Remembering Mary, Shaping Revolt: Reconsidering the Stono Rebellion," *Journal of Southern History* 67, no. 3 (August 2001): 518.

111. Ibid., 527, 531. see also Mark M. Smith, *Stono: Documenting And Interpreting a Southern Slave Revolt* (Columbia: University of South Carolina Press, 2005).

112. For a book-length study of this settlement, see the aforementioned Landers, *Black Society*.

113. Eugene Sirmans, *Colonial South Carolina: A Political History, 1663–1763* (Chapel Hill: University of North Carolina Press, 1966), 208, quote in Landers, *Black Society*, 34. For more information related to slave rebellions and uprisings in antebellum America, see Herbert Aptheker, *American Negro Slave Revolts* (New York: International Publishers, 1963); Eugene Genovese, *From Rebellion to Revolution: Afro-American Slave Revolts in the Making of the Modern World* (Baton Rouge: Louisiana State University Press, 1979); Douglas R. Egerton, *He Shall Go Out Free: The Lives of Denmark Vesey* (Madison, Wis.: Madison House, 1999); Douglas R. Egerton, *Gabriel's Rebellion: The Virginia Slave Conspiracies of 1800 and 1802* (Chapel Hill: University of North Carolina Press, 1993); Stephen B. Oates, *The Fires of Jubilee: Nat Turner's Fierce Rebellion* (New York: Harper-Perennial, 1990).

114. Landers, *Black Society*, 48, 113.

115. Ibid., 48. Mark Smith argues that the legacy of Catholicism in the Lowcountry can be discerned in more recent times. So Smith refers to George Cato, a former slave from Orangeburg, South Carolina, who informed Stiles Scruggs, an interviewer for the WPA slave narrative project in the 1930s. Cato, whose "granddaddy was a son of de son of de Stono slave commander," recalls the provocative though ambiguous words of his ancestor: "We don't lak slavery. We start to jine de Spanish in Florida. We surrender but we not whipped and we 'is not converted.'" Smith argues that Cato's determination not to be converted may very well constitute a resistance to Protestant theology in preference to the Catholicism with which he might have been familiar in his homeland. See George Rawick, ed., *The American Slave: A Composite Autobiography*, supplement, ser. 1 (Westport, Conn.: Greenwood, 1977), 11:100; Smith, "Remembering Mary," 526.

116. Alan Gallay, "Planters and Slaves in the Great Awakening," in *Masters and Slaves in the House of the Lord: Race and Religion in the American South, 1740–1870*, ed. John B. Boles (Lexington: University Press of Kentucky, 1988), 33.

117. Frey, *Water from the Rock*, 245, 246; Raboteau, *Slave Religion*, 143.

118. Frey, *Water from the Rock,* 246.

119. For a treatment that disputes the notion that missionaries generally failed in their attempts to convert slaves in the eighteenth century, see Olwell, *Masters, Slaves and Subjects,* 106–108.

120. Luther P. Jackson, "Religious Instruction of Negroes, 1830–1860, with Special Reference to South Carolina," *Journal of Negro History* 15 (1930): 79.

121. Slaveholders produced a litany of excuses on this point, including (1) slaves already had the gospel, (2) slaves were mentally unable to understand the gospel, (3) absentee owners were ill equipped to minister to the slaves, and (4) funds were lacking for such an enterprise. See C. C. Jones, *The Religious Instruction of the Negroes in the United States* (New York: Negro Universities Press, 1842), 175–185; Raboteau, *Slave Religion,* 121.

122. Jones, *Religious Instruction,* 100.

123. Frances Ann Kemble, *Journal of a Residence on a Georgian Plantation in 1838–1839* (1863; reprint, Athens: University of Georgia Press, 1984), 125. Translation of the French: "instructed in such a manner that would not give them any ideas."

124. James Andrew, "The Southern Slave Population," *Methodist Magazine and Quarterly Review* 13 (1831): 314.

125. Creel, *Peculiar People,* 170; C. C. Jones also noted planters' reluctance to instruct their slaves for fear of their own safety. See Jones, *Religious Instruction,* 109.

126. Jackson, "Religious Instruction of Negroes," 84.

127. William Capers, *Catechism for the Use of the Methodist Missions,* 3rd ed. (Richmond: John Early, 1852), 19. I Timothy 6:1–2.

128. John Hyrne Tucker Papers, 1818–1850 (43/518), SCHS; RWFA 12/6/22, SCHS. For a description of the catechism as performed on Kelvin Grove Plantation (Beaufort County, S.C.), see Celestine Lowndes writings, 1895 (43/1045), SCHS.

129. David Walker, *David Walker's Appeal to the Coloured Citizens of the World, but in Particular, and Very Expressly, to Those of the United States of America* (Baltimore: Black Classic Press, 1830), 58.

130. Jackson, "Religious Instruction of Negroes," 84.

131. Ibid.

132. After Nat Turner's uprising in Virginia, for example, various southern states passed laws aimed at curtailing the religious instruction of slaves. Carter G. Woodson connects this legislation to increasing abolitionist pressure. See Carter G. Woodson, *Education of the Negro Prior to 1861* (New York: G. P. Putnam's Sons, 1915); Jackson, "Religious Instruction of Negroes," 79.

133. Northern pressure on this issue could be quite significant as evidenced by a letter printed in the *Christian Advocate* in 1826, when a northern Presbyterian minister queried the poor state of religion among slaves. See letter to the editor, *Christian Advocate* 4 (January 1826): 96. This ambivalence is noted by Frances Kemble, the English wife of a southern planter who contributed much to abolitionist and missionary concerns through her observations of her husband's estate. She writes, "The outcry which has been raised... against the whole system has induced its upholders and defenders to adopt some appearance of religious instruction (such as it is)." Kemble, *Journal,* 92.

134. Barnwell Family Papers, 1824–1898 (25/184–186), 30–31, 86–87, SCHS.

135. Ibid., 40–41.

136. Creel, *Peculiar People*, 172, 180.

137. Ibid., 131.

138. Andrew, "Southern Slave Population," 320.

139. Bishop William Capers, T. Drayton Grimke, J. Grimke Drayton, and the Reverend Charles Colcock Jones all attended, along with others.

140. *Proceedings of Meeting in Charleston, S.C. on the Religious Instruction of the Negroes, Together with The Report of the Committee and the Address to the Public, May 13–15, 1845* (Charleston, S.C., 1845); see also Creel, *Peculiar People*, 187.

141. *Proceedings of Meeting in Charleston*, 7.

142. Jones, *Religious Instruction*, 125.

143. Allen Daniel Candler, *Colonial Records of the State of Georgia*, vol. 22, pt. 2 (Atlanta: Franklin, 1904–16), 233; see also Thornton, "On the Trail of Voodoo," 268; and Thornton, *Kongolese Saint Anthony*, 212.

144. Turpin, "Missionary Sketch."

145. Jones, *Religious Instruction*, 125.

146. See Erskine Clarke, *Wrestlin' Jacob: A Portrait of Religion in Antebellum Georgia and the Carolina Low Country* (Tuscaloosa: University of Alabama Press, 2000), 89, 90, 116, 132. Note also that the numbers of black Catholics increased during the postbellum period. In 1889, the First African American Catholic Congress was held at Washington, D.C. The federal census of the United States, conducted during the following year, reported approximately one hundred thousand black Catholics in the United States. See "Address of the Congress to Their Catholic Fellow-Citizens of the United States," in *Three Catholic Afro-American Congresses* (Cincinnati: American Catholic Tribune, 1893), 66–73; Sernett, *Religious History*, 296–299. At the conclusion of the conference, delegates addressed the participants: "Having learned in this Congress the admirable and remarkable efforts thus far accomplished for the benefit of the African race, either in this country or on the African continent, by the various religious orders of the Catholic Church, we tender these zealous and noble hearted pioneers of the Gospel the expression of our admiration and gratitude, and trust they will continue the work of devotion thus done for the regeneration of our people."

147. See table 1 of the introduction.

148. Brown, *From the Tongues of Africa*, 51.

149. Turpin, "Missionary Sketch."

150. Quoted in George Rawick, *The American Slave: A Composite Autobiography* (Westport, Conn.: Greenwood, 1972), 13:252. See also Olwell, *Masters, Slaves and Subjects*, 119.

151. Herskovits, *Myth of the Negro Past*, 224–234; Genovese, *Roll, Jordan, Roll*, 234–235; Creel, *Peculiar People*, 251; Mechal Sobel, *Trabelin' On: The Slave Journey to an Afro-Baptist Faith* (Princeton, N.J.: Princeton University Press, 1979), 79–80; Stuckey, *Slave Culture*, 33–35.

152. Herskovits, *Myth of the Negro Past*, 234. See also Stuckey, *Slave Culture*, 34–37. For a review of these arguments, see Gomez, *Exchanging Our Country Marks*, 272–274.

153. Herskovits, *Myth of the Negro Past*, 234.

154. Creel, *Peculiar People*, 45–54.

155. Ibid., 2.

156. Ibid., 231.

157. Thornton, *Kongolese Saint Anthony,* 56; Hilton, *Kingdom of Kongo,* 26–28.

158. Thornton, *Kongolese Saint Anthony,* 56–57.

159. Quoted in Hilton, *Kingdom of Kongo,* 196–197.

160. Stuckey, *Slave Culture,* 34.

161. Clifton Johnson, ed., *God Struck Me Dead* (Philadelphia: Pilgrim Press, 1969), ix.

162. Mary Ames, *A New England Woman's Diary in Dixie in 1865* (1906; reprint, New York: Negro Universities Press, 1969), 68.

163. John Work, *American Negro Songs and Spirituals* (New York: Bonanza Books, 1940), 22.

164. Johnson, *God Struck Me Dead,* 73; see also Zora Neale Hurston, *The Sanctified Church* (Berkeley, Calif.: Turtle Islands, 1983), 85, 87.

165. Johnson, *God Struck Me Dead,* viii, ix.

166. This state of being is beautifully described in the slave musical tradition in a song commonly sung in the Lowcountry: "Brudder George is a gwine to glory, take care the sin-sick soul." See William F. Allen, *Slave Songs of the United States* (1867; reprint, New York: Peter Smith, 1929), 49.

167. Johnson, *God Struck Me Dead,* 73. Note also that in its main features, this description applies also to Sarah with whom this chapter opened.

168. Ibid., 59, 91, 109, 110, 113, 114; WPA—Savannah Writers' Project, collection no. 1355, item 74, p. 7, GHS.

169. The work of Sterling Stuckey, Margaret Washington, Melville Herskovits, and Robert Farris Thompson is crucial here. To take but one example, Stuckey argues that the ubiquity of whiteness in slave baptisms recalls Kongolese cosmological conceptions in which the color white evoked the underworld whose inhabitants were commonly figured as white skinned. In Kongolese cosmology, the cosmos consists of two mountains opposed at their bases and separated by a barrier, the kalunga line—or the waters of parturition. Crossing these waters, one enters the realm of the dead, land of kaolin—of all things white. This world and the otherworld existed in perpetual mirror opposition, such that movement between the realms commonly occurred. See Stuckey, *Slave Culture,* 34–37; Georgia Writers' Project, *Drums and Shadows,* 92, 184; Parsons, *Folklore of the Sea Islands,* 204–205; Charles Lyell, *A Second Visit to the United States of North America* (London: John Murray, 1850), 363. See also Bunseki-Lumanisa, *Mukongo et le Monde;* Thompson, *Flash of the Spirit,* Sobel, *Trabelin' On.*

While Michael Gomez acknowledges these symbolic meanings of the color white as possible explanations for their use in the baptismal ritual, he does not preclude the fact that racism may have affected enslaved Africans' understanding not only of the faith but also of themselves. He writes: "It is an unassailable fact that American Christianity is directly responsible for the psychological impairment of many within the slave community. The white slaveholder's promotion of a white god aloft in white splendor, around whom stand the white heavenly host, was imagery sufficient to convey to the African a message of unmitigable disadvantage." See Gomez, *Exchanging Our Country Marks,* 244–245, 273; see also Blyden, *Christianity, Islam and the Negro Race,* 14–15.

170. Ambrose Gonzales, *The Black Border: Gullah Stories of the Carolina Coast* (1922; reprint, Columbia, S.C.: State Printing Company, 1964), 45; WPA—Savannah Writers' Project, collection no. 1355, item 74, p. 6, GHS.

171. William Allen, *Nation* 1 (December 14, 1865): 744, 745.

172. Edmund Ruffin, *The Private Diary of Edmund Ruffin, 1843: Agriculture, Geology, and Society in Antebellum South Carolina* (Athens: University of Georgia Press, 1992), 166. I learned of Ruffin's description of the cymbee in Ras Michael Brown, "West-Central African Nature Spirits in the South Carolina Lowcountry," paper presented at the Southeastern Regional Seminar in African Studies (SERSAS), Fall Meeting, October 2000, University of Tennessee, Knoxville.

173. Ruffin, *Diary,* 166.

174. Ibid., 167

175. Ibid.

176. Ruffin, *Diary,* 166, 167.

177. MacGaffey, *Religion and Society,* 43.

178. Adams, *Tales of the Congaree,* 79; E. C. L. Adams Papers, Folder c.14, SCL.

179. Clifton, *God Struck Me Dead,* 73.

180. William Barton, "Old Plantation Hymns," *New England Magazine,* January 1899, 95.

181. Georgia Writers' Project, *Drums and Shadows,* 113.

182. Warner-Lewis, *Central Africa,* 128

183. Peterkin, *Roll, Jordan, Roll,* 88.

184. Romans 6:3–4 and John 3:5–7.

185. Rawick, *American Slave* 3:108–110; John Bennet Papers, Box 21–126, Folders 14, 15, SCHS.

186. Michael Angelo and Denis de Carli, "A Curious and Exact Account of a Voyage to Congo, in the Years 1666 and 1667," in *A General Collection of the Best and Most Interesting Voyages and Travels in All Parts of the World,* vol. 16, by John Pinkerton (London: Longman, Hurst, 1814), 152; see also Sweet, *Recreating Africa,* 197.

187. Quoted in Sweet, *Recreating Africa,* 199.

188. Ibid., 202.

189. Moreau de Saint-Méry, *Description Topographique, Physique, Civile, Politique et Historique de La Partie Française de L'Isle Saint-Domingue* (Paris: Société de L'Histoire des Colonies Française, 1958), 53.

190. Warner-Lewis, *Central Africa,* 184–185.

191. Schuler, *Alas, Alas, Kongo,* 152.

192. L. Crookall, *British Guiana; or, Work and Wanderings among the Creoles and Coolies, the Africans and Indians of the Wild Country* (London: T. Fisher Unwin, 1898), 132.

193. Stuckey, *Slave Culture,* 35–37.

194. Ibid.; see also Thompson and Cornet, *Four Moments of the Sun,* 43–52.

195. Stuckey, *Slave Culture,* 35.

196. Gomez, *Exchanging Our Country Marks,* 273.

197. Ibid., 137–140, 150–151; Stuckey, *Slave Culture,* 12.

198. Leland Ferguson, *Uncommon Ground: Archeology and Early African America* (Washington, D.C.: Smithsonian Institute Press, 1992), 110–116; see also Joyner, *Down by the Riverside*, 75.

199. Thompson and Cornet, *Four Moments of the Sun*, 62–68.

200. See Gladys-Marie Fry, *Stitched from the Soul: Slave Quilts from the Ante-Bellum South* (New York: Dutton Studios Books, 1990), 84–91. See also Jane Livingston and John Beardsley, *Black Folk Art in America, 1930–1980* (Jackson: University Press of Mississippi, 1983), 34–35; Eva Ungar Grudin, *Stitching Memories: African American Story Quilts* (Williamstown, Mass.: Williams College Museum of Art, 1990), 6–7; For a reading of Powers's quilt that emphasizes the melding of different African traditions see Stuckey, *Slave Culture*, 91–92.

201. In fact, the sign of the cross is a graphic symbol of particular import for southern slaves as an emblem of protection against bad luck, "its original effectiveness probably being attributed to the fact that it pointed toward all four cardinal points; hence allowing nothing to get by it." Ben Washington, a former slave of the Sea Islands warns, "Ef yuh ebuh see a cross mahk in duh road, yuh nebuh walk obuh it. Das real magic. Yuh hab tuh go roun it. Duh cross is a magic sign an hab tuh do wid duh spirits." Georgia Writers' Project, *Drums and Shadows*, 135.

202. Georgia Writers' Project, *Drums and Shadows*, 177.

203. Ibid., 125.

204. Ibid., 131.

205. Ibid., 144.

206. Samuel Lawton, "The Religious Life of South Carolina Coastal and Sea Island Negroes," Ph.D. diss., George Peabody College for Teachers, 1939.

207. Puckett, *Folk Beliefs of the Southern Negro*, 569.

208. Georgia Writers' Project, *Drums and Shadows*, 185. Blacks in other parts of the world had similar concerns as regards baptism and the proper condition of the water. Among the Spiritual Baptists in Trinidad, baptism "must always take place in 'living' water." See Melville Herskovits and Frances Herskovits, *Trinidad Village* (1947; reprint, New York: Octagon Books, 1964), 203.

209. Parrish, *Slave Songs*, 363.

210. Ibid., 169.

211. Howard Thurman, *The Negro Spiritual Speaks of Life and Death* (New York: Harper and Row, 1969), 21.

212. Miles Mark Fisher, *Negro Slave Songs in the United States* (New York: Citadel Press, 1963), 100–101. This belief was quite widely held and can be found throughout the tradition of slave spirituals as in the notion that the "Jurdun's stream is cold and chilly, you got tuh wade it by yo'self; no one heah to wade it faw you, you got tuh wade it by yo'self." See Mary Allen Grissom, *The Negro Sings a New Heaven* (Chapel Hill: University of North Carolina Press, 1930) 3.

213. John Lomax and Alan Lomax, *Folk Song U.S.A.* (New York: Signet, 1947), 452. A similar sentiment is expressed in "Death Gwineter Lay His Cold Icy Hands on Me," in *The Books of American Negro Spirituals*, vol. 1, by James Weldon Johnson and J. Rosamond Johnson (New York: Viking Press, 1925), 93, 96.

214. Georgia Writers' Project, *Drums and Shadows*, 180. Writing in *Slaves Songs*, Lydia Parrish maintains that the use of the word "to" in this instance means "beside." Thus Parrish dismisses the assertion that the black faithful held any particular reverence for the power of the water itself. Even Parrish, however, acknowledges that the prayers were "punctuated in the African manner with encouraging responses, rhythmically delivered." Still, Parrish does not take into full account the importance of the African influence in the ritual and perhaps misses the meaning that slaves attached the baptism. See Parrish, *Slave Songs*, 168.

215. Georgia Writers' Project, *Drums and Shadows*, 122.

216. This would certainly be true for enslaved Africans who were not from West-Central Africa.

217. Alan Lomax, *The Folk Songs of North America* (Garden City, N.Y.: Doubleday, 1960), 463.

218. Creel, *Peculiar People*, 276–279.

219. For more on the ring shout, see Stuckey, *Slave Culture*, esp. chap. 1; Creel, *Peculiar People*, 277–302.

220. Charlotte Forten, "Life on the Sea Islands," pt. 1, *Atlantic Monthly* 13 (May 1864): 672.

221. Frederick Douglass, *Narrative of the Life of Frederick Douglass, an American Slave, Written by Himself*, ed. William Andrews and William McFeely (1845; reprint, New York: Norton, 1997), 75–76.

222. Creel, *Peculiar People*, 277.

223. Harriet Jacobs [Linda Brent], *Incidents in the Life of a Slave Girl, Written by Herself*, ed. Lydia Maria Child (1863; reprint, Cambridge: Harvard University Press, 1987), 93.

224. Elizabeth Ware Pearson, *Letters from Port Royal, 1862–1868* (New York: Arno Press, 1969), 20.

225. Ibid., 17–18.

226. Ibid., 18.

227. William J. Faulkner, *The Days When the Animals Talked: Black American Folktales and How They Came to Be* (1977; reprint Trenton, N.J.: Africa World Press, 1993), 54.

228. Frederick Law Olmsted, *The Cotton Kingdom: A Traveler's Observations on Cotton and Slavery in the American Slave States* (New York: Da Capo Press, 1996), 449.

229. T. J. Woofter, *Black Yeomanry: Life of St. Helena Island* (New York: H. Holt, 1930), 237.

230. Ibid., 148.

231. Du Bois, *Souls of Black Folk*, 156.

232. Ibid.

233. James L. Smith, *Autobiography of James L. Smith* (Norwich, Conn, 1881), 27.

234. Quoted in Creel, *Peculiar People*, 277.

235. Forten, "Sea Islands," 592.

236. Woofter, *Black Yeomanry*, 237.

237. Allen, *Slave Songs*, xii–xiv. Sterling Stuckey has written extensively on the ring shout and its role as an early incubator of racial and cultural unity among enslaved Afri-

cans from different areas of the continent. For that authoritative treatment, see Stuckey, *Slave Culture*, 12–13, 17–18, and passim.

238. Forten, "Sea Islands," 593–594.

239. Sernett, *Religious History*, 67.

240. Jacobs, *Incidents*, 69.

241. Lomax, *Folk Songs of North America*, 462–463.

242. Georgia Writers' Project, *Drums and Shadows*, 92, 203. Herskovits maintains that spirit possession attended water immersion rites in other New World locales. Possessions by the river spirits in Haiti brought the devotee thrashing into the stream near which the rituals were being held and where the deity was thought to reside. In Trinidad possession often attended the baptismal: "After you receive the Holy Ghos,' you cannot keep still at all. You feel a j'y within you, an' at the mention of God, the power shake you." Herskovits maintains that possession, as it occurred in the New World, was "almost indistinguishable from the possession brought on" in other African locales. Herskovits, *Myth of the Negro Past*, 234.

243. Faulkner, *Days When the Animals Talked*, 57–58.

244. Nella Larsen, *Quicksand; and, Passing*, ed. Deborah E. McDowell (New Brunswick, N.J.: Rutgers University Press, 1986), 111–114.

245. This recalls Frantz Fanon and his notion that "it is in his corporeality that the Negro is attacked." Fanon, *Black Skin, White Masks*, 163.

246. Frantz Fanon, *The Wretched of the Earth* (New York: Grove Weidenfeld, 1963), 57–58.

247. Genovese, *Roll, Jordan, Roll*, 163–164. It should be noted that many blacks, both slave and free, made use of Christianity in resistant and, at times, revolutionary ways in a manner that belies Genovese's notion of religion as ultimately passive. This would be true of Nat Turner, Frederick Douglass, and of David Walker treated above.

248. Anonymous, *Dwight's Journal of Music* 9, no. 7 (November 15, 1856): 51–52.

249. The literature for these methods of resistance are abundant and of crucial importance in slave studies. For a general overview see John Blassingame, *The Slave Community: Plantation Life in the Antebellum South* (New York: Oxford University Press, 1972), 192–223; Stampp, *Peculiar Institution*, 86–141; Herbert Aptheker, *American Negro Slave Revolts* (New York: International Publishers, 1943).

250. Cuvélier, *Relations sur le Congo*, 283.

251. For other treatments of slave religion as resistant, see Stuckey, *Slave Culture*, chap. 1; Gomez, *Exchanging Our Country Marks*, 1–4; Morgan, *Slave Counterpoint*, 648–651; for an international perspective, see João José Reis, *Slave Rebellion in Brazil*, trans. Arthur Brakel (Baltimore: Johns Hopkins University Press, 1993).

252. Doris Ulmann, *The Darkness and the Light* (New York: Aperture, 1974), 11.

NOTES TO CHAPTER 3

1. Anne McClintock, *Imperial Leather: Race, Gender, and Sexuality in the Colonial Contest* (New York: Routledge, 1995), 185–186.

2. Ibid., 186.

3. William Pietz, "The Problem of the Fetish IIIa: Bosman's Guinea and the Enlightenment Theory of Fetishism," *Res* 16 (Autumn 1988): 106.

4. Mudimbe, *Invention of Africa*, 45.

5. De Lucques, *Relations sur le Congo*, 146–147; emphasis added.

6. Edward Said, *Orientalism* (New York: Vintage Books, 1978), 121.

7. Caryl Phillips, *The European Tribe* (Boston: Faber and Faber, 1987), 121.

8. Said, *Orientalism*, 117.

9. Mudimbe, *Invention of Africa*, 190.

10. Ibid.

11. Herman Melville, *Moby-Dick; or, The Whale* (1851; reprint, New York: Modern Library, 2000), 31–33.

12. Dapper, *Description de L'Afrique*, 335.

13. Ibid., 372.

14. Ibid., 335, 372. See also John Barbot, *A Description of the Coasts of North and South Guinea; and of Ethiopia Inferior, Vulgarly Angola* (Henry Lintot and John Osborn, 1746), 477–478.

15. MacGaffey and Harris, *Astonishment and Power;* Wyatt MacGaffey, *Kongo Political Culture: The Conceptual Challenge of the Particular* (Bloomington: Indiana University Press, 2000); Wyatt MacGaffey, *Religion and Society in Central Africa: The Bakongo of Lower Zaire* (Chicago: University of Chicago Press, 1986); Wyatt MacGaffey, *Custom and Government in the Lower Congo* (Berkeley and Los Angeles: University of California Press, 1970); Thompson, *Flash of the Spirit*.

16. William Pietz, "The Problem of the Fetish I," *Res* 9 (Spring 1985): 6.

17. Pietz, "Fetish IIIa," 116.

18. MacGaffey and Harris, *Astonishment and Power*, 32.

19. For more on the *minkisi* complex and its role as a political theory, see MacGaffey, *Kongo Political Theory*.

20. Serafino da Cortona à José de Granada, gardien de Séville, Loanda, 6 March 1653, in Jadin, "Ancien Congo," 1453. See also Caltanisetta, *Diaire Congolais*, 184, 112–113.

21. Proclamation du Roi Garcia II à l'Occasion de la Mort du P. Georges de Geel, São Salvador, 2 March, 1653, in Jadin, "Ancien Congo," 1451. I treat more fully the relationship between the slave trade and the *minkisi* complex in a later section.

22. Louis Jadin, "Information sur le Royaume du Congo par le P. Raimondo da Dicomano, 1798," *Bulletin des Séances, Académie Royale des Sciences Coloniales* 2, no. 2 (1957): 324.

23. Jadin, "Ancien Congo," 1451.

24. See Karl Edward Laman, *The Kongo* (Uppsala, Sweden: Victor Petersons Bokindustri Aktiebolag, 1953), 1:vii–viii. *The Kongo* is an English translation of a portion of Laman's ethnographic materials. Despite some editorial drawbacks, the four-volume set is a valuable collection of source material regarding the life and culture of Kongolese at the end of the nineteenth century and the beginning of the twentieth century.

25. Jadin, "Rivalités Luso-Néerlandaises du Sohio," 231.

26. Janzen and MacGaffey, *Anthology of Kongo Religion*, 35, 37.

27. Anita Jacobson-Widding, *Red-White-Black as a Mode of Thought: A Study of Tri-*

adic Classification by Colours in the Ritual Symbolism and Cognitive Thought of the Peoples of the Lower Congo, (Uppsala: Univ., 1979), 132–135.

28. MacGaffey, *Kongo Political Culture,* 80.

29. MacGaffey, *Religion and Society,* 7.

30. For more on *kindoki,* see MacGaffey, *Kongo Political Culture,* 2–5; Hilton, *Kingdom of Kongo,* 17–19.

31. Wyatt MacGaffey, *Art and Healing of the Bakongo: Minkisi from the Laman Collection* (Bloomington: University of Indiana Press, 1991).

32. MacGaffey, *Kongo Political Culture,* 78–80.

33. Jacobson-Widding, *Red-White-Black,* 141–144.

34. Dapper, *Description de l'Afrique,* 336.

35. Janzen, *Anthology,* 36; MacGaffey, *Art and Healing,* p. 5.

36. MacGaffey, *Kongo Political Culture,* 86–89.

37. Dapper, *Description de l'Afrique,* 336.

38. Ibid., 335.

39. Wyatt MacGaffey, "The Personhood of Ritual Objects: Kongo *Minkisi,*" *Etnofoor* 3, no. 1 (1990): 45.

40. Robert Plant Armstrong, *Powers of Presence: Consciousness, Myth, and Affecting Presence,* (Philadelphia: University of Pennsylvania Press, 1981), 5.

41. Jacobson-Widding, *Red-White-Black,* 135.

42. Armstrong, *Powers of Presence,* 13.

43. MacGaffey and Harris, *Astonishment and Power,* 32; MacGaffey, "Personhood of Ritual Objects," 45.

44. Caltanisetta, *Diaire Congolais,* 82.

45. MacGaffey and Harris, *Astonishment and Power,* 95; MacGaffey, *Kongo Political Culture,* 97–99.

46. Caltanisetta, *Diaire Congolais,* 95.

47. Ibid. See also MacGaffey, *Religion and Society,* 266; Caltanisetta, *Diaire Congolais,* 19, 176.

48. Pero Tavares, "Le P. Pero Tavares au P. provincial du Portugal," in "Pero Tavares, Missionaire Jésuite, ses Travaux au Congo et en Angola," by Louis Jadin, *BIHBR* 38:370–372.

49. Notably, Christ's death and resurrection might not have been regarded as particularly unusual to many Kongolese, for whom movement between this world and the next was a normal experience for people specially invested with spiritual powers.

50. Louis Jadin, "Le Congo et la Secte des Antoniens: Restauration du Royaume sous Pedro IV et la 'Saint Antoine' Congolaise (1694–1718)," *BIHBR* 33 (1961): 90–91, 105.

51. MacGaffey, *Kongo Political Culture,* 99. The shift from banging to nailing was not necessarily uniform or total. Regional and temporal variations characterized ritual practice throughout Kongo. It seems clear, however, that ritual experts added nailing to their general repertoire during this time.

52. Dapper, *Description de l'Afrique,* 337; Jan Janzen, *Lemba, 1650–1930: A Drum of Affliction in Africa and the New World* (New York: Garland, 1982), 53–55.

53. Quoted in MacGaffey, *Religion and Society,* 205.

54. Jadin, "Information par Dicomano," 334.

55. Vansina, *Paths in the Rainforests*, 206.

56. Phyllis Martin, *The External Trade of the Loango Coast, 1576–1870: The Effects of Changing Commercial Relations on the Vili Kingdom of Loango* (New York: Oxford University Press, 1972), 70.

57. Jadin, "Information par Dicomano," 334.

58. Martin, *External Trade*, 119.

59. Ibid., 121.

60. This is true all the more when one considers that ritual objects were used throughout West and West-Central Africa. In the Americas, they represent the combined efforts of Africans from various regions to create meaning and ritual in a new circumstance. This chapter neither presumes Kongo hegemony over the arts of ritual objects in the Americas nor discounts the importance of other African traditions in this regard. Instead, it stands as an investigation into one of the prominent connections that link the ritual arts of Africa with those that developed in the Americas. Without minimizing the varied origins of ritual objects, this Kongo avenue, if you will, is of crucial importance for any understanding of the arts of ritual objects in the plantation societies of the New World.

61. Thompson, *Flash of the Spirit*, 123.

62. Ibid., 123, 127. For other treatments of ritual objects used by slaves, see Raboteau, *Slave Religion*, 80–86; Genovese, *Roll, Jordan, Roll*, 216–224, 719–720; Robert Farris Thompson, "Kongo Influences on African-American Artistic Culture," in Holloway, *Africanisms*; Stuckey, *Slave Culture*, esp. chap. 1; Gomez, *Exchanging Our Country Marks*, 283–289.

63. C. C. Jones, *Negro Myths from the Georgia Coast* (1888; reprint, Detroit: Singing Tree Press, 1969), 152.

64. Du Bois, *Souls of Black Folk*, 159, 161.

65. Lenora Herron and Alice Bacon, "Conjuring and Conjure Doctors in the Southern United States," *JAF* 9, no. 33 (April–June 1896): 143–147, 224–226. Along with Alice Bacon, Lenorra Herron was among the first to undertake a systematic and analytical study of slave conjure. At the end of the nineteenth century they formed the Hampton Folk-lore Society with the express aim to observe and collect: "To watch the little things peculiar to their own race, and to record them and place them where they can be made of permanent value . . . [and to] preserve a record of customs and beliefs . . . which connect the negro's African and American past with the present." *JAF* 11 (40): 17.

66. Philip A. Bruce, *The Plantation Negro as a Freeman* (Williamstown, Mass.: Corner House, 1970), 111.

67. Jones, *Religious Instruction*, 127–128.

68. "Folklore Scrapbook," *JAF* 10, no. 38 (1897): 241.

69. Bruce, *Plantation Negro*, 115.

70. Jones, *Negro Myths*, 151.

71. Ibid., see also Jones, *Religious Instruction*, 128.

72. Herron and Bacon, "Conjuring," 144–145. See also Hyatt, *Hoodoo*.

73. WPA—Savannah Writers' Project, collection no. 1355, item 74, p. 37, GHS.

74. "Concerning Negro Sorcery in the United States," *JAF* 3, no. 11 (1890): 286.

75. "Cures by Conjure Doctors," *JAF* 12, no. 47 (1899): 289.

76. Thompson, *Flash of the Spirit*, 142–145. See also Nancy Rhyme, *Slave Ghost Stories: Tales of Hags, Hants, Ghosts, and Diamondback Rattlers* (Orangeburg, S.C.: Sandlapper, 2002), 107.

77. Nkisi Nkondi Mungundu, before 1907, Bakongo, Zaire, glass bottle and other materials,12 inches high, National Museum of Ethnography, Stockholm, Sweden, pictured in MacGaffey and Harris, *Astonishment and Power*, 75–77.

78. Sweet, *Recreating Africa*, 126. For information on bottle trees, see Thompson, *Flash of the Spirit*, 142. For more on the role of conjure and witchcraft in Brazil, see Laura de Mello e Souza, *O diabo e a Terra de Santa Cruz: Feitiçaria e religiosidade popular no Brasil colonial* (Companhia das Letras, 1986), trans. Diane Grosklaus Whitty as *The Devil and the Land of the Holy Cross: Witchcraft, Slavery, and Popular Religion in Colonial Brazil* (Austin: University of Texas Press, 2004).

79. MacGaffey, *Religion and Society*, 266.

80. Roland Steiner, "Observations on the Practice of Conjuring in Georgia," *JAF* 14, no. 44 (1901): 179; Petrona McIver Papers (1071.01.01), SCHS.

81. Woofter, *Black Yeomanry*, 78.

82. Puckett, *Folk Beliefs of the Southern Negro*, 244; see also Sarah Hodgson Torian, "Antebellum and War Memories of Mrs. Telfair Hodgson," *Georgia Historical Quarterly* 27 (1943): 352.

83. Louis Pendleton, "Notes on Negro Folk-Lore and Witchcraft in the South," *JAF* 3, no. 10 (July–September 1890): 206.

84. Petrona McIver Papers (1071.01.01), SCHS.

85. "Cures by Conjure Doctors," 289.

86. "Superstitions and Beliefs from Central Georgia," *JAF* 12, no. 47 (1899): 263; Steiner, "Conjuring in Georgia," 180.

87. Georgia Writers' Project, *Drums and Shadows*, 39.

88. Puckett, *Folk Beliefs of the Southern Negro*, 175–176.

89. Rawick, *American Slave* 13:261–262; Rawick, *American Slave* 12:29; see also Georgia Writers' Project, *Drums and Shadows*,102.

90. "Concerning Negro Sorcery in the United States," *JAF* 3, no. 11 (1890): 281–282.

91. Roland Steiner, "Brazil Robinson Possessed of Two Spirits," *JAF* 13, no. 30 (1900): 228.

92. Herron and Bacon, "Conjuring," 145.

93. Ibid.

94. Puckett, *Folk Beliefs of the Southern Negro*, 221.

95. Georgia Writers' Project, *Drums and Shadows*, 93.

96. Parsons, *Folklore of the Sea Islands*, 212.

97. Georgia Writers' Project, *Drums and Shadows*, 84.

98. Ibid., 74, 77.

99. Boston King, "Memoirs of the Life of Boston King, a Black Preacher, Written by Himself, during his Residence at Kingswool-School" (1798), in *Unchained Voices: An Anthology of Black Authors in the English Speaking World of the Eighteenth Century*, by

Vincent Carretta (Lexington: University Press of Kentucky, 1996), 351; originally published in *Methodist Magazine,* March 1798.

100. Richard Parkinson, *A Tour in America in 1798, 1799, and 1800: Exhibiting Sketches of Society and Manners, and a Particular Account of the American System of Agriculture, with Its Recent Improvements* (London: J. Harding, 1805), 465.

101. Alan Watson, "North Carolina Slave Courts, 1715–1785," *North Carolina Historical Review* 60, no. 1 (January 1983): 31. The root doctor's name, Quash, is an apparent variation of Quashi or Kwesi, an Akan day name meaning "a son born on Sunday." For more on the use of Ghanaian day names in the slave community, see Rucker, *River Flows On,* 38–39.

102. Morgan, *Slave Counterpoint,* 620.

103. W. B. Hodgson, *The Gospels, Written in the Negro Patois of English, with Arabic Characters* (New York: Ethnological Society of New York, 1857), 8.

104. Zora Neale Hurston, "Hoodoo in America," *JAF* 44 (1931): 317; Morgan, *Slave Counterpoint,* 622; Turner, *Africanisms in the Gullah Dialect,* 193–204; also see Henry Middleton Hyatt, *Hoodoo, Conjuration, Witchcraft, Rootwork: Beliefs Accepted by Many Negroes and White Persons, These Being Orally Recorded among Blacks and Whites* (Washington, D.C.: Western Publishers, 1970).

105. Gwendolyn Midlo Hall, *Africans in Colonial Louisiana: The Development of Afro-Creole Culture in the Eighteenth Century* (Baton Rouge: Louisiana State University Press, 1992), 162–165, 302.

106. MacGaffey, *Kongo Political Culture,* 205.

107. Jeanette Robinson Murphy, "The Survival of African Music in America," *Popular Science Monthly* 55 (1899): 660–672.

108. John W. Roberts, *From Trickster to Badman: The Black Folk Hero in Slavery and Freedom* (Philadelphia: University of Pennsylvania, 1989), 71.

109. MacGaffey and Harris, *Astonishment and Power,* 134.

110. Native American communities would have been instructive here, because even as systems of regular and sustained contact between enslaved Africans and Native Americans may not have been readily available, there was certainly significant communion and contact between the two groups. We are reminded here of the black Seminoles of Florida, westward movements of Africans into Oklahoma, and any number of maroon communities in Louisiana, South Carolina, and other locales. Such was the case for one "old African . . . who claimed to be a conjurer and wizard, professing to have derived the art from the Indians after he arrived in the country from Africa." See Roland Steiner, "Observations on the Practice of Conjuring in Georgia," *JAF* 14, no. 3 (July–September 1901): 177.

111. Georgia Writers' Project, *Drums and Shadows,* 56.

112. Ibid.

113. Ibid. For an excellent discussion of enslaved Africans' notions of health and healing in the antebellum South, see Sharla Fett, *Working Cures: Healing, Health, and Power on Southern Slave Plantations* (Chapel Hill: University of North Carolina Press, 2002).

114. Georgia Writers' Project, *Drums and Shadows,* 57.

115. Zora Neale Hurston, "High John de Conqueror," in Hurston, *Sanctified Church*, 70; see also Rawick, *American Slave* 13:262.

116. Hurston, "High John de Conqueror," 70.

117. Ibid., 78.

118. Georgia Writers' Project, *Drums and Shadows*, 83–84.

119. Bruce, *Plantation Negro,* 115.

120. Georgia Writers' Project, *Drums and Shadows*, 177–178. Some have argued that the root doctor's influence depended primarily on the fear that he instilled in community members. In the example quoted above, it is important to note that Hunter is recalling an experience of his youth and it seems likely that his fear is, in large part, a product of that youth. Hunter certainly does not suggest that the root worker, himself, intended to frighten the boy. While it is true that the mysterious powers of the conjurers might very well have elicited fear, it should not be lost on the reader that the primary source of the root doctor's persuasive powers was not fear but the efficacy of his practice. In order to be highly regarded, a practitioner need be consistently effective. An ineffective root worker would enjoy neither the respect, admiration, nor fear of those around him.

121. Georgia Writers' Project, *Drums and Shadows*, 38–39.

122. Puckett, *Folk Beliefs of the Southern Negro*, 137.

123. Georgia Writers' Project, *Drums and Shadows*, 39.

124. Quoted in Richard Shryock, *Medicine in America: Historical Essays* (Baltimore: Johns Hopkins University Press, 1966), 63.

125. Regarding Africa as the final destination for the souls of the deceased, see Georgia Writers' Project, *Drums and Shadows,*18, 29, 79, 108, 150, 151, 154, 156, 169.

126. Bruce, *Plantation Negro,* 119.

127. Sweet, *Recreating Africa,* 171.

128. Bruce, *Plantation Negro,* 121.

129. Rawick, *American Slave* 3:78.

130. Ibid. 3:79.

131. Bruce, *Plantation Negro,* 118.

132. Jones, *Negro Myths*, 152.

133. Bruce, *Plantation Negro,* 118.

134. Ibid., 117–118.

135. Ibid., 118.

136. Thaddeus Norris, *Lippincott's Magazine* 6 (July 1870): 90–95.

137. Georgia Writers' Project, *Drums and Shadows*, 36.

138. Gonzales, *Black Border,* 244.

139. *Southern Workman* 23, no. 2 (January 1894): 26–27; South Carolina Writers' Program, *South Carolina Folktales* (University of South Carolina: Columbia, 1941), 45.

140. Henry C. Davis, "Negro Folk-Lore in South Carolina," *JAF* 27, no. 105 (July–September 1914): 247; R. Emmet Kennedy, *Mellows: A Chronicle of Unknown Singers* (New York: Albert and Charles Boni, 1925), 57.

141. Harris, *Complete Tales of Uncle Remus,* 104.

142. WPA—Savannah Writers' Project, collection no. 1355, item 74, p. 38, GHS.

143. "Superstitions Among the Negroes," 247; Petrona McIver Papers (1071.01.01), SCHS; John Bennet Papers, Box 21-126, Folders 14, 15, SCHS.

144. WPA—Savannah Writers' Project, collection no. 1355, item 74, p. 40, GHS; *Southern Workman* 23, no. 2, pp. 26–27; South Carolina Writers' Program, *South Carolina Folktales,* 90–93.

145. Parsons, *Folklore of the Sea Islands,* 63.

146. Dapper, *Description de l'Afrique,* 335.

147. Davis, "Negro Folk-Lore in South Carolina," 247.

148. Ibid.

149. *Southern Workman* 23:46–47.

150. Laura Towne, *Letters and Diary of Laura M. Towne: Written from the Sea Islands of South Carolina,* ed. Rupert Sargent Holland (1912; reprint, New York: Negro Universities Press, 1969), 186; see also Rose, *Rehearsal for Reconstruction,* 98–100; Georgia Writers' Project, *Drums and Shadows,* 34, 79.

151. Georgia Writers' Project, *Drums and Shadows,* 93.

152. Arna Bontemps, *Black Thunder* (1936; reprint, Boston: Beacon Press, 1963), 216.

153. Georgia Writers' Project, *Drums and Shadows,* 37.

154. Ibid.

155. WPA—Savannah Writers' Project, collection no. 1355, item 74, p. 37, GHS; South Carolina Writers' Program, *South Carolina Folktales,* 83.

156. Kemble, *Journal,* 119.

157. Ibid.

158. Ibid, 119.

159. Edmund Kirke [James Roberts Gilmore], *Southern Friends* (New York: Carleton, 1863), 154.

160. Ibid., 155.

161. Woofter, *Black Yeomanry,* 104.

162. Edward A. Pollard, *Black Diamonds Gathered in the Darkey Homes of the South* (1959; reprint, New York: Negro Universities Press, 1968), 118–119.

163. Ibid., 119.

164. *State of South Carolina v. Martin Posey* (1849), 4 Strobhart 103/142. In a rather dramatic turn of events, Posey hired Jeff to "doctor some of his Negroes." Jeff subsequently made a request to Posey that he be bought and brought permanently to Posey's plantation. To this Posey responded that "he would not buy the negro [Jeff] till he had first done something to put his wife out of the way." Hearing this, Appling, one of Posey's slaves, convinced Posey that he need not buy Jeff and that instead "he [Appling] could put Mrs. Posey out of the way." Mr. Posey agreed and promised further that Appling was to have his freedom for the murder. Mrs. Posey disappeared several days later and was eventually found drowned. In the end, Appling was not manumitted. Instead, Posey killed him to conceal the murderous plot. Posey was subsequently convicted as an accessory in the murder of his wife. See also Helen Catterall, *Judicial Cases concerning American Slavery and the Negro,* vol. 2 (New York: Octagon Books, 1968), 414.

165. Not only in the Lowcountry but also in other regions of the African Atlantic did whites make use of the ritual expertise of slaves. In Brazil, for example, slaveholders often

used African slaves to reveal the identities of slaves suspected of crime or to divine the whereabouts of a runaway. Sweet, *Recreating Africa,* 120, 135.

166. Fett, *Working Cures,* 153.

167. Ibid., 1, 16, 44, 47, 175.

168. Ibid., 1.

169. Todd L. Savitt, *Medicine and Slavery: The Diseases and Health Care of Blacks in Antebellum Virginia* (Urbana: University of Illinois Press, 1978), 171, 174; Richard Shryock, "Medical Practices in the Old South," in *Medicine in America: Historical Essays,* Richard Shryock (Baltimore: Johns Hopkins University Press, 1966), 58.

170. Fett, *Working Cures,* 38; see also Butler, *Awash in a Sea of Faith,* esp. chap. 3.

171. Carol Karlsen, *The Devil in the Shape of a Woman: Witchcraft in Colonial New England* (New York: W. W. Norton, 1988); John Demos, *Entertaining Satan: Witchcraft and the Culture of Early New England* (New York: Oxford University Press, 1983); Richard Godbeer, *The Devil's Dominion : Magic and Religion in Early New England* (New York: Cambridge University Press, 1994).

172. Butler, *Awash in a Sea of Faith,* 96.

173. Catterall, *Judicial Cases* 2:521.

174. Robert Starobin, ed., *Denmark Vesey: The Slave Conspiracy of 1822* (Englewood Cliffs, N.J.: Prentice Hall, 1970), 3, 5; Rucker, *River Flows On,* 164–166, 169, 182.

175. Zephariah Kingsley, *A Treatise on the Patriarchal, or Co-operative, System of Society as It Exists in Some Governments, and Colonies in America and in the United States, Under the Name of Slavery, with Its Necessity and Advantages,* 2nd ed. (Tallahassee, 1829), 13.

176. Ibid., 102.

177. Ibid., 45.

178. Ibid.

179. Starobin, *Great Lives,* 103.

180. Frederick Douglass, *Autobiographies,* ed. Henry Louis Gates (New York: Library of America, 1994), 586.

181. Douglass, *Autobiographies,* 586. Interestingly, neither Douglass nor Sandy suffered physical abuse at the hands of abusive masters after having utilized the protective root.

182. Jones, *Religious Instruction,* 128.

183. WPA—Savannah Writers' Project, collection no. 1355, item 74, p. 38, GHS.

184. Virginia Boyle, *Devil Tales* (Freeport, N.Y.: Books for Libraries Press, 1972), 201.

185. Harold Courlander, *A Treasury of Afro-American Folklore* (New York: Crown, 1976), 432–433.

186. William Wells Brown, *My Southern Home; or, The South and Its People* (Upper Saddle River, N.J.: Gregg Press, 1880), 70–80.

187. Jones, *Negro Myths,* 99.

188. From William Wells Brown, *Clotel,* quoted in Daryl Cumber Dance, *From My People: 400 Years of African American Folklore* (New York: W. W. Norton, 2002), 479.

189. Jones, *Negro Myths,* 99–102.

190. Bruce, *Plantation Negro,* 118.

191. Woofter, *Black Yeomanry,* 104.

NOTES TO CHAPTER 4

1. J. Van Wing, *Études Bakongo: Sociologie-religion et Magie* (Bruges, Belgium: Desclee de Brouwer, 1959), 284.

2. Jacobson-Widding, *Red-White-Black*, 307–309; Van Wing, *Études Bakongo*, 284–286.

3. F. Capelle, "Rapport de F. Capelle au Comte J.-M de Nassau et aux Directeurs de la Compagnie," in Jadin, "Rivalités Luso-Néerlandaises du Sohio," 234; Louis Jadin, "Le Clergé Séculier et les Capucins du Congo et d'Angola aux xvi et au xvii Siècles," *BIHBR* 36 (1964–66): 264.

4. M. Proyart, *Histoire de Loango, Kakongo, et autres Royaumes d'Afrique* (Paris: C. P. Berton, 1776), 199.

5. MacGaffey, *Kongo Political Culture*, 145.

6. F. Capelle, "Rapport de F. Capelle," 234; see also "Le Pero Tavares au P. Vogado," in Louis Jadin, "Pero Tavares, Missionaire Jésuite, ses travaux au Congo et en Angola," *BIHBR* 38 (1967): 319.

7. Da Gallo, "Relations," 453.

8. Cuvélier and Jadin, *Ancien Congo*, 123.

9. MacGaffey, *Kongo Political Culture*, 206.

10. South Carolina Writers' Program, *South Carolina Folktales*, 45

11. Caltanisetta, *Diaire Congolais*, 82. Dapper also reports the burial of *minkisi* between sacred trees. See Dapper, *Description de l'Afrique*, 338.

12. Proyart, *Histoire*, 199.

13. Dapper, *Description de l'Afrique*, 367; Hilton, *Kingdom of Kongo*, 10.

14. MacGaffey, *Kongo Political Culture*, 145.

15. Hilton, *Kingdom of Kongo*, 10–11.

16. Ibid., 11. John Weeks suggests that the resurrection of the deceased so described represents a form of spirit possession whereby the soul of the deceased takes possession of an individual. See John Weeks, "Notes on Some Customs of the Lower Congo People," *Folklore* 19, no. 4 (1908): 409–437; John Weeks, "Notes on Some Customs of the Lower Congo People (Continued)," *Folklore* 20, no. 1 (1909): 32–63.

17. Caltanisetta, *Diaire Congolais*, 62.

18. Hilton, *Kingdom of Kongo*, 12.

19. Ibid. 70.

20. Caltanisetta, *Diaire Congolais*, 62–63.

21. Tavares, "P. Tavares," 377.

22. Ibid.

23. Ibid.

24. W. H. Bentley, *Pioneering on the Congo*, vol. 1 (New York: Johnson Reprint, 1900), 236–237.

25. Ibid. In fact, when Protestant missionaries arrived in the region at the end of the nineteenth century they sought to retranslate many of the words that had formally been used to describe Christianity. They stopped using *nzo a nkisi* to mean "church" and replaced it with *esambilu,* which translated as "place of worship."

26. "Mort du Roi du Congo, Alvaro III, et election de Pedro duc de Bamba," in Louis Jadin, "Relations sur le Congo et l'Angola tirées des Archives de la Compagnie de Jésus," *BIHBR* 39 (1968): 374–375. Novel paths had to be taken to the church due to the belief that if the funeral procession followed the normal course to the church, then the successor would fall ill and die within the year.

27. Hilton, *Kingdom of Kongo,* 94–98.

28. De Lucques, *Relations sur le Congo,* 340–343.

29. Caltanisetta, *Diaire Congolais,* 111.

30. Tavares, "P. Tavares," 305.

31. Ibid.

32. "Rapport de Visite *ad limina* pour le diocès de São Salvador, présenté au Pape et à la Congregation du Concile par l'évêque Francisco de Soveral," in Jadin, "Relations sur le Congo et l'Angola," 436.

33. De Lucques, *Relations sur le Congo,* 127.

34. P. Mateus Cardoso, "Relation du Second Voyage du P. Mateus Cardoso," in Jadin, "Relations sur le Congo et l'Angola," 427.

35. De Lucques, *Relations sur le Congo,* 124.

36. Louis Jadin and Mireille Dicorato, *Correspondance de Dom Afonso, Roi du Congo* (Brussels: Académie Royale des Sciences d'Outre-Mer, 1974), 161.

37. Van Wing and Penders, *Dictionnaire Bantu,* 190; Cuvélier and Jadin, *Ancien Congo,* 123.

38. Warner-Lewis, *Central Africa,* 130–131.

39. MacGaffey, *Religion and Society,* 21, 23–24, 34; Fu-Kiau, *N'Kongo,* 106–109; Vansina, "Kongo Kingdom and Its Neighbors," 549.

40. Jadin, "Information sur le Royaume du Congo," 323.

41. Herbert S. Klein and David Richardson, "Long-Term Trends in African Mortality in the Transatlantic Slave Trade," in *Routes to Slavery: Directions, Ethnicity and Mortality in the Atlantic Slave Trade,* ed. David Eltis and David Richardson (London: Frank Cass, 1997), 38–40.

42. Gomez, *Exchanging Our Country Marks,* 163.

43. See MacGaffey, *Religion and Society,* 198; Fu-kiau, *Le Mukongo et Le Monde,* 118; and Hilton, *Kingdom of Kongo,* 50.

44. Miller, *Way of Death,* 4–6; John Thornton, "Cannibals, Witches, and Slave Traders in the Atlantic World," *William and Mary Quarterly* 60, no. 2 (April 2003); William Piersen, "White Cannibals, Black Martyrs: Fear, Depression, and Religious Faith as Causes of Suicide Among New Slaves," *Journal of Negro History* 62, no. 2 (April 1977): 147–159.

45. John Atkins, *A Voyage to Guinea Brasil and the West Indies* (1735; reprint, London: Frank Cass, 1970), 175.

46. Examples of similar sentiments may be found throughout West and West-Central Africa from Senegambia southward to Angola. Indeed, Philip Curtin argues that "all West Africans believed the Europeans practiced cannibalism." See Philip Curtin, ed., *Africa Remembered: Narratives by West Africans from the Era of the Slave Trade* (Madison: University of Wisconsin Press, 1967), 151n22, 92–93, 215, 313, 331; Mary

Karasch, *Slave Life in Rio de Janeiro, 1808–1850* (Princeton, N.J.: Princeton University Press, 1987), 39; Piersen, "White Cannibals, Black Martyrs," 147–150; and Miller, *Way of Death,* 4–5.

47. Quoted in Adam Potkay and Sandra Burr, eds., *Black Atlantic Writers* (New York: St. Martin's Press, 1995), 186.

48. Ibid., 134.

49. Marcus Wood, *Blind Memory: Visual Representations of Slavery in England and America, 1780–1865* (New York: Routledge, 2000), 17. For some treatment of aesthetic and artistic traditions in the black diaspora, see also Collins, *Art of History,* esp. chap. 4; and Grey Gundaker, *Signs of Diaspora, Diaspora of Signs: Literacies, Creolization, and Vernacular Practice in African America* (New York: Oxford University Press, 1998).

50. Wood, *Blind Memory,* 29.

51. John Newton, *Thoughts Upon the African Slave Trade* (London, 1788), quoted in Wood, *Blind Memory,* 23; emphasis added.

52. *Abstract of the Evidence Delivered before a Select Committee of the House of Commons in the Years 1790 and 1791 on the Part of the Petitioners for the Abolition of the Slave Trade* (Cincinnati: American Reform Tract and Book Society, 1855), 48–50.

53. James Stanfield, *Observations on a Guinea Voyage in a Series of Letters Addressed to the Rev. Thomas Clarkson* (London, 1788), quoted in Wood, *Blind Memory,* 15.

54. Adams, *Tales of the Congaree,* 277. For a reading of this tale that emphasizes black acculturation, see Stuckey, *Slave Culture,* 7

55. James Wright, "Monument to Slaves Produces Mysterious Story," *Washington Afro-American* 107 (August 6, 1999): 51; James Wright, "Participants Report their Experiences at Sea after Rituals of Remembering the Ancestors," *Michigan Citizen* 21 (August 14, 1999): 37.

56. Tom Feelings, "The Middle Passage," in *The Middle Passage,* by Tom Feelings (New York: Dial Books, 1995).

57. H. Carrington Bolton, "Decoration of Graves of Negroes in South Carolina," *JAF* 4:214. Similar practices were ubiquitous in the Lowcountry and throughout the slave South. Take for example the following description taken from St. Helena: "As elsewhere in the South, the St. Helena people put the things last used and most prized by a person upon his grave. These are usually china, glasses, pitchers, medicine bottles, and other inexpensive things, but sometimes articles of value are left on the graves—antique clocks, vases, and the like." See Woofter, *Black Yeomanry,* 78; WPA—Savannah Writers' Project, collection no. 1355, item 74, p. 56, GHS.

58. E. J. Glave, "Fetishism in Congo Land," *Century Magazine,* 1891, 825–836. The importance of broken vessels placed atop graves in Kongo is mentioned above and will be treated at length below.

59. Georgia Writers' Project, *Drums and Shadows,* 30–31.

60. Gonzales, *Black Border,* 129–130.

61. Puckett, *Folk Beliefs of the Southern Negro,* 104; Bolton, "Decoration of Graves," 214.

62. Georgia Writers' Project, *Drums and Shadows,* 93.

63. Thompson and Cornet, *Four Moments of the Sun,* 186.

64. Parsons, *Folklore of the Sea Islands,* 212; Georgia Writers' Project, *Drums and Shadows,* 93.

65. Petrona McIver Papers (1071.01.01), SCHS.

66. Georgia Writers' Project, *Drums and Shadows,* 58, 95, 117.

67. Warner-Lewis, *Central Africa,* 129, 135–136; Schuler, *Alas, Alas, Kongo,* 72; Landers, *Black Society,* 131.

68. Puckett, *Folk Beliefs of the Southern Negro,* 104–107. Ernest Ingersoll offers a comprehensive list of items placed atop burial mounds, including "bleached sea-shells, broken crockery and glassware, broken pitchers, soap-dishes, lamp chimneys, tureens, coffee cups, syrup jugs, all sorts of ornamental vases, cigar boxes, gun locks, tomato cans, teapots, flower pots, bits of stucco, plaster images, pieces of carved stone-work . . . glass lamps and tumblers in great number, and forty other articles are used." See Ernest Ingersoll, "Decoration of Negro Graves," *JAF* 5 (January–March 1892): 68–69.

69. Thompson, *Flash of the Spirit,* 132.

70. Ibid.

71. Roberta Wright Hughes and Wilber Hughes III, *Lay Down Body: Living History in African-American Cemeteries* (Detroit: Visible Ink, 1996), xiii.

72. WPA—Savannah Writers' Project, collection no. 1355, item 74, p. 55, GHS.

73. Woofter, *Black Yeomanry,* 79.

74. MacGaffey, *Kongo Political Culture,* 206–207.

75. See Hurston, "Hoodoo in America," 398.

76. Smith, *Slavery and Rice Culture,* 181 and 181n36.

77. Rawick, *American Slave* 13:267; Portia Smiley, "Folk-Lore from Virginia, South Carolina, Georgia, Alabama, and Florida," *JAF* 32, no 125 (July–September 1919): 382; Georgia Writers' Project, *Drums and Shadows,* 16, 141, 171, 192.

78. Georgia Writers' Project, *Drums and Shadows,* 16, 141, 171, 192.

79. Ibid.,122; WPA—Savannah Writers' Project, collection no. 1355, item 74, p. 575, GHS. For a treatment of similar themes in the Caribbean, see Warner-Lewis, *Central Africa,* 127.

80. Rawick, *American Slave* 13:330.

81. Petrona McIver Papers (1071.01.01), SCHS.

82. Warner-Lewis, *Central Africa,* 124.

83. Ibid.

84. Torian, "Antebellum and War Memories," 352.

85. The principal study of the ring shout is Stuckey's *Slave Culture,* 12, 24, 40, and passim; W. F. Allen, *Slave Songs of the United States* (1867; reprint, New York: Peter Smith, 1951), 101; WPA—Savannah Writers' Project, collection no. 1355, item 96, GHS; Smith, *Slavery and Rice Culture,* 180.

86. Georgia Writers' Project, *Drums and Shadows,* 180.

87. Thomas Wentworth Higginson, *Army Life in a Black Regiment* (1869; reprint, New York: W. W. Norton, 1984), 63; see also "You May Bury Me in de East," in Johnson and Johnson, *Books of American Negro Spirituals* 1:181.

88. Kemble, *Journal,* 147; WPA—Savannah Writers' Project, collection no. 1355, item 74, p. 54, GHS.

89. Quoted in Mechal Sobel, *Trabelin' On* (Princeton, N.J.: Princeton University Press, 1979), 200.

90. Georgia Writers' Project, *Drums and Shadows*, 58–59, 114.

91. Ibid., 53.

92. Thomas Fenner, *Religious Folk Songs of the Negro* (Hampton, Va.: Hampton Institute Press, 1909), 79.

93. Ibid., 114.

94. David Roediger, "And Die in Dixie: Funerals, Death, and Heaven in the Slave Community, 1700–1865," *Massachusetts Review* 22 (Spring 1981): 174.

95. Georgia Writers' Project, *Drums and Shadows*, 146–149.

96. Robert. L. Hall, "African Religious Retentions in Florida," in Holloway, *Africanisms*, 112.

97. Edmund Ilogu, *Christianity and Ibo Culture* (Leiden: E. J. Brill, 1974), 109, quoted in Hall, "African Religious Retentions," 112. For more on second burials in Africa and the American South, see Lorna McDaniel, "An Igbo Second Burial," *Black Perspective in Music* 6 (Spring 1978): 49–55; Clyde Vernon Kiser, *Sea Island to City; A Study of St. Helena Islanders in Harlem and Other Urban Centers* (New York: AMS Press, 1967), 84; Georgia Writers' Project, *Drums and Shadows*, 226–227; E. Franklin Frazier, "The Negro Slave Family," *Journal of Negro History* 15 (April 1930): 216–217; Edward Geoffrey Parrinder, *African Traditional Religion* (London: Sheldon Press, 1974), 99; Sweet, *Recreating Africa*, 196–199; Frances Leigh Butler, *Ten Years on a Georgia Plantation Since the War* (London: Richard Bentley & Son, 1883), 165; Blassingame, *Slave Community*, 41–45; and Genovese, *Roll, Jordan, Roll*, 198.

98. John Bennet, *Doctor to the Dead: Grotesque Legends and Folk Tales of Old Charleston* (New York: Rinehart, 1943), 193.

99. Bruce, *Plantation Negro*, 111.

100. Jones, *Negro Myths*, 153–155.

101. Ibid., 155.

102. Jones, *Negro Myths*, 155.

103. WPA—Savannah Writers' Project, collection no. 1355, item 74, p. 44, GHS.

104. Petrona McIver Papers (1071.01.01), SCHS.

105. Bennet, *Doctor to the Dead*, 169, 170.

106. This line was not at all unrelated to the line that separated the slave South from the free north. Note in the following spiritual the double entendre when slaves sang, "So free, so free—I done left this world behind; I done crossed the separatin' line . . . ain't you glad? ain't you glad? I done left this world behind; I done crossed the separatin' line." See Grissom, *Negro Sings a New Heaven*, 87.

107. Lomax and Lomax, *Folk Song U.S.A.*, 459; Fenner, *Religious Folk Songs*, 4.

108. Grissom, *Negro Sings a New Heaven*, 25.

109. Murphy, "Survival of African Music in America," 660–672.

110. Fisher, *Negro Slave Songs*, 144.

111. Adams, *Tales of the Congaree*, 48–49, 120–121. Stuckey's *Slave Culture* reintroduced the work of E. C. L. Adams to an entirely new generation of scholars. See Stuckey, *Slave Culture*, 9–10; WPA—Savannah Writers' Project, collection no. 1355, item 74, p. 9,

GHS; For more on the Ole Man Rogan and King Buzzard tales, see Stuckey, *Slave Culture*, 4–5, 46; and Brown, "Walk in the Feenda," 290–295.

112. See Stuckey, *Slave Culture*, esp. chap. 1; Brown, "Walk in the Feenda," 290–295; see also E. C. L. Adams's *Tales of the Congaree*.

113. Adams, *Tales of the Congaree*, 5.

114. Georgia Writers' Project, *Drums and Shadows*, 101.

115. Ibid., 171. Similar treatment is afforded the buzzard, which is also featured in Adams's *Tales of the Congaree*, 60; see also Stuckey, *Slave Culture*, 4.

116. Adams, *Tales of the Congaree*, 60.

117. Ibid., 9.

118. Georgia Writers' Project, *Drums and Shadows*, 4.

119. Ibid., 57.

120. Ibid., 32.

121. Ibid., 33.

122. Ibid.

123. WPA—Savannah Writers' Project, collection no. 1355, item 74, pp. 33–34, GHS.

124. Ibid., 72.

125. Brown, "Walk in the Feenda," 290.

126. Eli Shephard, "Superstitions of the Negro," *Cosmopolitan* 5 (March 1888): 47–50.

127. John Lovell Jr., *Black Song: The Forge and the Flame* (New York: Macmillan, 1972), 307–308.

128. Adams, *Tales of Congaree*, 278. For more on this tale, see Stuckey, *Slave Culture*, 17–20.

129. Stuckey, *Slave Culture*, 8. The persistence of African-derived words, cultural elements, and ritual practices in the Lowcountry certainly supports the contention that Africa continued to hold potent meanings for blacks enslaved in the Americas, even as they negotiated relations in the context of plantation life.

130. For more treatments on the "feenda," see Stuckey, *Slave Culture*, 8; Adams, *Tales of the Congaree*, liii; Brown, "Walk in the Feenda," 290.

131. Petrona McIver Papers (1071.01.01), SCHS.

132. Warner-Lewis, *Central Africa*, 130–131.

133. Ibid., 177.

134. Edward Pierce, "The Freedmen at Port Royal," *Atlantic Monthly* 12 (September 1863): 302.

135. So Car 393.1 78m, SCL, *Grave Matters* (Columbia, S.C.: Chicora Foundation, 1996).

136. Pierce, "Freedmen at Port Royal," 303.

137. Roediger, "Die in Dixie," 165.

138. Olmsted, *Cotton Kingdom*, 175.

139. Ibid.

140. Kemble, *Journal*, 147.

141. Ibid.

142. Ibid., 148; emphasis added.

143. Quoted in Creel, *Peculiar People*, 201.

144. Kemble, *Journal*, 147.

145. Quoted in Roediger, "Die in Dixie," 166–167.

146. Ibid., 167.

147. Catterall, *Judicial Cases* 1:48.

148. Ibid., 168.

149. Adams, *Tales of the Congaree,* 289.

150. Ibid., 297.

151. Ibid., 297.

152. Ibid., 296.

153. James Weldon Johnson, *God's Trombones* (New York: Penguin Books, 1955), 28, 29.

154. Patterson, *Slavery and Social Death,* 38.

NOTES TO CONCLUSION

1. Scott, "Common Wind," 60.

2. Michael Gomez, ed., *Diasporic Africa: A Reader* (New York: New York University Press, 2006), 2.

3. Ibid.

4. Ibid., 3.

5. Mintz and Price, *Birth of African-American Culture.*

6. Price and Price, *Maroon Arts,* 300.

7. See, for example, Richard Price, "On the Miracle of Creolization," in *Afro-Atlantic Dialogues: Anthropology in the Diaspora,* ed. Kevin A. Yelvington (Santa Fe: School of American Research Press, 2006).

8. Gwendolyn Midlo Hall, *Slavery and African Ethnicities in the Americas: Restoring the Links* (Chapel Hill: University of North Carolina Press, 2005), xxi.

9. Renée Stout, "Interview with author, Phillip Ravenhill and Bryna Freyer," Washington, D.C., June 1, 1990, quoted in MacGaffey and Harris, *Astonishment and Power,* 154.

NOTES TO EPILOGUE

1. Gloria Naylor, *Mama Day* (1988; reprint, New York: Vintage Books, 1993), 110–111.

2. Paul Gilroy, "Living Memory: An Interview with Toni Morrison," in *Small Acts: Thoughts on the Politics of Black Cultures,* by Paul Gilroy (New York: Serpent's Tail, 1993), 181.

3. For more on the antebellum sources of black nationalism and similar movements, see Sterling Stuckey, *The Ideological Origins of Black Nationalism* (Boston: Beacon Press, 1972); and Stuckey, *Slave Culture.*

4. Carrie Mae Weems, "Sea Island Series," in *In These Islands: South Carolina and Georgia,* by Carrie Mae Weems (Tuscaloosa: Sarah Moody Gallery or Art, University of Alabama, 1995).

5. Weems, "Sea Island Series."

6. Ibid.

SELECTED BIBLIOGRAPHY

UNPUBLISHED MATERIAL

Avery Research Institute, College of Charleston, Charleston, S.C.

Black Church Records Collection (B1F4)
Mcleod Plantation Cemetery Collection
Pease Collection

Georgia Historical Society, Savannah

C. C. Jones Papers
WPA Savannah Writers Project Collection 1355

Schomburg Center for Research in Black Culture, New York, N.Y.

Dupree African American Pentecostal and Holiness, 1876–1989, SC MG 325
First African Baptist Church Records, 1873–1977, SC Micro R-7087
Inventory of Second African Baptist Church, 1812–1979, SC Micro R-1090
Melville and Frances Herskovits Collection

South Caroliniana Library, University of South Carolina, Columbia

Christensen Family Papers
E. C. L. Adams Papers
Robert Grier Mss.
WPA Papers, D-4-27-A
WPA Papers, D-4-27-B
WPA Papers, D-4-27-B(1)

South Carolina Department of Archives and History, Columbia

Edgefield Est., Box 67, Martin Posey, ED38
Ga. Petition, 1842, no. 28, Fr. 409–411
Ga. Petition, 1844, no. 108, Fr. 745, 747, John G. Williams, ST1402
Ga. Petition, 1846, no. 81, Fr. 722–727, J. W. Tarrant, ST1404

Ga. Petition, 1846, no. 80, Fr. 716–721, J. W. Tarrant, ST1404
Ga. Petition, ND 1812, Fr. 65–73, Chester District, ST1430
Gen. Ass. Res., ND 564
Gen. Petition, 1849, no. 112, Fr. 393–395, H. R. Spram, ST1407
Gen. Petition, 1850, no. 3, Fr. 662–665, Dr. R. Fuller, ST1407
Gen. Petition, 1852, no. 114, Fr. 18–21, Josiah B. Fishbourne, ST1410
WPA Trans., no. A268, Edgefield County

South Carolina Historical Society, Charleston

Alexander Glennie Journal (34/0156)
Almira Coffin Letters (43/0979)
Barnwell Family Papers (25 186–4)
Celestine Lowndes Writings (43/1045)
Charleston Bible Society Records, Letters 1822 (239.01(c)01(1822)-01
Denmark Vesey Letters, Charleston Bible Society Records (0239.00)
John Bennet Papers (1176.00)
John Hyrne Tucker Papers, 1818–1850 (43/518)
Julia Mood Peterkin Papers (1271.00)
McTeer, Mary, Sukie Sue's Limit, n.d. (43/246)
Petrona McIver Papers (1071.01.01)
Robert F. W. Allston Papers (12/6/22)
Rutledge and Young Records (0308.01)
Samuel Gilman Letters (1084.01/19)

PUBLISHED PRIMARY MATERIAL

Abstract of the Evidence Delivered before a Select Committee of the House of Commons in the Years 1790 and 1791 on the part of the Petitioners for the Abolition of the Slave Trade. Cincinnati: American Reform Tract and Book Society, 1855.

Ames, Mary. *From a New England Woman's Diary in Dixie.* Norwood, Mass.: Plimpton Press, 1906.

Astley, Thomas. *A New and General Collection of Voyages and Travels; Consisting of the Most Esteemed Relations, which have been hitherto Published in any Language; Comprehending Everything Remarkable in its Kind, in Europe, Asia, Africa, and America.* London, 1745–47.

Atkins, John. *A Voyage to Guinea Brasil and the West Indies.* 1735. Reprint, London: Frank Cass, 1970.

Avary, Myrta Lockett. *Dixie After the War.* Boston: Houghton Mifflin, 1937.

Bal, Willy, ed. *Le Royaume du Congo aux XV et XVII Siècle: Documents d'Histoire.* Brussels: 1963.

Botume, Elizabeth. *First Days amongst the Contrabands*. 1893. Reprint, New York: Arno Press, 1968.

Brásio, António, ed. *História do Reino do Congo*. 1624. Lisbon: Centro de Estudos Históricos Ultramarinos, 1969. Edited and translated by François Bontinck and J. de Ségovia as *Histoire du Royaume de Congo* (Louvain: Études d'Histoire Africaine IV, 1972).

———, ed. *Monumenta Missionaria Africana*. Vol. 1. Lisbon: Agência-Geral do Ultramar, 1951.

Brown, William Wells. *My Southern Home; or, The South and Its People*. Upper Saddle River, N.J.: Gregg Press, 1880.

Butler, Frances Leigh. *Ten Years on a Georgia Plantation since the War*. London: Richard Bentley & Son, 1883.

Cadornega, António de Oliveira de. *História Geral das Guerras Angolanas, 1680–1681*. Edited by José Matias Delgado and Manuel Alves da Cunha. Lisbon: Agência-Geral do Ultramar, 1940.

Candler, Allen Daniel. *Colonial Records of the State of Georgia*. Atlanta: Franklin, 1904.

Capers, William. *Catechism for the Use of the Methodist Missions*. 3rd ed. Richmond, Va.: John Early, 1852.

Churchill, Awnsham. *A Collection of Voyages and Travels*. Vol. 5. London: H. Lintot, 1746.

Cuvélier, Jean, and Louis Jadin. *L'Ancien Congo d'après les Archives Romaines*. Brussels: Académie Royale des Sciences Coloniales, 1954.

Da Caltanisetta, Luca. *Diaire Congolais (1690–1701)*. Translated by François Bontinck. Kinshasa: Publications de l'Université Lovanium de Kinshasa, 1970.

Da Gallo, Bernardo. "Relations de Bernardo da Gallo." In "Le Congo et la Secte des Antoniens: Restauration du Royaume sous Pedro IV et la 'Saint Antoine' Congolaise (1694–1718)," by Louis Jadin, *BIHBR* 33 (1961).

Da Pavia, Francesco. "Temoinage du P. Francesco da Pavia." In "Le Congo et la Secte des Antoniens: Restauration du Royaume sous Pedro IV et la 'Saint Antoine' Congolaise (1694–1718)," by Louis Jadin, *BIHBR* 33 (1961): 432–440.

Dapper, Olfert. *Description de l'Afrique*. Amsterdam: Wolfgang, Waesberge, Boom & Van Someren, 1686.

De Lucques, Laurent. *Relations sur le Congo du Père Laurent de Lucques (1700–1710)*. Translated by Jean Cuvélier. Brussels: Institut Royal Colonial Belge, 1953.

Douglass, Frederick. *Autobiographies*. Edited by Henry Louis Gates. New York: Library of America, 1994.

Eltis, David, Stephen Brehendt, David Richardson, and Herbert Klein, eds. *The Trans-Atlantic Slave Trade: A Database on CD-ROM*. New York: Cambridge University Press, 1999.

Higginson, Thomas Wentworth. *Army Life in a Black Regiment*. 1869. Reprint, New York: W. W. Norton, 1984.

Jadin, Louis. "L'Ancien Congo et l'Angola, 1639–1655, d'après les Archives Romaines, Portugaises, Néerlandaises et Espangnoles." *BIHBR* 22 (1975).

———. "Le Clergé Séculier et les Capucins du Congo et d'Angola aux xvi et au xvii Siècles." *BIHBR* 36 (1964–66).

———. "Le Congo et la Secte des Antoniens: Restauration du Royaume sous Pedro IV et la 'Saint Antoine' Congolaise (1694–1718)." *BIHBR* 33 (1961).

———. "Pero Tavares, Missionaire Jésuite, ses travaux au Congo et en Angola." *BIHBR* 38 (1967).

———. "Relations sur le Congo et l'Angola tirées des Archives de la Compagnie de Jésus." *BIHBR* 39 (1968).

———. "Relations sur le Royaume du Congo du P. Raimondo de Dicomano." *BIHBR* 3, no. 2 (1957).

———. "Rivalités Luso-Néerlandaises du Sohio, Congo, 1600–1675." *BIHBR* 37 (1966).

Jadin, Louis, and Mireille Dicorato. *Correspondance de Dom Afonso, Roi du Congo, 1506–1543*. Brussels: Académie Royale des Sciences d'Outre-Mer, 1974.

Jones, C. C. *The Religious Instruction of the Negroes, in the United States*. New York: Negro Universities Press, 1842.

Kemble, Frances Ann. *Journal of a Residence on a Georgian Plantation in 1838–1839*. Athens: University of Georgia Press, 1961.

Larsen, Nella. *Quicksand; and, Passing*. Edited by Deborah E. McDowell. New Brunswick, N.J.: Rutgers University Press, 1986.

Lyell, Charles. *A Second Visit to the United States of North America*. London: John Murray, 1850.

Martin, Josephine, ed. *Dear Sister: Letters Written on Hilton Head Island*. Beaufort, S.C.: Beaufort Book Company, 1977.

Obilby, John. *Africa Being an Accurate Description of the Regions of Aegypt, Barbary, Lybia, and Billedulgerid, the land of Negroes, Guinee, Aethiopia and the Abyssines*. London, 1670.

Olmsted, Frederick Law. *The Cotton Kingdom: A Traveler's Observations on Cotton and Slavery in the American Slave States*. New York: Da Capo Press, 1996.

Parkinson, Richard. *A Tour in America in 1798, 1799, and 1800: Exhibiting Sketches of Society and Manners, and a Particular Account of the American*

System of Agriculture, with Its Recent Improvements. London: J. Harding, 1805.

Payne, Daniel. *Recollections of Seventy Years.* 1888. Reprint, New York: Arno Press, 1968.

Pearson, Elizabeth Ware. *Letters from Port Royal, 1862–1868.* New York, Arno Press, 1906.

Pinkerton, John. *A General Collection of the Best and Most Interesting Voyages and Travels in All Parts of the World.* Vol. 16. London: Longman, Hurst, 1814.

Proceedings of Meeting in Charleston, S.C. on the Religious Instruction of the Negroes, Together with The Report of the Committee and the Address to the Public, May 13–15, 1845. Charleston, S.C., 1845.

Proyart, M. *Histoire de Loango, Kakongo, et autres Royaumes d'Afrique.* Paris: C. P. Berton, 1776.

Rawick, George P., ed. *The American Slave: A Composite Biography.* Series 1, vols. 2–3 (South Carolina narratives), and series 2, vols. 12–13 (Georgia narratives). Westport, Conn.: Greenwood, 1972.

———. *The American Slave: A Composite Biography.* Supplement, series 1, vols. 3–4 (Georgia narratives) and vol. 11 (North and South Carolina narratives). Westport, Conn.: Greenwood, 1977.

Roma, Giovanni Francesco da. *Brève Relatione del Successo della Missione de Frati Minori Capuccini al Regno del Congo.* 1648. Translated by François Bontinck as *Brève Relation de la Fondation de la Mission des Frères Mineurs Capucins du Séraphique Père Saint François au Royaume du Congo, et des Particularités, Coutumes et Façons de Vivre des Habitants de ce Royaume* (Louvain: Éditions Nauwelaerts, 1964).

Saint-Méry, Moreau de. *Description Topographique, Physique, Civile, Politique et Historique de La Partie Française de L'Isle Saint-Domingue.* Paris: Société de l'Histoire des Colonies Française, 1958.

Sebastyen, Eva, and Jan Vansina. "Angola's Eastern Hinterland in the 1750s: A Text Edition and Translation of Manoel Correia Leitao's 'Voyage' (1755–1756)." *History in Africa* 26 (1999): 299–364.

Smith, James L. *Autobiography of James L. Smith.* Norwich, Conn., 1881.

Stanfield, James. *Observations on a Guinea Voyage in a Series of Letters Addressed to the Rev. Thomas Clarkson.* London, 1788.

Torian, Sarah Hodgson. "Antebellum and War Memories of Mrs. Telfair Hodgson." *Georgia Historical Quarterly* 27 (1943): 350–356.

Towne, Laura. *Letters and Diary of Laura M. Towne: Written from the Sea Islands of South Carolina.* Edited by Rupert Sargent Holland. 1912. Reprint, New York: Negro Universities Press, 1969.

Turpin, Thomas. "Missionary Intelligence." *Christian Advocate and Journal,* January 31, 1834.

Van Wing, J., and C. Penders. *Le Plus Ancien Dictionnaire Bantu.* Louvain: J. Kuyl-Otto, 1928.

Walker, David. *David Walker's Appeal to the Coloured Citizens of the World, but in Particular, and very expressly, to those of the United States of America.* Baltimore: Black Classic Press, 1830.

SELECTED SECONDARY MATERIAL

Andrew, James. "The Southern Slave Population." *Methodist Magazine and Quarterly Review* 13 (1831): 312–322.

Armstrong, Robert Plant. *Powers of Presence: Consciousness, Myth, and Affecting Presence.* Philadelphia: University of Pennsylvania Press, 1981.

Balandier, Georges. *Daily Life in the Kingdom of Kongo.* New York: Allen and Unwin, 1998.

Bascom, William. "Acculturation among the Gullah Negroes." *American Anthropologist* 43 (1941): 43–50.

Bates, Robert, V. Y. Mudimbe, and Jean F. O'Barr, eds. *Africa and the Disciplines: The Contributions of Research in Africa to the Social Sciences and Humanities.* Chicago: University of Chicago Press. 1993.

Birmingham, David. *Central Africa to 1870.* Cambridge: Cambridge University Press, 1981.

Blassingame, John. *The Slave Community.* New York: Oxford University Press, 1972.

Blyden, Edward. *African Life and Customs.* 1908. Reprint, Boston: Black Classics Press, 1994.

Bockie, Simon. *Death and the Invisible Powers: The World of Kongo Belief.* Bloomington: Indiana University Press, 1993.

Boles, John B., ed. *Masters and Slaves in the House of the Lord: Race and Religion in the American South, 1740–1870.* Lexington: University Press of Kentucky, 1988.

Bontinck, François. "Les Croix de Bois dans L'Ancien Royaume de Kongo." *Miscellania Historiae Pontificiae* 50 (1983): 199–213.

Brathwaite, Kamau. *Roots.* Ann Arbor: University of Michigan Press, 1993.

Broadhead, Susan. "Beyond Decline: The Kingdom of the Kongo in the Eighteenth and Nineteenth Centuries." *International Journal of African Historical Studies* 12, no. 4 (1979): 615–650.

Brown, Soi-Daniel W. "From the Tongues of Africa: A Partial Translation of Oldendorp's Interviews." *Plantation Society* 2, no. 1 (April 1983): 37–61.

Bruce, Philip A. *The Plantation Negro as a Freeman*. Williamstown, Mass.: Corner House, 1970.

Bunseki-Lumanisa, Fu-Kiau Kia. *African Cosmology of the Bântu-Kôngo: Tying the Spiritual Knot: Principles of Life and Living. Brooklyn*. New York: Athelia Henrietta Press, 2001.

———. *N'Kongo Ye Nza Yakun'zungidila: Nza Kongo*. Le Mukongo et le Monde Qui l'Entourait, Cosmogonie- Kongo no. 1. Kinshasa: Office National de la Recherche et de Developpement, 1969.

Butler, Jon, *Awash in a Sea of Faith: Christianizing the American People*. Cambridge: Harvard University Press, 1990.

Cate, Margaret, *Early Days of Coastal Georgia*. 1955. Reprint, St. Simons Island, Ga.: Fort Frederica Association, 1968.

Cavazzi, Giovanni Antonio, *Istorica Descrizione de tre Regni Congo, Matamba et Angola*. Bologne, 1687; Milan 1690. Translated by P. Graciano Maria de Leguzzano as *Descripção do Congo, Matamba et Angola* (Lisbon: Junta de Investigações do Ultramar, 1965).

Clarke, Erskine. *Wrestlin' Jacob: A Portrait of Religion in Antebellum Georgia and the Carolina Low Country*. Tuscaloosa: University of Alabama Press, 2000.

Collins, Lisa Gail. *The Art of History: African American Women Artists Engage the Past*. New Brunswick, N.J.: Rutgers University Press, 2002.

Cooley, Rossa B. *School Acres: An Adventure in Rural Education*. New Haven, Conn.: Yale University Press, 1930.

Creel, Margaret Washington. *A Peculiar People: Slave Religion and Community-Culture among the Gullahs*. New York: New York Universities Press. 1988.

Crookall, L. *British Guiana; or, Work and Wanderings among the Creoles and Coolies, the Africans and Indians of the Wild Country*. London: T. Fisher Unwin, 1898.

Crum, Mason. *Gullah: Negro Life in the Carolina Sea Islands*. 1940. Reprint, New York: Negro Universities Press, 1968.

Du Bois, W. E. B. *Black Folk Then and Now*. 1939. Reprint, Millwood, N.Y.: Kraus-Thompson, 1975.

———. *The Souls of Black Folk*. New York: Penguin Books, 1903.

———. *The World and Africa: An Inquiry into the Part Which Africa Has Played in World History*. New York: Viking Press, 1947.

Edwards, Brent Hayes. *The Practice of Diaspora: Literature, Translation, and the Rise of Black Internationalism*. Cambridge: Harvard University Press, 2003.

Egerton, Douglas R. *Gabriel's Rebellion: The Virginia Slave Conspiracies of 1800 and 1802*. Chapel Hill: University of North Carolina Press, 1993.

Selected Bibliography

———. *He Shall Go Out Free: The Lives of Denmark Vesey*. Madison, Wis.: Madison House, 1999.

Eltis, David, and David Richardson, eds. *Routes to Slavery: Directions, Ethnicity and Mortality in the Atlantic Slave Trade*. London: Frank Cass, 1997.

Fanon, Frantz. *Black Sins, White Mask*. New York: Grove Weidenfeld, 1967.

———. *The Wretched of the Earth*. New York: Grove Weidenfeld, 1963.

Featherstone, David. *Doris Ulmann, American Portraits*. Albuquerque: University of New Mexico Press, 1985.

Ferguson, Leland. *Uncommon Ground: Archaeology and Early African America*. Washington, D.C.: Smithsonian Institute Press, 1992.

Fett, Sharla. *Working Cures: Healing, Health, and Power on Southern Slave Plantations*. Chapel Hill: University of North Carolina Press, 2002.

Frazier, E. Franklin. *The Negro Family in the United States*. Chicago: University of Chicago Press, 1939.

Genovese, Eugene. *Roll, Jordan, Roll: The World the Slaves Made*. New York: Vintage Books, 1972.

Gilroy, Paul. *The Black Atlantic: Modernity and Double Consciousness*. Cambridge: Harvard University Press, 1993.

Glave, E. J. "Fetishism in Congo land." *Century Magazine* 19 (1881): 825–837.

Glissant, Eduoard. *Caribbean Discourse: Selected Essays*. Charlottesville: University Press of Virginia, 1989.

Gomez, Michael. *Exchanging Our Country Marks: The Transformation of African Identities in the Colonial and Antebellum South*. Chapel Hill: University of North Carolina Press, 1998.

———. *Reversing Sail: A History of the African Diaspora*. Cambridge: Cambridge University Press, 2005.

Gray, Richard. *Black Christians and White Missionaries*. New Haven, Conn.: Yale University Press, 1990.

Gundaker, Grey. *Signs of Diaspora, Diaspora of Signs*. New York: Oxford University Press, 1998.

Hall, Gwendolyn Midlo. *Africans in Colonial Louisiana: The Development of Afro-Creole Culture in the Eighteenth Century*. Baton Rouge: Louisiana State University Press, 1992.

———. *Slavery and African Ethnicities in the Americas: Restoring the Links*. Chapel Hill: University of North Carolina Press, 2005.

Hall, Stuart, David Held, Don Hubert, and Kenneth Thompson, eds. *Modernity: An Introduction to Modern Societies*. Cambridge: Blackwell, 1996.

Harris, Michael D. "Ritual Bodies-Sexual Bodies: The Role and Representation of the Body in African American Art." *Third Text* 12 (Autumn 1990): 81–95.

Hartman, Saidiya. *Scenes of Subjection: Terror, Slavery, and Self-Making in Nineteenth-Century America*. New York: Oxford University Press, 1997.

Hastings, Adrian. "The Christianity of Pedro IV of the Kongo, 'The Pacific' (1695–1718)." *Journal of Religions in Africa* 28, no. 2 (May 1998): 145–159.

Herron, Lenora, and Alice Bacon. "Conjuring and Conjure Doctors in the Southern United States." *JAF* vol. 9, no. 33 (April–June 1896), and vol. 11, no. 40.

Herskovits, Melville J. *The Myth of the Negro Past*. Boston: Beacon Press, 1941.

———. *The New World Negro: Selected Papers in Afroamerican Studies*. Edited by Frances S. Herskovits. Bloomington: Indiana University Press, 1966.

Herskovits, Melville J., and Frances S. Herskovits. *Trinidad Village*. 1947. Reprint, New York: Octagon Books, 1964.

Heywood, Linda. *Central Africans and Cultural Transformations in the American Diaspora*. New York: Cambridge University Press, 2001.

Hilton, Anne. *The Kingdom of Kongo*. Oxford: Clarendon Press, 1985.

Hine, Darlene Clark, and Jacqueline McLeod, eds. *Crossing Boundaries: Comparative History of Black People in the Diaspora*. Bloomington: Indiana University Press, 1999.

Holloway, Joseph, ed. *Africanisms in American Culture*. Bloomington: University of Indiana Press, 1990.

Horton, Robin. "African Conversion." *Africa: Journal of the International African Institute* 41, no. 2 (April 1971): 85–108.

Inikori, Joseph, *Africans and the Industrial Revolution in England*. Cambridge: Cambridge University Press, 2002.

Jackson, Luther P. "Religious Instruction of Negroes, 1830–1860, with Special Reference to South Carolina." *Journal of Negro History* 15 (1930): 72–114.

Jackson, Bruce. *The Negro and His Folklore in Nineteenth-Century Periodicals*. Austin: University of Texas Press, 1967.

Jacobson-Widding, Anita. *Red-White-Black as a Mode of Thought: A Study of Triadic Classification by Colours in the Ritual Symbolism and Cognitive Thought of the Peoples of the Lower Congo*. Uppsala: Univ., 1979.

Janzen, Jan. *Lemba, 1650–1930: A Drum of Affliction in Africa and the New World*. New York: Garland, 1982.

Janzen, John M., and Wyatt MacGaffey. *Anthology of Kongo Religion: Primary Texts from Lower Zaïre*. Lawrence: University of Kansas Press, 1974.

Johnson, Clifton. *God Struck Me Dead: Religious Conversion Experiences and Autobiographies of Ex-slaves*. Philadelphia: Pilgrim Press, 1969.

Jones, Norrece T. *Born a Child of Freedom, Yet a Slave: Mechanisms of Control and Strategies of Resistance in Antebellum South Carolina*. Middletown, Conn.: Wesleyan University Press, 1989.

Joyner, Charles W. *Down by the Riverside: A South Carolina Slave Community.* Urbana: University of Illinois Press, 1984.

———. *Remember Me: Slave Life in Coastal Georgia.* Atlanta: Georgia Humanities Council, 1989.

Kingsley, Zephariah. *A Treatise on the Patriarchal, or Co-operative, System of Society as It Exists in Some Governments, and Colonies in America and in the United States, Under the Name of Slavery, with Its Necessity and Advantages.* 2nd ed. Tallahassee, Fla., 1829.

Kolchin, Peter. *American Slavery, 1619–1877.* 1993. Reprint, New York: Hill and Wang, 2003.

Laman, Karl Edward. *The Kongo.* Uppsala, Sweden: Victor Petersons Bokindustri Aktiebolag, 1953.

Landers, Jane. *Black Society in Spanish Florida.* Urbana: University of Illinois Press, 1999.

Lawton, Samuel. "The Religious Life of South Carolina Coastal and Sea Island Negroes." Ph.D. diss., George Peabody College for Teachers, 1939.

Levine, Lawrence. *Black Culture and Black Consciousness: Afro-American Folk Thought from Slavery to Freedom.* Oxford: Oxford University Press, 1978.

Linebaugh, Peter, and Marcus Rediker. *The Many-Headed Hydra: Sailors, Slaves, Commoners, and the Hidden History of the Revolutionary Atlantic.* Boston: Beacon Press, 2000.

Littlefield, Daniel C. *Rice and Slaves: Ethnicity and the Slave Trade in Colonial South Carolina.* 1981. Reprint, Urbana: University of Illinois Press, 1991.

MacGaffey, Wyatt. "African Objects and the Idea of the Fetish." *Res* 25 (1994): 123–132.

———. *Art and Healing of the Bakongo Commented by Themselves.* Stockholm: Folkens Museum-Etnografiska, 1991.

———. "Cultural Roots of Kongo Prophetism." *History of Religions* 17, no. 2 (1977): 177–193.

———. *Custom and Government in the Lower Congo.* Berkeley and Los Angeles: University of California Press, 1970.

———. "Fetishism Revisited: Kongo Nkisi in Sociological Perspective." *Africa* 47, no. 2 (1977): 172–184.

———. *Kongo Political Culture: The Conceptual Challenge of the Particular.* Bloomington: Indiana University Press, 2000.

———. "The Personhood of Ritual Objects: Kongo *Minkisi.*" *Etnofoor* 3, no. 1 (1990): 45–61.

———. *Religion and Society in Central Africa.* Chicago: University of Chicago Press, 1986.

MacGaffey, Wyatt, and Michael D. Harris. *Astonishment and Power: The Eyes of Understanding Kongo Minkisi*. Washington, D.C.: National Museum of African Art. 1994.

Mann, Kristin, and Edna Bay, eds. *Rethinking the African Diaspora: The Making of a Black Atlantic World in the Bight of Benin and Brazil*. Portland, Oreg.: Frank Cass, 2001.

Martin, Phyllis. *The External Trade of the Loango Coast, 1576–1870: The Effects of Changing Commercial Relations on the Vili Kingdom of Loango*. New York: Oxford University Press, 1972.

Mbiti, John. *Introduction to African Religions*. New York: Praeger, 1975.

McClintock, Anne. *Imperial Leather: Race, Gender, and Sexuality in the Colonial Contest*. New York: Routledge, 1995.

Meillasoux, Claude. *The Anthropology of Slavery: The Womb of Iron and Gold*. Chicago: University of Chicago Press, 1991.

Mercer, Kobena. *Welcome to the Jungle: New Positions in Black Cultural Studies*. New York: Routledge, 1994.

Miller, Joseph. *Way of Death: Merchant Capitalism and the Angolan Slave Trade*. Madison: University of Wisconsin Press, 1988.

Mintz, Sidney, and Richard Price. *The Birth of African-American Culture: An Anthropological Perspective*. Boston: Beacon Press, 1992.

Morgan, Philip. *Slave Counterpoint: Black Culture in the Eighteenth-Century Chesapeake and Lowcountry*. Chapel Hill: University of North Carolina Press, 1998.

Mudimbe, V. Y. *The Invention of Africa: Gnosis, Philosophy, and the Order of Knowledge*. Bloomington: Indiana University Press, 1988.

Mullin, Michael. *Africa in America: Slave Acculturation and Resistance in the American South and the British Caribbean, 1736–1831*. Urbana: University of Illinois Press, 1992.

Naef, Weston, ed. *In Focus: Doris Ulmann*. Los Angeles: J. Paul Getty Museum, 1996.

Nassau, Rev. Robert Hamill. *Fetichism in West Africa*. New York: Charles Scribner's Sons. 1904.

Newton, John. *Thoughts Upon the African Slave Trade*. London, 1788.

Nsondé, Jean. "Christianisme et Religion Traditionelle en pays Kongo aux XVII–XVIII Siècle." *Cahiers d'Études Africaines* 128, nos. 32–34 (1992): 705–711.

Okpewho, Isidore, ed. *The African Diaspora: African Origins and New World Identities*. Bloomington: Indiana University Press, 1999.

Olwell, Robert. *Masters, Slaves and Subjects: The Culture of Power in the South Carolina Lowcountry, 1740–1790*. Ithaca, N.Y.: Cornell University Press, 1998.

Patterson, Orlando. *Slavery and Social Death: A Comparative Study*. Cambridge: Harvard University Press, 1982.

Peek, Phillip. *African Divination Systems: Ways of Knowing*. Bloomington: Indiana University Press, 1991.

Peterkin, Julia. *Roll, Jordan, Roll*. New York: Robert A. Ballou, 1933.

Pietz, William. "The Problem of the Fetish I." *Res* 9 (Spring 1985): 5–17.

———. "The Problem of the Fetish IIIa: Bosman's Guinea and the Enlightenment Theory of Fetishism." *Res* 16 (Autumn 1988): 105–123.

Pollard, Edward. *Black Diamonds, Gathered in the Darkey Homes of the Old South*. New York: Pudney & Russell, 1859.

Powers, Bernard E., Jr. *Black Charlestonians: A Social History, 1822–1885*. Fayetteville: University of Arkansas Press, 1994.

Price, Richard, ed. *Maroon Societies: Rebel Slave Communities in the Americas*. 3rd ed. Baltimore: Johns Hopkins University, 1996.

Price, Richard, and Sally Price. *Maroon Arts: Cultural Vitality in the African Diaspora*. Boston: Beacon Press, 1999.

Puckett, Newbell Niles. *Folk Beliefs of the Southern Negro*. New York: Negro Universities Press, 1926.

Raboteau, Albert. *Slave Religion: The "Invisible Institution" in the Antebellum South*. New York: Oxford University Press, 1978.

Randles, W. G. L. *L'Ancien Royaume du Congo: Des Origines à la fin du XIX siècle*. Paris: Mouton, 1968.

Rattray, Robert. *The Tribes of the Ashanti Hinterland*. Oxford: Clarendon Press, 1932.

Reis, João Jose. *Slave Rebellion in Brazil*. Translated by Arthur Brakel. Baltimore: Johns Hopkins University Press, 1993.

Richardson, David. "Slave Exports from West and West-Central Africa, 1700–1810: New Estimates of Volume and Distribution." *Journal of African History* 30, no. 1 (1989): 1–22.

Roach, Joseph. *Cities of the Dead: Circum-Atlantic Performance*. New York: Columbia University Press, 1996.

Roberts, John W. *From Trickster to Badman: The Black Folk Hero in Slavery and Freedom*. Philadelphia: University of Pennsylvania, 1989.

Roediger, David. "And Die in Dixie: Funerals, Death, and Heaven in the Slave Community, 1700–1865." *Massachusetts Review* 22 (Spring 1981): 163–183.

Rose, Willie Lee. *Rehearsal for Reconstruction: The Port Royal Experiment*. 1964. Reprint, New York: Oxford University Press, 1976.

Rucker, Walter. *The River Flows On: Black Resistance, Culture, and Identity Formation in Early America*. Baton Rouge: Louisiana State University Press, 2006.

Savitt, Todd L. *Medicine and Slavery: The Diseases and Health Care of Blacks in Antebellum Virginia,* Urbana: University of Illinois Press, 1978.

Schuler, Monica. *Alas, Alas, Kongo: A Social History of Indentured African Immigration into Jamaica, 1841–1865.* Baltimore: Johns Hopkins University Press, 1990.

Scott, David. *Refashioning Futures: Criticism after Postcoloniality.* Princeton, N.J.: Princeton University Press, 1999.

———. "That Event, This Memory: Notes on the Anthropology of African Diasporas in the New World." *Diaspora* 1, no. 3 (1991): 261–284.

Scott, James C. *Domination and the Arts of Resistance: Hidden Transcripts.* New Haven, Conn.: Yale University Press, 1990.

Scott, Julius Sherrard, III. "The Common Wind: Currents of Afro-American Communication in the Era of the Haitian Revolution." Ph.D. diss., Duke University, 1986.

Sernett, Milton. *African American Religious History: A Documentary Witness.* Durham, N.C.: Duke University Press, 1999.

Shryock, Richard. "Medical Practices in the Old South." In *Medicine in America: Historical Essays.* Baltimore: Johns Hopkins University Press, 1966.

Smith, Julia Floyd. *Slavery and Rice Culture in Lowcountry Georgia, 1750–1860.* Knoxville: University of Tennessee Press, 1985.

Smith, Mark M. "Remembering Mary, Shaping Revolt: Reconsidering the Stono Rebellion." *Journal of Southern History* 67, no. 3 (August 2001): 513–534.

———. *Stono: Documenting and Interpreting a Southern Slave Revolt.* Columbia: University of South Carolina Press, 2005.

Smythe, Augustine, Herbert Ravenel Sass, Alfred Huger, Beatrice Ravenel, Thomas Waring, Archibald Rutledge, Josephine Pinckney, Caroline P. Rutledge, DuBose Heywood, Katharine C. Hutson, and Robert W. Gordon, eds. *The Carolina Low-Country.* New York: Macmillan, 1931.

Sobel, Mechal. *Trabelin' On.* Princeton, N.J.: Princeton University Press, 1979.

Southern, Eileen. *The Music of Black Americans.* New York: W. W. Norton. 1971.

Souza, Laura de Mello e. *O Diabo e a Terra de Santa Cruz: Feitiçaria e Religiosidade Popular no Brasil Colonial.* Companhia das Letras, 1986.Translated by Diane Grosklaus Whitty as *The Devil and the Land of the Holy Cross: Witchcraft, Slavery, and Popular Religion in Colonial Brazil* (Austin: University of Texas Press, 2004).

Stampp, Kenneth. *The Peculiar Institution: Slavery in the Ante-bellum South.* 1956. Reprint, New York: Vintage, 1989.

Starobin, Robert, ed. *Denmark Vesey: The Slave Conspiracy of 1822.* Englewood Cliffs, N.J.: Prentice Hall, 1970.

Stuckey, Sterling. *Going Through the Storm: The Influence of African American Art in History* (New York: Oxford University Press, 1994).

———. *Slave Culture: Nationalist Theory and the Foundations of Black America.* New York: Oxford University Press, 1987.

———. "Through the Prism of Folklore: The Black Ethos in Slavery." *Massachusetts Review* 9, no. 3 (Summer 1968).

Sweet, James. *Recreating Africa: Culture, Kinship, and Religion in the African-Portuguese World, 1441–1770.* Chapel Hill: North Carolina Press, 2003.

Thomas, Hugh. *The Slave Trade: The Story of the Atlantic Slave Trade, 1440–1870.* New York: Simon and Schuster, 1997.

Thompson, Robert Farris. *Face of the Gods: Art and Altars of Africa and the African Americas.* New York: Museum for African Art. 1993.

———. *Flash of the Spirit: African and Afro-American Art and Philosophy.* New York: Random House, 1983.

———. *The Four Moments of the Sun.* Washington, D.C.: National Art Gallery, 1981.

Thompson, Vincent. *The Making of the African Diaspora in the Americas, 1441–1900.* Harlow, Essex: Longman, 1987.

Thornton, John. *Africa and Africans in the Making of the Atlantic World, 1400–1800.* 2nd ed. Cambridge: Cambridge University Press, 1998.

———. "African Dimensions of the Stono Rebellion." *American Historical Review* 96, no. 4 (October 1991): 1101–1113.

———. "The African Experience of the '20 and Odd Negroes' Arriving in Virginia in 1619." *William and Mary Quarterly*, 3rd ser., 55, no. 3 (July 1998): 421–434.

———. "The Development of an African Catholic Church in the Kingdom of Kongo, 1491–1750." *Journal of African History* 25, no. 2 (1984): 147–167.

———. "I am the Subject of the King of Congo: African Political Ideology and the Haitian Revolution." *Journal of World History* 4 (1993): 181–214.

———. *The Kingdom of Kongo: Civil Wars and Transition, 1641–1718.* Madison: University of Wisconsin Press, 1983.

———. *The Kongolese Saint Anthony: Dona Beatriz Kimpa Vita and the Antonian Movement, 1684–1706.* Cambridge: Cambridge University Press, 1998.

———. "On the Trail of Voodoo: African Christianity in Africa and the Americas." *Americas* 44, no. 3 (1988): 261–278.

Turner, Lorenzo Dow. *Africanisms in the Gullah Dialect.* 1949. Reprint, Columbia: University of South Carolina Press, 2002.

Ulmann, Doris. *The Darkness and the Light.* New York: Aperture, 1974.

Vansina, Jan. *Art History in Africa: An Introduction to Method.* New York: Longman, 1984.

———. "Deep-Down Time: Political Tradition in Central Africa." *History in Africa* 16 (1989): 341–362.

———. *Kingdoms of the Savanna*. Madison: University of Wisconsin Press, 1966.

———. *Paths in the Rainforests: Toward a History of Political Tradition in Equatorial Africa*. Madison: University of Wisconsin Press, 1990.

Van Wing, J. *Études Bakongo: Sociologie-religion et Magie*. Desclee de Brouwer, 1959.

Vass, Winifred Kellersberger. *The Bantu Speaking Heritage of the United States*. Los Angeles: Center for Afro-American Studies at the University of California at Los Angeles, 1979.

Warner-Lewis, Maureen. *Central Africa in the Caribbean: Transcending Time, Transforming Cultures*. Barbados: University of West Indies Press, 2003.

Waters, Donald J. *Strange Ways and Sweet Dreams: Afro-American Folklore from the Hampton Institue*. Boston: G. K. Hall, 1983.

Williams, Eric. *Capitalism and Slavery*. 1944. Reprint, Chapel Hill: University of North Carolina Press, 1994.

Wood, Betty. *Slavery in Colonial Georgia, 1730–1775*. Athens: University of Georgia Press, 1984.

———. *Women's Work, Men's Work: The Informal Slave Economies of Lowcountry Georgia*. Athens : University of Georgia Press, 1995.

Wood, Marcus. *Blind Memory: Visual Representations of Slavery in England and America, 1780–1865*. New York: Routledge, 2000.

Wood, Peter H. *Black Majority: Negroes in South Carolina from 1670 through the Stono Rebellion*. New York: Knopf, 1974.

ART AND FOLKLORE

Abrahams, Roger D., ed. *African American Folktales: Stories from the Black Tradition in the New World*. 1985. Reprint, New York: Pantheon Books, 1999.

Adams, E. C. L. *Tales of the Congaree*. Chapel Hill: University of North Carolina Press, 1987.

Allen, William F. *Slave Songs of the United States*. 1867. Reprint, New York: Peter Smith, 1929.

Bascom, William. *African Folktales in the New World*. Bloomington: Indiana University Press, 1992.

Bastide, Roger. *African Civilizations in the New World*. London: C. Hurst, 1972.

Bennet, John. *Doctor to the Dead: Grotesque Legends and Folk Tales of Old Charleston*. 1946. Reprint, Columbia: University of South Carolina Press, 1995.

Bontemps, Arna. *Black Thunder: Gabriel's Revolt, Virginia, 1800.* 1936. Reprint, Boston: Beacon Press, 1963.

Bontemps, Arna, and Hughes Langston, eds. *The Book of Negro Folklore.* New York: Dodd, Mead, 1958.

Boyle, Virginia. *Devil Tales.* New York: Harper & Brothers, 1900.

Brown, Sterling A., Arthur P. Davis, and Ulysses Lee, eds. *The Negro Caravan.* 1941. Reprint, New York: Arno Press, 1969.

Carawan, Guy. *Ain't I Got a Right to the Tree of Life?* New York. Simon and Schuster, 1967.

Chambers, H. A. *The Treasury of Negro Spirituals.* 1959. Reprint, New York: Emerson Books, 1963.

Chatelain, Heli. *Folk Tales of Angola.* Boston: Houghton Mifflin, 1894.

Christensen, A. M. H. *Afro American Folklore.* Freeport, N.Y.: Libraries Press, 1971.

Clews, Elsie Parsons. *Folk-lore of the Sea Islands, South Carolina.* New York: American Folk-lore Society, 1923.

Courlander, Harold. *Terrapin's Pot of Sense.* New York: Holt. 1957.

———. *A Treasury of African Folklore.* New York: Crown, 1975.

———. *A Treasury of Afro-American Folklore.* New York: Crown, 1976.

Dance, Daryl Cumber. *From My People: 400 Years of African American Folklore.* New York: Norton, 2002.

Dett, R. Nathaniel. *Religious Folk-songs of the Negro as Sung at Hampton Institute.* Hampton, Va.: Hampton Institute Press, 1927.

Dorson, Richard. *American Negro Folktales.* Greenwich, Conn.: Fawcett, 1967.

———. *Buying the Wind.* Chicago: University of Chicago Press, 1964.

Faulkner, William J. *The Days When the Animals Talked: Black American Folktales and How They Came to Be.* 1977. Reprint, Trenton, N.J.: Africa World Press, 1993.

Feelings, Tom. *The Middle Passage: White Ships/Black Cargo.* New York: Dial Books, 1995.

Fenner, Thomas. *Religious Folk Songs of the Negro as Sung on the Plantations.* Hampton, Va.: Hampton Institute Press, 1909.

Fisher, Miles Mark. *Negro Slave Songs in the United States.* Ithaca, N.Y.: Cornell University Press for the American Historical Association, 1953.

Georgia Writers' Project. *Drums and Shadows: Survival Studies among the Georgia Coastal Negroes.* Athens: University of Georgia Press, 1940.

Gilmore, James [Edmund Kirke]. *My Southern Friends.* New York: Tribune Association, 1863.

Gonzales, Ambrose. *The Black Border: Gullah Stories from the Carolina Coast.* 1922. Reprint, Columbia, S.C.: State Company, 1964.

———. *With Aesop along the Black Border.* Columbia, S.C.: State Company, 1924.

Grissom, Mary Allen. *The Negro Sings a New Heaven.* Chapel Hill: University of North Carolina Press, 1930.

Harris, Joel Chandler. *The Complete Tales of Uncle Remus.* Compiled by Richard Chase. Boston: Houghton Mifflin, 1955.

Heyward, DuBose. *Mamba's Daughters: A Novel of Charleston.* 1929. Reprint, Columbia: University of South Carolina Press, 1995.

Hodgson, W. B. *The Gospels, Written in the Negro Patois of English, with Arabic Characters.* New York: Ethnological Society of New York, 1857.

Hurston, Zora Neale. *Mules and Men.* 1935. Reprint, New York: Negro Universities Press, 1969.

———. *The Sanctified Church.* Berkeley, Calif.: Turtle Islands, 1983.

Jacobs, Harriet [Linda Brent]. *Incidents in the Life of a Slave Girl, Written by Herself.* Edited by Lydia Maria Child. 1863. Reprint, Cambridge: Harvard University Press, 1987.

Johnson, James Weldon. *The Book of American Negro Poetry.* New York: Harcourt, Brace, 1931.

———. *The Book of American Negro Spirituals.* New York: Viking Press, 1940.

———. *God's Trombones.* New York: Penguin Books, 1955.

Jones, C. C. *Negro Myths from the Georgia Coast.* 1888. Reprint, Detroit: Singing Tree Press, 1969.

Kennedy, R. Emmet. *Mellows: A Chronicle of Unknown Singers.* New York: A. and C. Boni, 1925.

Landeck, Beatrice. *Echoes of Africa in Folk Songs of the Americas.* New York: D. McKay, 1961.

Lomax, Alan. *The Folk Songs of North America.* Garden City, N.Y.: Doubleday, 1960.

Lomax, John, and Alan Lomax. *American Ballads and Folk Songs.* 1934. Reprint, New York: Dover, 1994.

———. *Folk Song U.S.A.* New York: Columbia University Press, 1963.

Lovell, John. *Black Song: The Forge and the Flame.* New York. Macmillan, 1972.

McIlhenny, E. A. *Befo' de War Spirituals.* New York: AMS Press, 1973.

Naylor, Gloria. *Mama Day.* 1988. Reprint, New York: Vintage Books, 1993.

Parrish, Lydia. *Slave Songs of the Georgia Sea Islands.* Hatboro: Folklore Associates, 1965.

Parsons, Elsie. *Folklore of the Sea Islands, South Carolina.* New York: American Folklore Society, 1969.

Rhyme, Nancy. *Slave Ghost Stories: Tales of Hags, Hants, Ghosts, and Diamondback Rattlers.* Orangeburg, S.C.: Sandlapper Publishing, 2002.

Scarborough, Dorothy. *On the Trail of Negro Folk Songs*. Cambridge: Harvard University Press, 1925.

South Carolina Writers' Program. *South Carolina Folktales*. Columbia: University of South Carolina, 1941.

Weems, Carrie Mae. *In These Islands: South Carolina and Georgia*. Tuscaloosa: Sarah Moody Gallery of Art, University of Alabama, 1995.

Woofter, T. J. *Black Yeomanry: Life of St. Helena Island*. New York: H. Holt, 1930.

Work, John. *American Negro Songs and Spirituals*. New York: Bonanza Books, 1940.

INDEX

CPSIA information can be obtained
at www.ICGtesting.com
Printed in the USA
LVHW052053171120
671949LV00014B/483